Laurel & Thorn

The Athlete in American Literature

Robert J. Higgs

THE UNIVERSITY PRESS OF KENTUCKY

For Reny, Julie, and Laura

Library of Congress Cataloging in Publication Data

Higgs, Robert J., 1932–
    Laurel & thorn : the athlete in American literature.

    Includes bibliographical references.
    Includes index.
    1. American literature—History and criticism.
2. Athletes in literature.   3. Sports stories—
History and criticism.   I. Title.   II. Title:
Laurel and thorn.
PS173.A85H5   810'.9'355   80-51014
ISBN 0-8131-1412-8   AACR2

The publication of this book received financial support
from the University of Tennessee Better English Fund,
established by John C. Hodges.

Contents

Preface

FROM Christmas day 1621, when William Bradford admonished young men for playing in the streets of Plymouth, to this year's Super Bowl Sunday, sports in America have been almost completely transformed. Increased leisure time and technology have wrought changes in our attitudes toward sports (and toward ourselves) that the old Puritans could not have imagined. Among the technological innovations, none has had so profound an influence upon sports as television. Indeed its impact has been so great that its long-range effects upon sports and all society cannot even yet be envisioned. In its relentlessness television is like reality. Game shows grind on and on throughout the week, athletic competition dominates the weekend, and morning and evening sports reports keep us up to date on the latest scores and trade transactions. Television has helped to make sports as ubiquitous as the weather and as important as the news of catastrophe, war, and politics. Where once men, or at least some men, engaged in matins and vespers, today we begin and end our day by listening to the news, sports, and weather—a new sort of trinity.

Television is a marvel, even a miracle. It can do much, but it is not all-powerful. It can show us the action of sports and provide instant replay with commentary. It can capture the beauty of sport, the skill of the athlete, and the enthusiasm of the fan. It can tell us more accurately how the game was played than we could discover if we ourselves were there. It can bring the drama and genuine excitement of the world's best competition right into our living rooms. Television cannot, however, reveal to us the meaning of what we watch. The primary purpose of television is not to mirror a game for better understanding of it but to extend it to a larger audience. Admittedly, television can (and does) provide different points of view, that is, different angles of the camera, but camera angles are not interpretations. Television is not an art but a medium, and the medium is not always the message.

Television has other limitations. It cannot tell us everything about the social and cultural significance of the athlete hero whose deeds it records in minutest details at the time of occurrence. Television can evaluate the deed but falls far short in its potential for evaluation of the person who performed it. For a more complete picture of the individual we must still turn to the written word, to the sporting press to be sure, but also to literary art. On a television screen all players look alike, excepting numbers and colors of uniforms, but literature takes us behind the scenes and provides comparison and contrast of players so that the best among them can be identified. Television will show us who is the strongest and fastest on the field, but it cannot locate other qualities we look for in the strong of arm and fleet of foot. Television thus provides only part of the story; for the rest we look either to the sports pages or to the literature of sports. The sportswriter, like the television camera, can also tell us much. but he too is limited, not by his intelligence, knowledge, or skill, but by the mode of writing and the extent of coverage. For the most part, the sportswriter reports; or if he does interpret, his interpretation usually does not extend beyond the boundaries of the playing field. It is true that in the last few years a number of sportswriters have looked at the role of sports in society with a rather critical eye, but they form the exceptions rather than the rule. By and large, the sporting press is no more critical of what it surveys than is the television industry. For the most comprehensive and pluralistic view of the athlete, at least of his life off the field, literature is still the champion. This is not to say that the literature tells the whole story either, but it does remind us of some important points—that winning is not the only thing, that victory on the playing field may often be gained at a cost far too high for the general good of society.

This work therefore deals with literature, but it is not by any means a traditional literary study. It does not undertake to assess the authors aesthetically, to examine form and content; rather the approach is cultural. The concern here is not primarily with

how well the author has done his job, how artistic a product he
has created in the athletic hero, but with the view he takes of this
figure and his milieu. As a popular hero, the athlete has anthropological and mythological importance, and the values he
represents are quite indicative of the tastes, attainments, beliefs,
and ideals of his society. Whenever the athlete has prospered
previously, notably in ancient Greece and Victorian England, he
has figured prominently in the literature of his time. The same is
true today, and this work is nothing more or less than an attempt
to show how the athlete has fared in modern American literary
art, not as an artistic creation, but as a symbol, in the eyes of the
authors, of American culture.

Explanations of a number of limitations are necessary. I have
excluded more popular literature (subliterature often) and
juvenile fiction in which the athlete remains a hero à la Frank
Merriwell and the Rover boys, nor have I considered the boy
athlete of serious fiction who is not a full-fledged hero. The
criteria for selection of authors and works were that the author
have literary or social significance and that the work treat of the
athlete in some significant way. Many of the authors are univer-
sally recognized as our best, but I do not wish to imply that there
is not other good fiction about the athlete by writers not included. Indeed to discover what all American writers of consequence have had to say would be quite unnecessary for the
purposes here. I am convinced that I have uniformly chosen a
sufficient number of major authors to prove my thesis. I should
also point out that I do not presume to discuss all the athletes of
the authors selected but only those I feel best reflect their attitudes toward the athlete. Almost invariably these athletes are the
authors' most famous: Busher Keefe in Ring Lardner, Robert
Cohn in Ernest Hemingway, Tom Buchanan in F. Scott
Fitzgerald, Jim Randolph and Nebraska Crane in Thomas
Wolfe, Labove in William Faulkner, Tom Stark in Robert Penn
Warren, Biff Loman in Arthur Miller, and Brick Pollit in Tennessee Williams, to name a few.

Though I have attempted briefly to trace some influences and
ideals back to their origins in the ancient world, the time covered
by this study is essentially the first three quarters of the twentieth
century, the period in which sports have flourished as never

before in all history. Chronologically the first writer dealt with is Jack London; the last, Walker Percy. The intent, once again, has not been to treat as many authors as possible but to arrive at a composite view of the athlete in all his roles and manifestations.

The main body of the study is devoted to particular types of athlete hero. Most of the terms are common in everyday use and in themselves carry some definition. When necessary, however, the definition is expanded to attempt to clarify the discussion. It has been necessary to limit the number of athletes illustrative of each type, and in doing so I have kept in mind an observation of Thoreau: "If you are acquainted with a principle, what do you care for a myriad of instances and applications?" How many boxers from London, Lardner, Hemingway, Farrell, and Schulberg might one include in a discussion on the bromide, beast, or natural? Several indeed, but to do so would overstate a point.

Also the fact that an athlete is discussed under one type does not necessarily mean that he does not possess traits common to other types. Classification is never a simple matter, but I will let the reader judge if I have been fair in the broad categories I have established and in the selection of the athletes representative of the types. Also, the classification of athletes is a means and not an end. The purpose of the study is not merely to catalog recognizable types of athletic heroes; rather, the attempt is to interpret the wide variety of athletic models as symbols of American culture.

By way of acknowledgment, I wish first of all to pay tribute to my father for teaching me early the joys of sports. I wish to thank F. DeWolfe Miller and Ralph Haskins, members of my doctoral committee at the University of Tennessee, for their assistance in preparation of the dissertation out of which the present work evolved. I am grateful to Richard Beale Davis, who directed both my M.A. thesis on this subject and the dissertation as well. His own scholarship has always been a source of inspiration. I would like to pay special thanks to my friend Neil Isaacs, also a member of my doctoral committee, for continuing to encourage me over the years in the study of the literature of sports and to Bain T. Stewart for his wise counsel at several points in my academic career.

I am indebted to the entire staff of the Charles Sherrod Li-

brary, East Tennessee State University, for their assistance in so
many ways and especially to Hal Smith, former Head Librarian,
Ed Walters, current Head Librarian, Edith Keys, Reference Li-
brarian, Berney Burleson, retired Acquisitions Librarian, and
David Parsley, current Acquisitions Librarian. I am grateful to
the ETSU Research Advisory Council for the assistance of
Katherine Honour and to the chairman of the Department of
English John Tallent, East Tennessee State University, for providing me the opportunity to attend symposia and to teach
classes in this field of interest. I wish to express my gratitude to
Joseph Traherne, Head of the Department of English at the
University of Tennessee, and the Trustees of the John C.
Hodges Better English Fund at the University of Tennessee for
their support of the publication of this book. Thanks are due to
Don Johnson for reading portions of the manuscript and making helpful comments, to Betty Branscomb for her aid in edit-
ing, to Elizabeth Hunter for typing, to Professors Helen Hol-
lingsworth and Anne Lecroy for help in selection of title, and to
Laura and Julia Higgs for typing and proofreading. My other
familial debt is indicated in the dedication.

1. Game Plan

A study of anything must begin in dissection; before a new understanding of the whole can be reached there must be an analysis of the parts. An examination of the athlete or, more specifically, the athlete in American literature is no exception. Who is the athlete? In Greek and Roman antiquity, he was "one who competed for a prize in public games," especially games requiring strength and stamina, and the definition is as relevant today as in classical times. There are a number of key words in this definition, but none more important than the word *one*. Who is this *one*? He is one, like all men, with a body *and* a self; and when he competes publicly, he places himself, literally "him" plus "self," before spectators for judgment and evaluation with all the consequences involved for the self.

A natural and understandable tendency is to regard the athlete principally as a body. Even Paul Weiss, one of the leading speculative philosophers of our time, has made the statement in *Sport: A Philosophic Inquiry* that "the athlete comes to accept his body as himself." This of course is not wholly true. The athlete accepts the importance of the body in relation to self but he never equates the two unless he becomes hopelessly narcissistic. Weiss himself realizes this since he devotes much attention to the athlete's pursuit of physical excellence and concludes his work with a "metaphysical excursus" on the significance of sport. The body is always an object to be overcome by the self, as Ernest Becker has so brilliantly shown in *The Denial of Death,* and it is in this agon that the athlete becomes what Weiss calls "a representative of all." He achieves this symbolic significance not because he "accepts his body as himself" but because he knows instinctively that the body is the natural enemy of self. Though there have been many notable victories by the athlete, the battle is inevitably a losing one since the body eventually deteriorates and dies. Nevertheless, the athletic endeavor is heroic for both winner and loser.

It is the heroism inherent in the transcendence of the body that underlies the philosophical limitations of a study of sport and of the athlete in his athletic role. The heroics of the athlete simply cannot be confined to the playing field since the self manifested in the physical struggle is the same self that directs the body in activities off the field.

Whatever that mystical force is that moves the sprinter in the hundred yard dash to overcome the inertia of his body is the same force that directs all other aspects of the athlete's life. In other words, an athlete is an athlete off the field as well as on. Sport is but one way of "partializing" life so that nature or the body can be reshaped in a more pleasing image. This "partializing," however, has significance for the person not only when he is intensely engaged in the game but, just as important, when he is not.

The first and most crucial question of all in a study of the meaning of the athlete in literature is this: What is the *self*? There is a tendency to equate it with what has traditionally been called "the soul," but Ernest Becker warns against such simplistic analogy. Michael Murphy in *Golf in the Kingdom* seems to like the phrase "inner body" in his discussion of the flamelike mystery of man, but, after citing Madame Blavatsky and other theosophists, he leaves the reader in essentially the same state of confusion as others have in discussing the soul. What is the soul? Who knows? No one, but by way of a feeble attempt at definition I will refer to Socrates, who is the first speaker in the following dialogue, the other being Glaucon.

"And as there are two principles of human nature, one the spirited and the other the philosophical, some God, as I should say, has given mankind two arts answering to them (and only indirectly to the soul and body), in order that these two principles (like the strings of an instrument) not to be relaxed or drawn tighter until they are duly harmonized."

"That appears to be the intention."

"And he who mingles music with gymnastic in the fairest proportions, and best attempers them to the soul, may be rightly called the true musician and harmonist in a far higher sense than the tuner of the strings."[1]

Obviously, the dichotomy that Socrates identifies is "mind and body," and the soul is that mysterious and unknowable entity which insists on some sort of truce between the two. A lost soul would be one who either indulges his animal nature excessively or is hopelessly entrapped in airy abstractions; in short, one who has lost a sense of limits and the saving knowledge of the golden mean, which, incidentally, does not equate with mediocrity. Socrates implies a distinction between mind and soul but for purposes of this study I would like to place both of these abstractions under the broader abstraction of *self*. There is the *body* and the *self*. If the soul is that which drives us toward wholeness or holiness, the two having the same root meaning, what is the mind, the other part of self? As far as I know, no one has the slightest idea. We are surrounded by utter mystery in an effort to determine who we are as thinking beings. All we know is that we are more than bodies and that we are driven toward self-esteem and joy. Michael Novak in *The Joy of Sports* writes:

The root of human dissatisfaction and restlessness goes as deep into the spirit as any human drive—deeper than any other drive. It is the human spirit [or soul]. Nothing stills it. Nothing fulfills it. It is not a need like a hunger, a thirst, or an itch, for such needs are easily satisfied. It is need even greater than sex; orgasmic satisfaction does not quiet it. 'Desire' is the word by which coaches call it. A driveness. Distorted, the drive for perfection can propel an ugly and considerably less than perfect human development. True, straight, and well-targeted, it soars like an arrow toward the proper beauty of mankind." (p. 27)

The soul is the holy (or wholly) spirit; to deny this is death though the body may live on.

If the soul is the impulse toward order, toward a healing of the cosmic crack, the mind appears to be that side of self which is conscious of the crack or flaw in the first place. It is also the side of self which envisions things "nearer to the heart's desire." It is the generator of "eidólons," to use Whitman's term, but it is both more and less than that. If a mistake is made in assuming that

the athlete accepts his body as himself, a mistake of equal mag-
nitude lies in the myth that athletics constitute a "mindless" endeavor. The athlete uses his mind as much as a scholar or scientist; he merely uses a different part of the mind. Essentially, he
uses intelligence while the intellectual uses intellect. It is impossible to separate the two completely, but Richard Hofstadter has
provided us with the "nub of distinction."

Intelligence is an excellence of mind that is employed within a fairly
narrow, immediate, and predictable range; it is a manipulative, adjust-
ive, unfailingly practical quality—one of the most eminent and endearing of the animal virtues. Intelligence works within the framework of
limited but clearly stated goals, and may be quick to shear away questions of thought that do not seem to help in reaching them.
    Intellect, on the other hand, is the critical, creative, and contempla-
tive side of the mind. Whereas intelligence seeks to grasp, manipulate,
reorder, adjust, intellect examines, ponders, wonders, theorizes,
criticizes, imagines. Intelligence will seize the immediate meaning in a
situation and evaluate it. Intellect evaluates evaluations, and looks for
the meanings of situations as a whole. Intelligence can be praised as a
quality in animals; intellect, being a unique manifestation of human
dignity, is both praised and assailed as a quality in men.[2]

The equation of intelligence with "the endearing quality of animals" is an important consideration here. The less intelligence
required in a sporting endeavor, the more the tendency to regard the participant in that activity as an animal. Hence, linemen
in football are often referred to jokingly as "animals," "beasts,"
"neanderthals," while quarterbacks, for example, are considered
more intelligent.
    Sports require intelligence though not necessarily intellect. In
any event, the athlete has both, and he has a soul, all of which
make the self. It cannot be overemphasized: the athlete is like
everyone else, but he is different. In his youth he relies on intelligence to overcome the body, but when the body has made its
inevitable counterattack and forced him to retire, he then begins
to rely on intellect in order to discover new ways of transcending
nature. In fact, everyone in the world is an ex-athlete, since
somewhere along the line, if only during childhood, we engaged
in games or exercises seeking approval of witnesses, usually a

parent or a friend. We tried to "show off" and we continue showing off for the rest of our lives. What many, if not most of us, discover is that sports is not our interest or talent, and we turn, often sadly I suspect, to more abstruse endeavors. This is why growing up is difficult, and so is growing old, because most of us have neither mind nor body to do anything spectacular during our three score years and ten. What is there left for us? Transference. We pay tribute to those who have overcome. Man, said Dr. Johnson, is "a worshipping animal." Hence, we watch, imitate, render praise, and strive to do the best we can. We want wholeness and when we cannot achieve it, we admire others who can.

The wholeness we seek is the mastering of nature by the self, by the created self, by the artificial self. What we want is wholesome artificialness in which we can rejoice, directly or vicariously, in the victory over nature or death while we are in the "magic circle" of life. Nature is our eternal foe and what is needed in our world is a sense of good sportsmanship and fair play in the contest. There is in fact only one contest, man against nature, and to rape the earth in the manner we do is no different from kicking an opponent in the groin in a boxing match— hence, the obvious universal significance of sports.

The athlete, like his admirers, seeks wholeness, and the manner in which he seeks this wholeness makes all the difference. After the athlete has retired, he then makes one of three choices. He places his athletic accomplishments in perspective and with the rest of us comes to live in what Freud called "the common misery of mankind." Or he adds to his normal misery and that of others by becoming paranoid in one of two ways: he retreats into the past and thrives on the glory of yesteryear or, overestimating his intellect, capitalizes on his heroic achievements in sport in an attempt to extend self in other directions. The self always wants to expand but to ignore one's limitations is to become neurotic or self-deceived. Northrop Frye has called this character in literature the *Alazon* and his besetting sin is hubris or pride. In one way or another he engages in self-glorification and establishes himself as a model of wholeness. Hence the long and familiar parade of bromides of every stripe, the all-round man, student athlete, the muscular Christian, the booster alumnus, the sporting gentleman, and so on, in short he who has not achieved distinguished wholeness but only the shadow of it. In his own eyes this true believer sees himself as a splendid representative of a sound mind in a sound body and, like Apollo, begins to render laws and prophecies that establish platitudinous cultural attitudes affecting the entire course of history.

What is emerging is a picture of the athlete as a human being with, like everybody else, mind, body, and soul, the mind and soul constituting the self. Once more, where he differs from others is in the manner of transcending the body. Generally speaking, the athlete in his efforts of transcendence relies on intelligence which, as Hofstadter said without reference to sports, "lies within the framework of limited but clearly stated goals." The immediate goal for the athlete is simply winning the game. If he wins, he gains self-esteem and recognition, which must eventually be subjected to self-evaluation. The consequence of this evaluation is that the athlete will either choose or not choose to join others in the other various routes to self-worth: making high grades, writing good books, raising nutritious vegetables, erecting beautiful buildings, making money in order to engage in philanthropy, running for public offices, fighting holy wars, saving souls, and building "a better world" in which to live. We know the varieties of tunes, but the theme is always the same: *the conquest of nature*. It is not so much versatility that the athlete and nonathlete alike are seeking as what we all must seek through either intelligence or intellect or both, and that is the transcendence of the body. *Mens sana in corpore sano* (sound mind in a sound body) is neither an archaic nor a trivial epithet; it is, as Juvenal tells us, the one goal worth praying for and what it means requires emphasis at the expense of redundancy: mental sanity and physical health, a health that in addition to whatever role luck may play derives from control, direction, care, and rational concern for the body.

I hope, then, to have established at this point that the athlete is not merely a body performing but a self engaged in heroic transcendence of the body. With this in mind, we can now move to the major theme with which this book is concerned: the quality of athletic heroism in American literature. I would like to qualify this immediately by saying that the real subject is the quality of athletic heroism in life since literature, like sport, does not exist in a vacuum. It invariably reflects the *Zeitgeist* of a society in much the same manner as sports and games and the heroes emerging from those events. What, then, is quality? It is, says Robert Pirsig in *Zen and the Art of Motorcycle Maintenance,* the coming together of mind and matter, the third event in the universe, and it is also the goal of all heroic action.

Man, Ernest Becker shows, is either a hero or a hero worshiper, or, by implication, a vegetable, a nonbeing. I have been aware for many years of D. H. Lawrence's dictum "Give homage and allegiance to a hero and you yourself become heroic; it is the law of men,"[3] but it remained for Becker to confirm for me Lawrence's intuitive proclamation with his stunning survey of psychoanalysis and religion. Perversity is averted as much as possible by acceptance of both the body and the need for transcendence; thus is implied a sort of middle way analogous to Robert Pirsig's synthesis of nature and art. Quality, the third event, the union of energy and form, Pirsig equates with the Greek term *Areté,* or excellence, a pervasive concept applicable to every aspect of life. I propose here to examine the manner in which athletic excellence or heroism is transferred from the playing field to *Areté* in society. According to the poet Wallace Stevens in "The Pure Good of Theory," "There is always the thing and the version of the thing." As a student of literature, I intend to examine the version of the thing, the myths of the athlete, principally in his nonathletic role.

The basic questions in regard to athletics in the modern world come down to these: what is the quality of athletic heroism, not in terms of mere physical accomplishments, in numbers of passes thrown, home runs hit, or feet jumped, or in terms of isolated parts, health, speed, strength, and endurance, but in relation to the whole social mythos? What does the athlete hero expect for his accomplishments and why and what praise by hero-worshipers is rendered him and why? These are formidable issues, and I believe that American literature provides some valuable insights toward the understanding of the athlete as a highly symbolic hero intensely engaged in the human drama between self and nature. The athlete in literature comes in a wide variety of splendid shapes and it is not an easy task to find a common thread. Even to begin the search it is first necessary to gain some understanding of the major myths that surround and motivate the athlete in his time off the field as well as on.

Apollo, Dionysus, & Adonis

The athlete in American literature assumes one of two basic roles, that of conformist or that of rebel. With obvious indebtedness to Nietzsche, I have designated these tendencies Apollonian and Dionysian or "artificial" and "natural." I am quite familiar with the Procrustean dangers inherent in any categorization and I know full well that matters are never a simple either/or. In *Sex in History* G. Rattray Taylor reminds us that this is especially true in the case of the Apollonian-Dionysian dichotomy.

As Euripides strove to show, the central problem is control of . . . powerful instinctive forces by the conscious mind. As Kind Penthus discovered, to try and suppress them is entirely suicidal. The attempt provokes an explosion in which all barriers are overthrown. The conscious mind must ride these forces as a man rides a powerful horse. This explains, what has puzzled so many, why the worship of Apollo at Delphi was combined with the worship of Dionysus. It was Nietzsche who started the confusion with his false antithesis between Apollonian and Dionysiac religions. Since then numerous writers have classified not only theoleptic religions, but periods such as Romanticism, as Dionysiac; and have treated religions and periods of cerebral control (including Classicism) as being Apollonian. But Apollo was the symbol of moderation, the golden mean, the Greek concept of measure. The extremes of patrist Puritanism are not Apollonian, while on the other hand, the Romantics never abandoned themselves to group orgies. Apollo did not deny the unconscious in a state of trance, and the Delphic sibyl, who spoke from the unconscious in a state of trance, was under his aegis. Apollo and Dionysus are not opponents but partners.[4]

Indeed Apollo and Dionysus are partners or ought to be, and I have only maintained the division in order to examine in some detail the disproportionate combinations reflected in fictional athletes. When I talk about Apollo and Dionysus in this study, I do not wish to imply that either by itself is good or bad; I employ them merely to indicate conformity to some fixed code, that is, to the artificial in the case of Apollonian, or the degree of revolt against society and the indulgence of the body or the return to nature in the case of the Dionysian. Each type always suggests its opposite and each always raises the question of emphasis on body or self, nature or art. Apollo and Dionysus are "the two hands of God," to borrow the title of Alan Watts's book on oriental dichotomies and unity.

The word Apollonian can be defined in many ways, but the manner in which I apply it is described by Otto Rank. The Apollonian world view, says Rank, "rests on likeness to others and leads in the sense of the Greek mentality to the acceptance of the universal ideal; it contains implicitly the morality worked out by Socrates, which still lies at the basis of psychoanalytic therapy: Know thyself, in order to improve thyself (in terms of universal norms). It is, therefore, not knowledge for the sake of the self, but knowledge for the sake of adaptation."[5] In a study of the athlete it is especially appropriate to refer to Apollo since the god himself, in addition to whatever else he was, "heartily believed in youth, and was the sponsor of athletic contests, himself drawing a strong bow."[6] The Apollonian types in American literature, however, are not Olympic youth schooled in music and gymnastics; rather, they are, in the Rankian sense, those attempting to conform to some stereotyped conception of completeness. They are the know-it-alls, the true believers who have panaceas for the dispensation of knowledge, the banishment of evil, and the control of nature. They are unrealistic, immature, though giving the illusion of maturity, and, if given enough prominence, tyrannical and oppressive. Familiar types in literature and life, as I will illustrate, are the busher, the sporting gentleman, the apotheosized WASP, the booster alumnus, the muscular Christian, and the brave new man. Each in a different way attempts to embody or uphold some concept or code of the unity of body and self. Each fails or is made to appear either ridiculous or in some way autocratic. We ought never to forget that Apollo is the patron god not only of games but of tyranny as well. He may be beautiful on the outside but underneath the surface he may be a Nero, which was precisely the case with the great statue that stood outside history's most famous stadium, as

John Pearson points out on the first page of *Arena* (Keltshire, 1973):

Officially the arena was called the Flavian Amphitheatre, after the dynastic name of the Emperor, but several centuries ahead it would pick up its simpler and more lasting title. Ironically this name, which would erase all mention of the Flavians from popular memory, had originated with their hated predecessor, Nero. His colossal statue stood near the site of the arena. Rather than demolish it, Vespasian had ingeniously changed its head and its identity to that of Apollo, the sun god. And it was this colossus, with Apollo's head, but built by Nero, that gave the arena its enduring name, the Colosseum.

Who is the Dionysian type? Following Rank's classification, he is the neurotic who wants to be himself. He is the true "natural" who has accepted his body as himself and feels no need to conform to an Apollonian order of any sort. He is, in fact, narcissistic in that he worships his own body as an end in itself. He seeks not to become at all but regresses instead. We recognize him in life as the familiar babe, bum, or beast. He, like the Apollonian figures, is invariably guilty of hubris, but he is not self-deceived as the Apollonians are because he has no self to deceive.

There is another type of Dionysian figure, however, that is almost the antithesis of that described above. I shall refer to him as Adonis, though it is virtually impossible to make significant distinctions between some ancient versions of Dionysus and Adonis. Was Dionysus persecuted by Apollo? So was Christ or the Phoenician "Lord" or "Adon." Did Adonis suffer? So did Dionysus. "He is the suffering and dying god, the god of tragic contrast."[7] Was Adonis the favorite of women? So was Dionysus. "He, the confidant of women, he whose majesty is complete in the intoxicated gaze of the most beautiful of women, claims the queen of Athens, when he comes."[8] Adonis was the god of youthful beauty and so was Dionysus, at least in the *Bacchae*: "Dionysus is a human youth, lovely, with curled hair, but in a moment he is a Snake, a Lion, a Wild Bull, a Burning Flame."[9] Thus we think of Dionysus as the god of sexual energy just as we do Adonis. "Dionysus is considered, like Adonis, to be the founder of orgiastic festivals,"[10] a myth that Freud noted.[11] Clearly there is a need for interpretation on different levels, to do battle against what Leslie Fiedler has called "the endemic disease of our time, the inability to see relationships."

This other Dionysus, or Adonis, as I shall call him, is a rebel who reminds us of greater "beyonds" than all those little "beyonds" with which most of us rest content. He does not kill himself on the one hand, nor does he uncritically conform on the other. He does not seek knowledge for the sake of adaptation, but knowledge for the sake of self. It is an approach to life that Rank has called "the Kantian," a sort of middle way between Dionysian and Apollonian or animal indulgence on the one hand and authorized forms of behavior on the other. Invariably he is the sacrificial figure who is eternally harassed by Apollo or authority. He is "natural" man, in one sense, but never so natural as Dionysus the Bull or eternal youth that he does not seek transcendence in some way. He is a divided being who reminds us that body and self must be united on the side of nature and not on the side of control and conformity as Apollo would have us believe. Adonis in contrast to Dionysus the transformed Bull defies both authority and nature. He does not conform to temporal codes on the one hand nor hedonistically indulge his body on the other. Hence he lives in a world of tension, pain, struggle, and hope. Through his revolt he reminds us of the imperfectibility of man and of the hubris of those who would assume to spell out the best manner of reconciling body and mind. Athletic types that fall under this classification are the folk hero, the fisher king, the scapegoat, the absurd athlete, and the "secret" Christian. Adonis is the *revolté* not because he desires the sexual ecstasy that society frequently prohibits but because he cannot accept stereotyped definitions of what it means to be a man.

The Touchstone

If the athlete, fictional or real, is to be evaluated as a cultural symbol, it is necessary to establish the ideal by which he is to be measured; and to do that one must look briefly to ancient Greece.

While epic heroes are invariably athletic, they are not considered athletes, though to be sure Odysseus, Achilles, Aeneas, and

Beowulf probably could have performed as such. Instead, we
regard as athletes the subjects of the art of Myron and Polyclitus,
specifically the Discus Thrower and the Canon. Through these
statues and the brief commentaries of philosophers one can
come to some understanding of the athletic ideal of fifth-century
B.C. Greece, the essence of which was strength and beauty in
harmony, or, in other words, Dionysus and Apollo, energy and
form. These opposites were best combined in the pentathlete or
all-round athlete, which is why Aristotle admired him more than
participants in single events. Since "beauty" suggests an aesthetic
limitation, the athletic ideal in art was directly related to the ideal
of Greek education, the balance of "gymnastic" and "music,"
which has an obvious kinship with the epic code *sapientia et fortitudo* (strength and wisdom) and Juvenal's *mens sana in corpore
sano*. Whatever the nuances of differences in these related ideals,
all share one common characteristic, the need for synthesis of
mind and matter or idea and energy. If *Aretê*, or excellence, is
the goal of that union, then what is the moral aspect of the trinity
that makes one care about quality at all? One way of understanding this concern for wholeness is through the Greek term *aidos*,
that trait classically associated with the athlete. It is *aidos*, according to E. Norman Gardiner, which wins the athlete the favor of
the gods and averts their jealousy.

That jealousy is excited by all excess, by pride, by insolence. Aidos is
the exact opposite of insolence. . . . it is the feeling of respect for what
is due to the gods, to one's fellow men, to oneself; the feeling of reverence, modesty, honor. It distinguishes the athlete from the bully.
Strength may tempt a man to abuse it; success may beget "braggart
insolence." But aidos puts into the heart "valour and the joy of battle."
No sport demands so high a standard of honour as boxing and wrestling
and none are so liable to corruption. But aidos makes a man "a straight
fighter," the epithet by which Pindar describes Diagoras of Rhodes
"who walks in the straight path that abhors insolence." It is a feeling
incompatible with the commercial spirit, for "aidos is stolen away by
secret gain." It is akin to that typical Greek virtue of self-control,
Sophrosyne, but is something more subtle and more indefinite.[12]

   The connotations of *aidos* are distinctly positive. It is not a
pejorative shame, but rather, says Edith Hamilton, "that shame

which holds men back from wrongdoing."[13] It is "reverence" but also the "feeling a prosperous man should have in the presence of the unfortunate—not compassion, but a sense that the difference between him and those poor wretches is not deserved." According to Werner Jaeger, it is dedication to an ideal, a sort of noblesse oblige. "In Homer, the real mark of the nobleman is his sense of duty. He is judged and proud to be judged by a severe standard. And the nobleman educates others by presenting to them an eternal ideal to which they have a duty to conform. His sense of duty is 'aidos.' "[14]

Sense of duty to an eternal ideal, restraint from wrongdoing, abhorrence of insolence, delight in the toil of the agon, all add a moral dimension to strength and beauty as well as a certain charisma and even divinity; and there appears to be little difference between what the Greeks aspired toward and what the Psalmist ascribed to the Lord: "Honor and majesty are before him; Strength and beauty are in his sanctuary" (Psalm 96:6 KJV). It is not surprising that in Michelangelo's *Creation of Adam* the influences of Hebrew religion and Greek art appear so congruous. If you wish to see strength and beauty, look upon Adam's body in that divine work; if you wish to see *aidos,* look upon his face.

In this study it will be noted that the athletes who possess *aidos* are the Adonic types, the cripples, who are inwardly persecuted by the hubris-ridden Apollos, the fixed idealists and true believers. It should be emphasized that *aidos* is not humility per se, though it comes close to it. Certainly it is not arrogance, but it is not self-effacement, either. It is a sort of middle way between the two. The athlete possessing *aidos* is a fighter, but he is a "straight fighter." Hence the universal significance of rules, law, and justice. We want to control our lives and we wish for others to have control of theirs. We respect ourselves and we try to respect others, to promote goodness, the essence of which is the fair fight. This is *aidos.* No one has said it better than Robert Frost.

Prowess of course comes first, the ability to perform with success in games, in the arts and, come right down to it, in battle. The nearest of kin to the artists in college where we all become bachelors of arts are their fellow performers in baseball, football and tennis. That's why I am so particular college athletics should be kept from corruption. They are

close to the soul of culture. At any rate the Greeks thought so. Justice is
a close second to prowess. When displayed toward each other by an-
tagonists in war and peace, it is known as the nobility of noble natures.
And I mustn't forget courage, for there is neither prowess nor justice
without it. My fourth if it is important enough in comparison to be
worth bringing in, is knowledge, the mere information we can't get too
much of and can't ever get enough of, we complain, before going into
action.[15]

The athletic ideal, then, is a severe one. It suggests not only the
very essence of the concept of *aidos* but *Aretê* as well.

The Fragmentation

There was of course a remarkable disparity between Greek
ideals and Greek practice, as several students of ancient athletics
have pointed out. The Greeks hated to lose, and much more was
often given victors by way of reward than the mere wreath.
Moreover, "the chivalrous generosity" which we often see today
extended to the loser is, says Gardiner, a contribution of the
English, and Erich Segal argues that de Coubertin's philosophy,
"it is not the winning, but the taking part, not the conquering,
but the playing fair," is a distinct improvement over the Greek
attitude.[16]

There are, however, other matters to consider, especially
when viewing sport as part of culture. Since the Greek
philosophers neglected sport in general, one should not expect
to find in the corpus of ancient writings a manual on the art of
losing. Moreover, one does not think of the ideal athlete as losing anyway; and even if one persists in imagining such a case,
surely he would avoid insolence in defeat as well as in victory.
Whether we have improved over the Greeks in the practice of
sport is a matter of opinion. Undoubtedly modern athletes are
generally stronger and faster than those of the time of Socrates,
and more "sportsmanship" is evident after contests today than
was after the Olympic events in Greece. If, however, we have
surpassed them in these respects we are too much like them in
other ways, the wrong ways, especially in the lack of willingness
to uphold ideals.

There even appears to be a common pattern of fragmentation of ideals in western cultures, from epic qualities of strength
and wisdom to the more sophisticated but related ideal of
strength and beauty, from bromidism, brutality, and professionalism on the one hand and darlingness, preciousness, and
absurdity on the other—not that all of these cannot be mixed in
strange and endless ways. After the Homeric ideal of *sapientia et
fortitudo*,[17] one finds in sixth-century Greece the worship of
strength, in fifth-century the glorification of strength and
beauty, and thereafter a specialization noted by Plato and Aristotle.[18] In Anglo-Saxon culture the ideal of Beowulf is vitiated by
Appollonius of Tyre, Chaucer's Squire, and Troilus, all of whom
are darlings. Excluding perhaps Rupert Brooke, "the modern
Sidney," a memorable combination of strength and beauty was
never attained in England. There was not, in other words, a
happy cross between the strength and wisdom of Chaucer's
Knight ("And evermore he hadde a sovereyn prys./And though
that he were worthy, he was wys") and the prettiness of his son.
Philip Sidney, of course, following the Code of Castiglione's
Courtier, strove for versatility. "The darling of mankind," to use
Emerson's phrase, was Christian, poet, athlete, scholar, and soldier, but the portraits and engravings we have of him somehow
evoke pity instead of admiration.[19] The healthy and humanistic
recommendations of Roger Ascham, Montaigne, and Milton
seem to have met with little success, and Dr. Arnold's noble
attempts finally brought about a situation that Arnold himself
could probably never have imagined.

As Leslie Stephen predicted, the 1870's did not see the end of athleticism. In a sense athleticism as we are familiar with it today was only
then beginning. As the intellectuals lost interest in the controversy, *mens
sana in corpore sano* was abandoned to specialists: zealous headmasters
and physical culturists, physicians and professional sports promoters.
Not until the writers of the twentieth century began their revolt against
victorian ideals did the issue again become alive in any sense important
to the historian of ideas. The Bloomsbury intellectuals, using the public
schools as the focus for their attack upon the late victorian culture, held
the worship of games responsible for the failure of these institutions to
turn out truly enlightened young men.[20]

America has not had an Odysseus, Aeneas, or Beowulf, but we do have Natty Bumppo; and though in some places in the Leatherstocking novels he becomes a romantic type, he remains an epic hero, a good example of *sapientia et fortitudo*. Natty himself is well aware of these heroic qualities. Contrasting himself with the Bushes in *The Prairie*, he says, "The law is needed, when such as have not the gifts of strength and wisdom are to be taken care of." After Leatherstocking little is heard about strength and wisdom but a great deal about strength and beauty. Hawthorne was quite taken up with the matter as can be seen in *The Marble Faun*, but Donatello, "so handsome, so physically well developed" with "no impression of maimed or stinted nature," is not the combination of strength and beauty one admires. He is too faunish. For the ideal, one would choose instead Melville's "Handsome Sailor."

Invariably a proficient in his perilous calling, he was also more or less of a mighty boxer or wrestler. It was strength and beauty. Tales of his prowess were recited. Ashore he was the champion; afloat the spokesman; on every suitable occasion always foremost. Close-reefing topsails in a gale, there he was, astride the weather yardarm-end, foot in the Flemish horse as stirrup, both hands tugging at the earing as at a bridle, in very much the attitude of a young Alexander curbing the fiery Bucephalus. A superb figure, tossed up as by the horns of Taurus against the thunderous sky, cheerily hallooing to the strenuous file along the spar.[21]

The moral nature of the "Handsome Sailor," a black, is in keeping with his physical nature, and, as in the classic ideal, the two are finally indistinguishable. Black, then, can be beautiful but so can white when done up right, for Billy Budd was also a "Handsome Sailor":

[He] showed in face that humane look of reposeful good nature which the Greek sculptor in some instances gave to his heroic strong man, Hercules. But this again was subtly modified by another and pervasive quality. The ear, small and shapely, the arch of the foot, the curve in mouth and nostril, even the indurated hand dyed to the orange-tawny of the toucan's bill, a hand telling alike of the halyards and tar bucket; but, above all, something in the mobile expression, and every chance attitude and movement, something suggestive of a mother eminently favored by love and the Graces; all this strangely indicated a lineage in direct contradiction to his lot. (p. 51)

What Melville is describing is the quality of *aidos*, that humility and modesty which does not degenerate into self-effacement, the same spiritual attribute that informs so much of the poetry of Walt Whitman, who called himself "the teacher of athletes" and who rhapsodized unabashedly:

> Thou, thou, the ideal Man,
> Fair, able, beautiful, content, and loving
> Complete in body and dilate in spirit,
> Be thou my God.[22]

There is little difference between the ideal of Melville and Whitman and that of Mark Twain, who, in *Roughing It,* also announced "myriad of youths, beautiful, gigantic, sweet blooded."

It was a curious population. It was the only population of the kind that the world has ever seen gathered together, and it is not likely that the world will ever see its like again. For, observe, it was an assemblage of two hundred thousand young men—not simpering, dainty, kid-gloved weaklings, but stalwart, muscular, dauntless young braves, brimful of push and energy, and royally endowed with every attribute that goes to make up a peerless and magnificent manhood—the very pick and choice of the world's glorious ones. No women, no children, no gray and stooping veterans—none but the erect, bright-eyed, quick-moving, strong-handed young giants—the strangest population, the finest population, the most gallant host that ever trooped down the startled solitudes of an unpeopled land.[23]

Mark Twain's description of the California miners, because it is exaggerated, provides an excellent summary of the characteristics of the ideal of manhood in the latter half of the nineteenth century. Mark Twain's image is masculine, but one should note how ingeniously he has used certain terms, "young," "royally endowed," "peerless," "magnificent," "bright-eyed," and "glorious," to soften the image and give it beauty. These young men are closer to the Discus Thrower than they are to actual prospectors.

But if Mark Twain has lied in his picture of the miners, he has done so nobly and with great skill, for maintaining that delicate balance between strength and beauty is perhaps the most difficult tightrope act in writing. After Mark Twain only a few succeeded, and F. Scott Fitzgerald is not one who did. Note, for instance, how in "The Ice Palace" the host tries to impress a southern belle by pointing out to her some of the Ivy League stars from the Midwest. "They're a good looking crowd, don't you think? . . . Just look around. There's Spud Hubbard, tackle at Princeton last year, and Junie Morton—he and the red-haired fellow next to him were both Yale hockey captains; Junie was in my class. Why, the best athletes in the world come from these states around here. This is a man's country, I tell you."[24] Had Mark Twain been around he would have laughed at the host's idea of "a man's country." One of his muscular, dauntless, erect, bright-eyed, quick-moving, strong-handed young giants could have licked a whole room full of "Junies," "Spuds," and "red-haired fellows," just as Beowulf could have taken thirty Christian knights, excepting Galahad who had the strength of ten, and Achilles, a whole gymnasium full of fifth-century Greek youths oiling and massaging themselves and listening to flute players as they exercised in the nude.

Between the time of *Roughing It* and that of "The Ice Palace" the concept of masculinity underwent significant change. Ironically, the ideal of strength and beauty lost credence at the same time that the athlete began to challenge the western hero in popularity. It is difficult to generalize and exceptions are numerous, but these statements can, I believe, be substantiated fairly well.

In many ways the ideal of the superman of strength and beauty died with Nietzsche; and Victorian intellectuals have by this time allowed *mens sana in corpore sano* to be taken over by professionals. Jack London can be cited here for examples of support. In *The Game* (1905) Joe Fleming, symbol of strength and beauty, though not a very good one, is killed by a bruiser, and in *The Abysmal Brute* (1913) the blond, blue-eyed young god, "the last hope of the white race," retires to the hills after knocking out the world's heavyweight champion in a very unusual encounter.

Mark Twain also saw what was happening. In *Roughing It* he

could express his ideal, but by 1906 he could only tell what was not his ideal.

I am Buffalo Bill's horse. I have spent my life under his saddle—with him in it, too, and he is good for two hundred pounds, without his clothes; and there is no telling how much he does weigh when he is out on the war path and has all of his batteries belted on. He is over six feet, is young, hasn't an ounce of waste flesh, is straight, graceful, springy in his motions, quick as a cat, and has a handsome face, and black hair dangling down on his shoulders, and is beautiful to look at; and nobody is braver than he and nobody is stronger, except myself.[25]

Nowhere in history perhaps has strength and beauty been so distorted as in William Cody, and it is doubtful if anyone has captured his darlingness so well as Mark Twain. By the turn of the century Cody's fortunes began to wane,[26] at approximately the same time that another star was appearing on the horizon—Frank Merriwell. Created in 1896, Frank to some extent replaced Cody and other heroes of the plains as a popular ideal, a fact that, according to Frank's creator, was deliberately planned.

Believing the old-fashioned dime novel was on its way out, I decided to set a new style with my stories and make them different and more in step with the times. As the first issues were to be stories of American school life, I saw in them the opportunity to feature all kinds of athletic sports, with baseball, about which I was best informed, predominating.
     Such stories would give me the opportunity to preach—by example—the doctrine of a clean mind in a clean and healthy body.[27]

Since Frank properly belongs to juvenile literature, he is not included in the study; but because of the influence he has had upon the athlete hero in America, he deserves a few remarks here. "Of all the athletic heroes who have ever appeared on the American scene," says Robert Boyle, "probably none ever aroused the admiration or left so enduring an impression [as Frank Merriwell]."[28] Frank was, quite simply, the most all-round man that ever appeared in American print. "He was a whiz at boxing, baseball (his 'double shoot,' which curved in both directions, was always good in the clutch); football, hockey, lacrosse, crew, track, shooting, bicycle racing, billiards, golf—in fact any sport he deigned to play" (p. 241). Moreover, he stood for "truth, faith, justice, the triumph of right, mother, home, friendship, loyalty, patriotism, the love of alma mater, duty, sacrifice, retribution and strength of soul as well as body. Frank was manly; he had 'sand'" (p. 242).

It has been estimated that sales of Merriwell novels approached 500 million.[29] In addition Frank has been on radio as well as in the movies and comics. Among his many admirers have been Franklin P. Adams, Jess Willard, Floyd Gibbons, Jack Dempsey, Christy Mathewson, Woodrow Wilson, Al Smith, Wendell Willkie, Babe Ruth, George Jean Nathan, and Westbrook Pegler.[30] American authors who admittedly read Patten's works were James T. Farrell and Sinclair Lewis, and from the following description of Andy Lockheart in "The Captured Shadow" one can probably assume that F. Scott Fitzgerald did also. "Winner of the western Golf Championship at eighteen, captain of the freshman baseball team, handsome, successful at everything he tried, a living symbol of the splendid glamorous world of Yale."[31] Throughout the study one will see shades of Frank, but never another quite like him.

Around the turn of the century, then, the fragmentation of the ideal of strength and beauty was increasingly remarked in fiction, *mens sana in corpore sano* was popularized in subliterature—and hence vitiated—by a young athlete specifically created to replace the western heroes of dime novels. The White House was occupied by a scholarly president who proclaimed values of athletic training and called a conference to correct abuses in football. Crowds at athletic events grew year by year and the athletic hero began to experience an adulation that equaled, if not surpassed, that bestowed upon the western hero. In short, the trends were such as to continue to evoke the reaction of American writers over the coming decades. The thrust of this reaction, as I will demonstrate, is both condemnation and praise of the athlete and his admirers, condemnation because of adherence to shallow forms of the union of mind and body and also of mindless merging with nature, and praise for the heroic endurance that suggests infinite becoming and hence infinite possibilities. The encompassing and controlling myths through which this blame and praise are registered and by which the athlete is measured and understood are the Apollonian, Dionysian, and Adonic. Let me begin with the Apollonians, and among the most familiar of all seekers of glory, power, and prestige are Ring Lardner's bushers, especially Busher Keefe.

2. Apollo

The Dumb Athlete

For whatever reason, spoofing of spurious heroes and their codes has almost consistently appeared after the particular convention ridiculed had become obsolete or was becoming so. As has frequently been remarked, Falstaff and Don Quixote came onto the scene after chivalric pretense had had its day; Samuel Butler appears to have waited for the comparative safety of the Restoration to debunk the Presbyterian knight; and Henry Fielding with *Tom Thumb* was, according to Bonamy Dobree, "whipping a dying dog" with his satire of bombast in the age of Dryden. Similarly, Buffalo Bill was on his way out when Mark Twain showed the superiority of his horse.

In his abhorrence of sham Ring Lardner had much in common with these authors, but unlike them he did not wait until the material for his satire had become dated. When Jack Keefe made his first appearance in the *Saturday Evening Post* in 1914, the concept of the all-round man, symbolized so magnificently by Frank Merriwell in fiction and by Teddy Roosevelt and Jack London in real life, had become something of a cult; and Lardner's work, instead of being a coup de grace, was more of a coup de main.

Those were the days when the manager of a baseball team was regarded as a combination of captain of finance . . . A Freud, and an unborn Einstein. A fine body of college graduates, clean-living, sport-loving, well-read boys were the players, and a sport-loving game-for-the-game's sake body of men the enthusiasts. Hughie Fullerton and Paul Elmer More might be seen any day in the same column, and John J. McGraw, who allowed himself to be called Muggsy to show what a good democrat he was, lunched daily at the President's table. Into this pretentious parade Mr. Lardner injected the busher—and baseball has never recovered.[1]

The influence of Frank Merriwell on the image of the baseball hero, as Seldes suggests, had been enormous, as can be seen in the phrases "clean-living," "sport-loving," "well-read," and "game-for-the-game's sake"; but the influence of Lardner's bushers became even greater. "Dizzy Dean wasn't born," Heywood Broun said, "Ring Lardner invented him."[2] With this one must agree in part, for the following quatrain by Ogden Nash could not be fully appreciated had not Lardner long before made famous the archetype of the bragging, ungrammatical hurler:

> D is for Dean
> The Grammatical Diz
> When they asked, who's the tops?
> Said correctly I is.[3]

In a sense Lardner's Busher actually replaced Frank; for in 1914, the year of Busher's debut in the *Saturday Evening Post*, Frank disappeared from the pages of *Tip Top Weekly* after a run of eighteen years. Though fortuitous, this change of heroes was partly symbolic. Frank and the eastern college hero were to be around for some years to come, but in Lardner's stories the uneducated man, usually from the South or the Midwest, is seen stepping forth for his share of the applause. Lardner dealt with the busher almost exclusively, seeming in fact to have been almost unaware of the type of college athlete about whom his neighbor Fitzgerald was to write.[4] Jack Keefe tells a Red Cross nurse overseas that he had been to Harvard on two different occasions, but surely no one could mistake Jack for an Ivy Leaguer.

To many critics, however, Keefe with all his pretensions is not so comic as insidious. Stuart Sherman calls him "the all-American 'boob,' two-fisted, pig-headed, a liar, braggart in victory, whining in defeat, greedy for money, callous, brutal, intemperate in food and drink, and gorgeously pleased with himself in every relation of life."[5] Clifton Fadiman says that he is not only "slow-witted" and "conceited" but "heartless" as well.

To Gilbert Seldes, Busher was "simply a roughneck and a fool, a braggart and a liar." From these comments one might conclude that the White Sox right-hander is depicted as unfavorably as any character in American fiction. Such a view, however, must be tempered.

That Busher has his faults of character is certain as any one of his letters to friend Al will make plain, but he does have some redeeming qualities. He pays his debts, though slowly, loves his child (even though the child is a left-hander), is faithful to his wife—no small virtue in his eyes since he considers himself irresistible to women—and he would not throw a game. Moreover, he is quite funny. His braggadocio demands a certain license and to look too closely at his many faults is perhaps a bit unfair. In "Champion" Lardner will reveal a viciousness in dealing with boxers, but the manner of his treatment of baseball players, with rare exceptions, is no closer in tone to Swift than to Cervantes. Perhaps in all the literature of satire no writer has ever been so consistently detached from his material as Lardner.

The characteristic of Busher lampooned most by Lardner is Busher's versatility. In his own eyes at least, Busher is unsurpassable, especially on the mound.[6] But his talents are not limited to the diamond. After his celebrated exploits in *You Know Me Al* Busher in *Treat 'em Rough* and *The Real Dope* goes overseas and in the tradition of the braggart soldier of Plautus and Shakespeare considers himself a born leader and a great strategist. In the regimental newspaper published "somewheres in France" he writes an article entitled "War and Baseball: Two Games Where Brains Win." Such a stir is caused by the article that Busher receives a letter supposedly from General Pershing asking for his advice. Busher, of course, is glad to help in any way, and he concludes his letter to the general on a note of optimism. "I note what you say about our name being both Jack and I was thinking to myself that lots of time in a poker game a pair of jacks is enough to win and maybe it will be the same way in the war game and anyway I guess the two of us will put up a good bluff and bet them just as if we had them. Eh gen?"[7] Fortunately for the allied cause Jack never gets a chance to confer in person with the general.

Busher loses some of his humor when Lardner takes him out of the ball park. Like Huck Finn he is never quite the same when away from his natural surroundings, but neither his vanity nor his ability to rationalize ever diminishes. In Busher's view there is no field of endeavor in which he cannot excel; and those undertakings in which he falls short, like learning French and making the Camp Grant football team are not, in his opinion, worth doing anyway. Busher is a megalomaniac who is as often disturbing as he is funny, mainly because he is a new literary figure in America, the buffoon traveling around the world without his aristocratic master. Lord Raglan, for instance, points out abundant evidence of the comic braggart in Greek, Arab, and Indian mythology, and in medieval literature.[8] Basically the same character appears in the tall tales of the old Southwest, especially as seen in the unmitigated world-beater Mark Twain writes about in *Life on the Mississippi* and the aspiring country bumpkin as portrayed in some of the versions of Davy Crockett. The bloodlines, though with mutations, extend down to Lardner's cockalorum athletes, who are seen in a different light from that of any fools preceding them. Whereas no one ever took the braggart soldier and the master of the tall tale for anything other than what they ostensibly were, many critics have found in Lardner's self-inflated semiliterate not so much a humorous character as a sobering symbol of American culture. Nothing can quite compare with the concern expressed by Maxwell Geismar, whose view is fairly typical, in his evaluation of the Lardner hero. "Conceit is the center of Lardner's humanity. The U.S. Champion, master of one field, believed himself master of all, and the U.S. Mediocrity believed himself a champion. In Lardner's view the bombastic American ego always aspired to exceed its own potentialities and all other potentialities too. Beside this contemporary conqueror, Marlowe's mighty Tamburlaine was an Elizabethan ne'r do well."[9]

In Busher Keefe especially, one sees not only the bombastic American ego attempting to exceed all potentialities but also the usurpation of the powers and privileges of the extinct royal hero. One should not be sorry that the buffoon has survived, but it is perhaps unfortunate that his companion is no longer around to make his limitations so comically obvious by contrast that no critic could fail to laugh at all his grandiose undertakings.

All Lardner's characters appear to be conceived from what might be called a Hobbesian point of view, which holds that man in his natural state is a rather deplorable creature, laughable as a "rube" or "hayseed" when his aspirations obviously exceed his abilities but nevertheless vicious underneath and perhaps harmless only in make-believe situations such as games. It is a satiric view that has virtually disappeared in the literature of sports since the creations of Lardner, Runyon, and Thurber. In more recent years it can be noted only in the treatment of such minor characters as Hut Sut Sutter in Mark Harris's *Bang the Drum Slowly* and T. J. (for "Torn Jock") Lambert in Dan Jenkins's *Semi-Tough*. Both Hut Sut and Torn Jock are football players from southern universities and are obviously intended as comical parodies (which they are) of the student athlete in their particular forms of specialization, Hut Sut being an expert in hunting up whorehouses and Torn Jock, a champion wind-breaker.

Such satire is not the manner of Lardner, and not simply because he abhorred smutty tales. Jenkins, and Mark Harris on occasion, are irreverent, but Lardner was indifferent. T. J.'s prowess reminds one of the outrageous tales of Rabelais, Swift, and Mark Twain. Indeed the huge end would have been right at home in the Elizabethan court of Mark Twain's *1601*. Few writers, with the notable exception of Dan Jenkins, are writing satire of sport anymore, and the situation is especially obvious in the case of baseball. Is it that the game and players are no longer subjects for humor or is it merely that no one has the sustained satiric vision of Ring Lardner? Mark Harris is not entirely wrong when he challenges Donald Elder's statement that Ring Lardner's stories exhibit "strict realism in their language and conception of character," but he is not entirely right when he goes on to say that "caricature renders people and the scene unreal."[10] Caricature may not provide verisimilitude, but it does provide meaning, as anyone who has read the novels of Flannery O'Connor will agree. What Mark Harris in his astute evaluation of Lardner fails to do fully is to grant Lardner his donnée.

Lardner employed what Northrop Frye calls "the ironic mode," in which the hero is "inferior in power and intelligence to ourselves, so that we have a sense of looking down on a scene of bondage, frustration, and absurdity." What Mark Harris does in his own baseball novels is to use the "low mimetic mode," in which, according to Frye, "the hero is one of us: we respond to a sense of his common humanity and demand . . . the same canons of probability that we find in our own experience." Thus Mark Harris gives us highly credible and endearing characters such as Henry Wiggen, as does Jim Brosnan who wrote from personal experiences.

Lardner succeeded so well that no one could top him in baseball fiction in the ironic mode; hence the flowering in the last quarter of a century of other modes, Malamud's *The Natural* (the mythic mode), Robert Coover's *The Universal Baseball Association* (the romantic mode), and Philip Roth's *The Great American Novel* (a combination of both). Certainly baseball needed to be expanded in other directions from that begun by Lardner, but one wonders now if it is not time for a return to the ironic, if sentiment and nostalgia have not had their turns, and if there is not a need to determine if modern baseball is as devoid of humor and absurdity as we are led to believe by the sports pages and television commentators. I suspect that baseball is as rich in ironic material as it always has been, but it will take a perceptive intelligence indeed to uncover the wealth, and it will take more than the talent of a Jim Bouton to report it, though Bouton should be applauded for reminding us in *Ball Four* that the lore is still there. It is a lore that will yield to many methods of mining, but when the ironic is tried again, those doing so will still find the man from Niles, Michigan, standing astride the genre like a colossus, casting an intimidating shadow that demands lasting respect if not plain awe. A variety of other approaches have now been tried, but as yet no one has surpassed Lardner in the one that he chose. What we need to keep in mind in evaluating the overall scene is that no one mode has a monopoly on meaning, that realism, sentiment, or myth do not guarantee any more understanding of the human condition than irony, and sometimes perhaps not as much, as is often the case when Lard-

ner's stories are placed beside the efforts of those who have
followed him, regardless of the mode adopted.

There is undeniably a decline in quality of Lardner's sports
writing over the years, but it came about when Lardner, for
whatever reason, began to allow sentiment to replace irony. For
over thirteen years after the last of the Busher stories Lardner
wrote little about athletes, and when he returned to baseball with
Lose with a Smile (1932), he was a different Lardner. The enigmatic quality and toughness are still there, but the mask is now thin.
The whole novel in fact is slightly sentimental and sad, and
Danny Warner, the hero in search of the American dream, is, in
the southern idiom, "plumb pitiful." Pathetic as he is, however,
he too has a distorted view of his capacities. Like Keefe he thinks
himself as a lover, and throughout the novel he considers leaving baseball and becoming a crooner. He is not, however, good
enough for either major league ball or the "crooning business,"
but through one of his lyrics he comes up with the best advice
that his creator can give.

> Some people take life serious
> in stead of a game to play
> If they only would not take it so serious
> But more like a game to play.
> I try and laugh at the hard knocks
> like you get in a base ball game
> so wether your with St. Louis or the red Sox
> smile and don't be a shame.[11]

One can laugh at Danny, as can be seen from the song, but
most of the time he has a way of making the reader a little glum,
unless he is talking about or quoting one of the game's most
famous figures, Casey Stengel. In fact Casey seems at times to
serve the function of comic relief. Here is one way in which
Casey, who is always "sane things like that witch don't make no
sense," manages to dispel some of the gloom and mawkishness
of Danny's letters: "Stengel told me that he was acquaint it with
the mgr of Irving Berlins music Company and promise he would
take me there and see what they thot of that song I wrote Life is
just a game of base ball. So we stopped there yesterday noon and
Stengel ast to see Mr. Schwartz and the girl says they didn't have

no Mr. Schwartz and Stengel says what the hell kind of a music publishing Company is this?" (p. 102)

Not only is Casey humorous in his unique form of double talk (Stengelese) but he is also kind. His treatment of Danny is generous throughout. He throws the gold digger Vivian Duane off Danny's trail and attempts to get Danny to marry Jessie and to make a career of baseball. But even when giving advice of the most serious nature, Casey cannot refrain from displaying his comic powers, as Danny reveals in one of his most despondent letters. "I says she aint libel to want me now that Brooklyn says I aint good enough and Stengel says she is just the kind of a girl that would want you all the more and what aint good enough for Brooklyn is good enough for any body" (pp. 170–71). If there is a genuine hero in Lardner's work, it is Casey, a man who appears to have taken baseball for what it is, not as a Big Deal, but as a "game to play."

In order better to understand Lardner's attitude toward the athlete hero in America one should also look at his nonfiction, particularly at his essay "Sport and Play," for here too Lardner lashes out at the foolish adoration of mere reflexes. With Stuart Sherman he agrees obviously that "we do not know how to play [mainly] because (1) we lack imagination, and because (2) we are a nation of hero-worshippers."[12] Lardner thus became one of the first major critics of American life to deplore that form of hero-worship which exalts Babe Ruth and Jack Dempsey but neglects men whose contributions to society have been far more significant. Dixon Wecter was in effect only echoing Lardner (and in a sense Isocrates) two decades later when he wrote: "No doctor has ever become a first-class hero to the American people. Walter Reed and William Gorgas as victors over yellow fever, Osler as a brilliant adopted son, Harvey Cushing as the pioneer of brain surgery, and among the older generation even Oliver Wendell Holmes as the innovator of asepsis to check puerperal fever—these men have received less personal adoration than Lindbergh or Jack Dempsey or Babe Ruth."[13]

At the heart of the problem, Lardner realized, were the people. A society is and always has been defined best by its heroes; and if our heroes range from Thomas Jefferson to outlaws, then we are, as has been remarked many times, a diverse

people but on the whole rather decadent, as indicated by the
number of "surface heroes" and "celebrities"[14] now held in esteem.

Lardner simply distrusted the taste and judgment of the masses, who long for the miraculous and sensational in sports as well
as in religion, drama, fiction, and movies. His most trenchant
satire in fact is directed not at the heroes but at the worshipers,
the faithful fans. In "Take a Walk" he compares them to wolves,
but in *Lose with a Smile* he compares them to another animal.

Some of the boys has got nick names like wear they come from like 1 of
the pitchers Clyde Day but they call him Pea ridge Day because he come
from a town name Pea ridge and he was the champion hog caller of
Arkansaw and when he use to pitch in Brooklyn last year he use to give
a hog call after every ball he throwed but the club made him cut it out
because the fans come down on the field every time he gave a call and
the club had to hire the champion of Iowa to set up in the stand and call
them back.[15]

Where, may I ask, is such satire today?

If Lardner found so much wrong with sports, why did he not
turn to something else altogether? Why after more than a decade of comparative silence did he bring out Danny Warner, Max
Carey, and Casey Stengel and take another vicious sock at fan-
dom? These questions are formidable, but well-known writers
and critics have attempted answers that show how inextricably
sports and society in America are related. Clifton Fadiman
thought that sports provided Lardner a way to draw together
"bonehead and sharper" in order to indict "large areas of
American life." Virginia Woolf's view did not greatly differ,
being only more politely phrased: "It is no coincidence that the
best of Mr. Lardner's stories are about games, for one may guess
that Mr. Lardner's interest in games has solved one of the most
difficult problems of the American writer; it has given him a
clue, a centre, a meeting place for the divers activities of people
whom a vast continent isolates, whom no tradition controls.
Games give him what society gives his English brother." Later
Woolf adds, but not insultingly, "In America there is baseball
instead of society."[16]

Fitzgerald seems to have hit closest to the heart of the matter.

It was never that he was completely sold on athletic virtuosity as the be-all and end-all of problems; the trouble was that he could find nothing finer. Imagine life conceived as a business of beautiful muscular organization—an arising, an effort, a good break, a sweat, a bath, a meal, a love, a sleep—imagine it achieved; then imagine trying to apply that standard to the horribly complicated mess of living, where nothing, even the greatest conceptions and workings and achievements, is else but messy, spotty, tortuous—and then one can imagine the confusion that Ring faced on coming out of the ball park.[17]

What Fitzgerald says here of Lardner holds true for many athlete heroes. Not being able to face the tribulations of off-field living, they try to go back to athletics but inevitably fail. This is part of their tragedy. Being a writer, Ring Lardner could go back to the ball park, but his tragedy was that the world of baseball had become too much like the rest of the world, had in fact become "tortuous." Sometime before the end of his life Lardner was caught between businessmen and bridge players on the one hand and dull, uninteresting, mammon-minded ball players and their worshipers on the other. Finally, he was left with no place to turn. Somehow all the novels of despair of the lost generation do not affect one so much as the thought of tough-minded Ring Lardner weeping over his typewriter. One believes with Sherwood Anderson that there was in him not only a "quick sharp stinging hunger for beauty" but also, as Fitzgerald implies, a hunger for strength and beauty, as there was in Melville; and one also believes that Lardner would have agreed with E. M. Forster, who, before Busher Keefe burst on the American scene, wrote, "There is no abiding home for strength and beauty among men. The flower fades, the seas dry up in the sun, the sun and all the stars fade as a flower. But the desire for such things, that is eternal."[18] In the athlete Lardner found a fraction of the eternal ideal. In him he at least found physical strength, a prowess, and perhaps the shadow of the real thing.

If Ring Lardner invented the dumb pitcher from the boonies, James Thurber might well be the inventor of the dumb tackle with the foreign-sounding name in Bolenciecwcz, one of the "outstanding stars" at Ohio State. In order to remain eligible to play, Bolenciecwcz must keep up his grades, "a very difficult matter, for while he was not dumber than an ox he was not any smarter." Everyone supports Bolenciecwcz, however, so there is little chance of his failing. In economics class he is asked only to name "one means of transportation"; and when it appears that he is stumped, the professor, Mr. Bassum, adds, "any agency or method of going from one place to another." Still Bolenciecwcz finds no clue, and Mr. Bassum finds himself saying "Choo-choo-choo" and "ding, dong, ding, dong," while a student imitates a locomotive letting off steam. In spite of all, Bolenciecwcz cannot come up with the answer, and Mr. Bassum must lead him out of the maze.

"How did you get to college this year, Mr. Bolenciecwcz?" asked the professor. "Chuffa chuffa, chuffa chuffa."
"M' father sent me," said the football player.
"What on?" asked Bassum.
"I git an 'lowance," said the tackle, in a low husky voice, obviously embarrassed.
"No, no," said Bassum. "Name a means of transportation. What did you ride here on?"
"Train," said Bolenciecwcz.
"Quite right," said the professor.[19]

While this dialogue is unquestionably funny, it is also sad, for in it can be seen everything that is wrong with athletics in the schools. At the heart of the problem is the marriage of the concept of the all-round man with the philosophy of winning at all cost. Bolenciecwcz illustrates the problem well. Ohio State must beat Illinois so that the coaches can keep their jobs and make the alumni happy. Bolenciecwcz must be eligible to play, for he is an outstanding star; but he is also a student. Thus between football and school Bolenciecwcz must be an all-round man. Football demands that he be strong, which he is; school demands that he display a certain amount of knowledge, a task in which he must be assisted. If, however, beating Illinois were not so important, if other values were held in esteem, the demands upon Bolenciecwcz would be correspondingly reduced. First Bolenciecwcz would quit football to concentrate on his studies in which, even with the assistance of Mr. Bassum, he would fail. Then he would leave Ohio State and take up some occupation more commensurate with his intelligence. What happens, however, is that Bolen-ciecwcz will somehow graduate, go into coaching, and, remembering his own experiences, will tell his boys how important it is to study hard in order to remain eligible. Eligibility, not excellence, becomes the touchstone.

But Bolenciecwcz is not really to blame. He is a victim. He has been told no doubt that he "must keep up his grades," that he must be a "student-athlete," that, as a football player, he must set an example for others. In any event Bolenciecwcz simply is not equipped for such a task; he thus takes shortcuts that corrupt the ideal of the philosopher-athlete. Bolenciecwcz's shortcuts consists of help from Mr. Bassum and other students, but his counterpart today may take advantage of private tutors and courses that seem to have been created for him. Bolenciecwcz's own schedule sounds relatively respectable, botany, physics, and economics, but like Thurber, he gets the classes mixed up.

Now what about *Mr. Bassum*? Both the name and the man are significant. The first letter of the professor's name is, like the consonant p, made with closed lips, the difference being that p is voiceless and b is not. Thus one can easily imagine the name of Bolenciecwcz's professor being "Passum." If this were not intended by Thurber, it is Mr. Bassum's intent to "passum." This Thurber tells us. "Most of the professors were lenient and helped him along." Carrying possibilities still further by using the British broad "a" in pronunciation, one obtains "Possum," thereby indicating one who has closed his eyes to the dangers around him. Let him, then, be called "Mr. Possum."

Mr. Possum is nothing less than a symbol of the American professor who has either closed his eyes to, laughed at, or actively promoted the burlesque represented by Bolenciecwcz. He is, then, more reprehensible than Bolenciecwcz: He saw what was happening and yet he deliberately contributed to the breakdown of standards. Why then did he do it? There are a number of possible answers, but the chances are that Mr. Possum is simply a victim of the great American philosophy of Helping Hand, which holds that education is a type of obstacle course that must be run by everyone. Since then it is required of all, it does not seem too immoral—almost virtuous in fact—to help the crippled around some of the more difficult hurdles. This philosophy, though ruinous, is actually Christian in spirit and communal in outlook, facts that might well explain why America's greatest athlete hero was also a Mr. Possum. Specifically, reference is made to Frank Merriwell whose first day at Yale was, as Robert Boyle notes, anything but exemplary.

Frank's conduct on entering Yale is strangely out of character. Before kicking the dog, he helps Rattleton cheat on the entrance exam: "Harry and Frank were seated close to each other, and the latter saw that the boy from Ohio was completely stumped over some question whereupon Frank took to writing the answers on tiny pieces of paper and snapping them across in the form of wads. Harry caught on in a moment and skillfully secured each wad, opening them as fast as they came. When the right one came along he nodded a bit and looked satisfied." Informed of this shocking behavior, Joseph Graham, the president and beloved founder of the Friends of Frank Merriwell, said, "Rattleton was known as a nervous type, and Frank probably only slipped him hints. I'm sure that Frank wrote in one of the notes 'Calm down, Harry. You knew the answers last night.' " But when told that this was the first time Frank had seen Rattleton and that the two did not meet and become roommates until *after* the exam, Graham exclaimed, "Gee Whiz!"[20]

Like Frank, Mr. Possum is an understanding person, a sincere human being. He genuinely wants to make a contribution and never sees himself as a subverter of values. There are many professor possums, far more than anyone realizes.

Sometimes, a professor possum may wake up, see the error of his ways, and repent. Gary Shaw speaks of such a one in *Meat on the Hoof*. "I [the anonymous professor quoted] have since found it necessary to completely divorce myself from any connections with the football program at Texas. I have realized that my aim of aiding in the education of students is in direct conflict with the football program's aims of bypassing an education. The football program at Texas has absolutely nothing to do with a university's proper function, and I am saddened by the fact that the university professors are among those this program smoothly uses to its own ends."[21]

But what can be done in the way of change? Very little it seems, for Bolenciecwcz has become one of America's inverted heroes. Jokes about dumb tackles who have trouble passing to stay eligible are part of our way of life. There is a healthy need for the buffoon, even in college. While comic enough, Bolen-ciecwcz, dumb tackle, and Keefe, dumb pitcher, nevertheless symbolize the inversion of an ideal of completeness. Keefe believes that he can do the impossible; Bolenciecwcz finds that he must. He must pass in order to play, must be something of an all-round man if only a caricature, which is precisely what he is. Both he and Keefe are monumental jokes who have grown out of an area of our life that we take entirely too seriously—our games.

The Sporting Gentleman

When F. Scott Fitzgerald lamented Ring Lardner's long association with a "few dozen illiterates," it was almost a case of the pot calling the kettle black. Never would Fitzgerald have thought of writing about athletes with the intelligence of bushers, but his fascination with the Ivy League football players makes Lardner's attachment to the White Sox pale by comparison. Between the two, they virtually destroyed the image of the athlete as a hero of strength, intelligence, depth, and feeling. If in Lardner's works the busher moves into the province of the aristocratic hero, in Fitzgerald's is seen a major reason why: the general disappearance of this hero. Basil Lee Duke, Andy Lockheart, Ted Fay, Brick Wales, Amory Blaine, Allenby, Dudley Knowleton, and Samuel Meredith, all these clean-living, all-round, upperclass heroes and would-be heroes are superseded and overshadowed by Tom Buchanan of *The Great Gatsby*, who betrays their class. Just as Keefe towers over Lardner's other bushers, so Buchanan, "one of the most powerful ends that ever played for New Haven," dwarfs the rest of Fitzgerald's players and relegates them to Fitzgerald's fairyland.

An understanding of Buchanan is crucial to the understanding of the titular hero. A symbol of the worldly ideal and the moral and cultural vacuity of one type of American dream, he has everything Gatsby longs for: a home in East Egg, family background, a degree from a famous university, wealth, athletic prowess, Daisy, and, in sum, the green light Gatsby worshiped. Everything about him is designed to make Gatsby and others run faster, work harder, and cheat more, but at the same time he is too formidable to be overcome. During the hotel party in which Gatsby states his claim, Buchanan overwhelms him with insult after insult which his physique and social position allow him to make. "I suppose the latest thing is to sit back and let Mr. Nobody from Nowhere make love to your wife," and "you must have gone there [Oxford] about the time Biloxie went to New Haven."[22] His scorn of Gatsby never abates. Addressing Daisy in the hotel before the accident, he says, "Go on. . . . He won't annoy you. I think he realizes that his presumptuous little flirtation is over." Gatsby's flirtation is over, both with Daisy and the Bitch Goddess of Success. "I have an idea," says Carraway, "that Gatsby himself didn't believe it [the message from Daisy] would come, and perhaps he no longer cared. If that was true he must have felt that he had lost the old warm world, paid a high price for living too long with a single dream" (p. 194).

The point of the novel is that Buchanan, the dream, is a nightmare; the green light, a false one. A surface hero, Buchanan has everything but soul and intelligence. He beats Daisy, breaks Mrs. Wilson's nose with his open hand, worries constantly over the rise of the Negro, and in the face of tragedy is revoltingly mawkish. "And if you think I didn't have my share of suffering," he says to Carraway in reference to Mrs. Wilson's death, "look here, when I went to give up that flat and saw that damn box of dog biscuits sitting there on the sideboard, I sat down and cried like a baby. By God it was awful" (pp. 216–17). The irony in this speech cannot be put into words, and Carraway no doubt would agree. "I couldn't forgive him or like him," Carraway says, "but I saw that what he had done was, to him, entirely justified. It was all very careless and confused. They were careless people, Tom and Daisy—they smashed up things and creatures and then retreated back into their money or their vast carelessness, or whatever it was that kept them together, and let other people clean up the mess they had made" (p. 216). If there is a term that can with accuracy be applied to the class of gridders represented by Buchanan, it is indeed "carelessness." It was no doubt this carelessness, this cruel cavalierism, that Maxwell Perkins recognized. "I would know Tom Buchanan," he said, "if I met him on the street and would avoid him."

Buchanan is certainly a person to avoid. In addition to all his

other negative traits, he is the legendary Ivy League hero gone
to seed. With his "great pack of muscle" and his "cruel body" he
suggests the Farnese Hercules and the professional athletes of
the Roman Empire. Stripped, he, along with so many weight-
lifting college and professional gridders, would not be out of
place among the athletes on the mosaic found in the baths of
Caracalla at Rome. Physically and morally he is the antithesis
of the ideal of strength and beauty.

The truth is that there is not in Fitzgerald anywhere a good
example of strength and beauty. He himself worshiped the ideal
but could not personify it in his fiction. In his characterization of
athletes he moves from the boyishness of Amory Blaine to the
brutality of Buchanan without capturing at any point the golden
mean. Fitzgerald was perhaps too tender, too mercurial, too
concerned with his own masculinity to create a character who
even comes close to resembling Billy Budd or the ideal of Whitman or Mark Twain. But though none of his boy heroes embody
the ideal, they constantly suggest it and possess qualities that are
indeed admirable. These are best enumerated by John Davies,
who in describing Hobie Baker describes the athlete hero
Fitzgerald most admired.

To a generation brought up on Frank Merriwell this [Baker's incredible
athletic ability] was heady wine: a combination of Tom Brown and Sir
Galahad, a clear case of life imitating art: the superb athlete, mannered,
modest, handsome, who was actually a gentleman and an amateur and a
sportsman. His Princeton contemporary, F. Scott Fitzgerald, remembered him as "an ideal worthy of everything in my enthusiastic admiration, yet consummated and expressed in a human being who stood
within ten feet of me." [Davies points out that Fitzgerald patterned
Allenby and to some extent Amory after Baker in *This Side of Paradise*.]
When he was killed in France in 1918, the "old-fashioned" virtues he
personified took on a legendary, eternal quality.[23]

Baker, the Philadelphia aristocrat and All-American in the same
backfield with Jim Thorpe, seems more fictional than real and
Buchanan more real than fictional. What has happened, ironically, is that the Tom Buchanans have survived in reality while
the Bakers with their "old-fashioned virtues" have passed on to
the realm of the good and the great. Perhaps the Buchanans

have become less common in the East but not elsewhere. There is, for instance, not a great deal of difference between Tom Buchanan and Tom Stark of *All the King's Men*; and if the type were not so common in life, one could accuse Robert Penn Warren of literary plagiarism.

In the Basil Lee Duke stories, written after *Gatsby,* Fitzgerald continued to reveal his enthrallment with the Ivy League ideal and his own dreams of athletic glory, but the result of such great expectations is already known. Fitzgerald, as these stories confirm, could not free himself from football, a view with which "Fritz" Crisler, head football coach at Princeton from 1932 to 1937, would no doubt agree.

During this period Crisler received a call from Fitzgerald before every home game. The calls came from Miami, Saint Paul, Chicago, Alabama, Hollywood, and New York during the years marked by Zelda's illness and Fitzgerald's own deteriorating stability. "It got so I sort of expected him to call," Crisler says,

It seemed to me that the fellow felt an uncommon amount of devotion toward Princeton, for which he had to find a release of some kind. And for some personal reason of his, as head coach of the football team, I guess I was in line for it.

After a while, though, I began to realize that with him it wasn't just a matter of the habitual Old Grad spirit and enthusiasm. There was something beyond comprehension in the intensity of his feelings. Listening to him unload his soul as many times as I did, I finally came to the conclusion that what Scott felt was really an unusual, a consuming devotion for the Princeton football team.[24]

Eventually Fitzgerald must have realized that his particular type of loyalty was old-fashioned. Certainly he realized that his hero-worship was, but he defended it and indicted instead the unimaginative world in which he lived.

The old dream of being an entire man in the Goethe-Byron-Shaw tradition, with an opulent American touch, a sort of combination of J. P. Morgan, Topham Beauclerk, and St. Francis of Assisi, has been relegated to the junk heap of the shoulder pads worn for one day on the Princeton freshman football field and the overseas cap never worn overseas.

So what? This is what I think now: that the natural state of the sentient adult is a qualified unhappiness. . . . My own happiness in the past often approached such an ecstasy that I could not share it even with the person dearest to me but had to walk it away in quiet streets and lanes with only fragments of it to distil into little lines in books—and I think that my happiness or talent for self-delusion or what you will, was an exception.[25]

Indeed Fitzgerald's "self-delusion" was an exception. No one worshiped the aristocratic athlete more than he, and no one fell harder when Götterdämmerung was complete. Sherwood Anderson recovered from the early disappointment of being a swipe, and even Ring Lardner, after the "live ball" and the Black Sox scandal, could stay away from the ball park; but Fitzgerald, deprived even of his dreams of glory, was transformed into an animal, into the very thing he found the heartless Buchanan to be. "Life will never be very pleasant again, and the sign *Cave Canem* is hung permanently just above my door. I will try to be a correct animal though, and if you throw me a bone with enough meat on it, I may even lick your hand" (p. 84).

Over and over in his fiction Fitzgerald expressed a loss of faith in the ideal of the all-round man. Amory Blaine attempted to perfect himself "socially," "physically," and "mentally" but concluded finally that life was "a damned muddle . . . a football game with everyone offside and the referee gotten rid of—everyone claiming the referee should have been on his side."[26] Carraway in the very beginning of *Gatsby* speaks of the "well-rounded man" as the "most limited of all specialists," and Jimmy Gatz's schedule found on the flyleaf of *Hopalong Cassidy* and dated September 12, 1906, is designed to prove Carraway's thesis that "life is much more successfully looked at through a single window."

The theme of Ernest Hemingway's *The Sun Also Rises* is that of *Gatsby:* the person of extreme romantic imagination cannot survive. Jimmy Gatz had perhaps taken Horatio Alger too seriously; Robert Cohn, "W. H. Hudson" and Castiglione.

In Renaissance Urbino, Robert Cohn would have been right at home, but he is lost in postwar Paris. He is not so much a case of arrested development as an enigmatic anachronism, a survival of the code of gentleman, who causes reflection on manners.

"Why do you follow Brett around? Haven't you any manners?" Mike asks him. "You're a splendid one to talk about manners! Brett said. You've such lovely manners."[27] Cohn's manners, Brett suggests, are better than Mike's, which is precisely the case, until Cohn loses all manners and becomes a sentimental brute like Tom Buchanan. Until that moment, however, he is the gentleman fashioned after Castiglione's courtier, practicing the "arts of defense and attack,"[28] playing tennis, "a game very befitting a man at court" (p. 23), reading many books and writing novels in order to be thought "well versed in the poets . . . orators and historians" and "proficient in writing" (p. 45). Also like the courtier, Cohn is "nobly born and of gentle race" (p. 21), being "a member, through his father, of one of the richest Jewish families in New York, and through his mother one of the oldest" (p. 4). Thus by endowing Cohn with an aristocratic background and so many courtly ways Hemingway individualizes him, but at the same time elucidates a syndrome described a quarter of a century earlier by Veblen, by whom Hemingway may have been influenced in the creation of Cohn.

Sports of all kinds are of the same general character, including prize-fights, bull-fights, athletics, shooting, angling, yachting, and games of skill, even where the element of destructive physical efficiency is not an obtrusive feature. Sports shade off from the basis of hostile combat, through skill, to cunning and chicanery, without its being possible to draw a line at any point. The ground of an addiction to sports is an archaic spiritual constitution—the possession of the predatory emulative propensity in a relatively high potency. A strong proclivity to adventuresome exploit and to the infliction of damage is especially pronounced in those employments which are in colloquial usage specifically called sportsmanship. . . . The addiction to sports . . . in a peculiar degree marks an arrested development in the man's moral nature. This peculiar boyishness of temperament in sporting men immediately becomes apparent when attention is directed to the large element of make-believe that is present in all sporting activity.[29]

Because of his "archaic spiritual constitution" and his indulgence in make-believe, Cohn takes a courtly view of women. He cannot see Brett as Circe, but imagines her instead as a sort of Beatrice d'Este. "There's a certain quality about her, a certain fineness. She seems to be absolutely fine and straight," he says.

"I don't know how to describe the quality.... I suppose it's breeding" (p. 38). Brett herself does not hesitate to play up this particular quality. "Shut up, Michael," she says after one of Mike's numerous insults directed at Cohn, "try and show a little breeding." To this Mike replies: "Breeding be damned. Who has any breeding anyway, except the bulls? Aren't the bulls lovely? Don't you like them, Bill? Why don't you say something, Robert? Don't sit there looking like a bloody funeral. What if Brett did sleep with you? She's slept with lots of better people than you" (pp. 141–142).

Cohn takes offense at Mike's outburst and prepares for a duel (with fists) not because Mike says Cohn lacks breeding but because he says that Brett does. Cohn can take all sorts of abuse himself—indeed he is almost a glutton for punishment—but he will throw down the gauntlet when he hears the truth about his "lady love," a lady who shows so little breeding as to offer his letters to Michael to read.

Cohn forgets his breeding, as Mike says, when he follows Brett around, but in the very act of making a fool of himself raises questions not only of manners but of morals as well. In a sense the novel is a retelling of the Maypole of Merrimount theme with Cohn filling the role of Endicott. "Do you think you amount to something, Cohn?" Mike asks him. "Do you think you belong among us? People who are out to have a good time?" (p. 177) Brett says that "he doesn't add much to the gayety," that she hates "his damned suffering," and Jake says that he has "a quality of bringing out the worst." But is it a matter of bringing out the worst or of reminding others of what they are? Jake, the court eunuch, is uncertain. "Mike was a bad drunk. Brett was a good drunk. Bill was a good drunk. Cohn was never drunk. Mike was unpleasant after he had passed a certain point. I liked to see him hurt Cohn. I wished he wouldn't do it, though, for afterwards it made me disgusted at myself. That was morality; things that made you disgusted afterward. No, that must be immorality" (pp. 148–149).

The fact that Cohn is a Jew affects his heroism in the most direct way. Castiglione advocated the art of self-defense but did not include boxing as part of that defense. Whether this is because boxing was not popular in the Renaissance is difficult to say, but it should be noted that while Cohn boxes, he does not like to. This form of *goyim nochas* (gentile pleasures) he had begun at Princeton in reaction to anti-Semitism. Learning to box and becoming middleweight champion provided him "a certain inner comfort in knowing he could knock down anybody who was snooty to him." Ironically, it is his boxing to which he resorts in order to bring about his separation from "everything." Also to be taken into account is Cohn's "hard, Jewish stubborn streak," which perhaps as much as anything accounts for the persistence with which he tries to get "in" at the wrong court.

Though Hemingway does not like Cohn, he nevertheless illustrates through him the difficulty in applying "a good break, a sweat, a bath, a love" to the "horribly complicated mess of living." Cohn tries to qualify as a Renaissance man, a gentleman of sport and leisure like Tom Buchanan, but history has conspired to make him anything but a finely tempered spirit. The Great War, centuries of anti-Semitism, and deep psychological aberrations all combine and come to bear on him, causing him to yield to the brute within. He is turned into a shell of a man, a being deprived of faculties and, especially, of manners. His tragedy is both personal and universal, for in it is seen the staggering problems not only of being heroic in the modern world but also of being human.

Hubris has been a theme in literature since the days of the epic. Hrothgar's famous harangue in *Beowulf*, among other things, is advice to the young hero to avoid this pitfall of so many heroes and warriors. That Beowulf did not develop arrogance is the reason he is remembered as a good king; that Macbeth did is the reason he is called tyrant. To a lesser degree Jim Randolph of Thomas Wolfe's *The Web and the Rock* suffers from and is overcome by Macbeth's malady, excessive pride.

Wolfe in "The Promise of America" (*You Can't Go Home Again*, chapt. 31) excluded football as a means of achieving fame; in *The Web and the Rock* he had gone to some length to show that football is more apt to contribute to vainglory. In Jim Randolph, Wolfe reflects not only the changing attitude in hero worship after World War I but also the workings of that egocentricity which separates man from man.

When Monk Webber first meets Jim at Pine Rock College, the

young athlete is hardly a human being at all but rather an Olympian god who had descended momentarily at Catawba. In his youth, Wolfe would have us believe, he is the closest thing to a real hero in our fiction, at least during his days at Pine Rock. Indeed Wolfe is guilty of one-upmanship in making Jim the apotheosis of strength and beauty and strength and intelligence.

He was a man who had done brilliant and heroic things, and he looked the part. It seemed that he had been especially cast by nature to fulfill the most exacting requirements of the writers of romantic fiction. He was a Richard Harding Davis hero, he was the hero of a book by Robert W. Chambers, he was a Jeffery Farnol paragon, he was all the Arrow collar young men one had seen in pictures, all the football heroes from the covers of the *Saturday Evening Post,* he was all the young men in the Kuppenheimer clothing ads—he was all of these rolled into one, and he was something more than all of these. His beauty was conformed by a real manliness, his physical perfection and natural and incomparable grace, his handsome perfection and regularity of his features by qualities of strength, intelligence, tenderness, and humor that all the heroes of romantic fiction can counterfeit but do not attain.[30]

Jim has many other romantic characteristics. Having come from a good but impoverished South Carolina family, he had learned responsibility early and "had accumulated a variety of experience that few men know in the course of a whole lifetime. To Monk Webber, it seemed that his hero had done everything and been everywhere." He had been a country schoolteacher, a seaman, a traveling salesman, in which role he had "had" women in every state but Oregon, "a deficiency which troubled him no little." In addition to all these awe-inspiring accomplishments Jim had played baseball for a mill town down in Georgia and had been paid in a manner which apparently never entered the mind of poor Jim Thorpe or his unimaginative employer.

He had played under an assumed name in order to protect as best he could his amateur standing and his future as a college athlete. His employer had been the owner of a cotton mill. His salary had been $140 a month and traveling expenses. And for this stipend it had been his duty to go to the mill offices once a week and empty out the waste paper baskets. In addition to this, every two weeks the manager of the team would take him to a pool room, carefully place a ball exactly in front of the pocket and two inches away from it, and then bet his young first baseman $75 that he could not knock it in. (p. 203)

The height of Jim's career comes with his winning touchdown against Madison and Monroe, the old rival of Pine Rock. "That was the apex of Jim Randolph's life, the summit of his fame. Nothing that he could do after that could dim the perfect glory of that shining moment." Thereafter Jim goes downhill all the way. Even the war is anticlimactic. Presumably he does well in the war—after fighting around Château-Thierry he is made a captain—but when his admirers see him again in 1920, they realize that something has happened. Jim is "handsome as ever, magnificent in his captain's bars and uniform," but the physical wound he has received in his spine has, like that of the Hemingway hero, caused a spiritual death. "It would have been better for him had he died in France. He had suffered the sad fate of men who live to see themselves become a legend. And now the legend lived. The man was just a ghost to them" (p. 212).

One could not expect a Jim Randolph to be able to live in a world in which all gods are dead and all battles fought. When Monk meets him again in New York, Jim, now thirty, is a newsman who longs not so much for a war to report as one in which he would play a "central and heroic part." Living in the romantic days of his youth, he cannot adjust to a staid life.

Jim was lost. The period of his fame was past. The brightness of his star had waned. He had become only a memory to those for whom he once had been the embodiment of heroic action. His contemporaries had entered life, had taken it and used it, had gone past him, had forgotten him. And Jim could not forget. He lived now in a world of bitter memory. He spoke with irony of his triumphs of the past. He spoke with resentment against those who had, he thought, deserted him. He viewed with bitter humor the exploits of the idols of the moment, the athletic heroes who were now the pampered favorites of popular applause. He waited grimly for their disillusionment, and, waiting, unable to forget the past, he hung on pitifully to the tattered remnants of his greatness, the adoration of a group of boys. (p. 299)

Jim begins to drink and carouse more and more and at one of the parties he disintegrates before the body of retainers he had presided over at Pine Rock College. "If anyone don't like my way of doing," he tells them, "he knows what he can do about it! He can pack up his stuff right now and cart his little tail right out of here! I'm boss here, and as long as I stay I'm going to keep on being boss! I've played football all over the South! They may not remember me now, but they knew who I was seven or eight years ago, all right!" (pp. 302–3) Dismissing or perhaps not even hearing remarks telling him to "grow up" and to remember that he is a "southern gentleman," he continues to break up (pp. 302–3).

Wolfe has a number of literary faults, but among his excellences is his ability to capture with an episode the tendencies of an age. In the writing, one sees not only Götterdämmerung but also the dissolution of the comitatus and the abandonment of manners, morals, and ideals, without which there is only loneliness and chaos. Like Robert Cohn, the Renaissance courtier, Jim, a child of Sir Walter Scott, is separated from everything, and like Cohn he has no choice but to go away, not to Valhalla but to some syrupy place "where romance was in the air and where . . . he could have the easy love of easy women. . . . There he went and lived a while [in bunnyland] and there he died" (p. 281). Like Tom Buchanan, the Aryan plutocrat, he is reduced to sentimental drivel. The message we are left with in the case of all three would-be aristocrats of the lost generation is simple: if one aspires to be a gentleman, he should at least have the humility and sense of limits that "gentilesse" since Chaucer has clearly implied.

Like all fictional leisure-class gentlemen, Lancelot Andrewes Lamar in Walker Percy's *Lancelot* is a romantic with a sentimental fixation on the past. Like Tom Buchanan he had been a star athlete, holding the record for the longest punt return in history, a 110-yard runback against Alabama, a record indeed, since, as he points out, no one can break it. Like Robert Cohn he tends to idealize and idolize women and like Jim Randolph he drinks.

Though he has much in common with other sporting gentlemen, Lancelot is quite different. In contrast to Tom Buchanan, he has a sense of social responsibility and in contrast with Cohn and Randolph, he plans not merely to run away but to begin a new order of men and women in the Shenandoah Valley of Virginia. Why does Lancelot wish to start over? Simply because the world has fallen apart. Lancelot, like so many athletes in American literature, is the "type who reaches the peak of his life in college and declines thereafter: prominent on campus, debater, second-string all-S.E.C. halfback [for Tulane], Rhodes scholar."[31]

Lancelot and his family had once "lived for great deeds" and he has trouble finding meaning in life after his days of youthful glory, not that he doesn't try. He becomes a lawyer, though a "half-assed" one in his view, takes up in the sixties the cause of blacks and civil rights, partly to shock his white friends, and writes, as did his father, a few articles on local history, partly out of boredom: "So what was my discovery? that for the last few years I had done nothing but fiddle at law, fiddle at history, keep up with the news (why?), watch Mary Tyler Moore, and drink myself into unconsciousness every night" (p. 60).

The shock of recognition of this routine is, he states, "quite a discovery." Lancelot realized that he had ceased "to feel" and had come to live in a state of "comfort and abstraction." There are several other discoveries, the chief being the affair of his wife Margot with Merlin, the movie director using Belle Isle plantation, Lancelot's ancestral home. Just as Lancelot du Lac's adultery was confirmed by blood on sheets, so Lancelot Lamar finds blood to be the telling clue of Margot's infidelity: the blood type of his daughter shows that she cannot be his child; and Margot uses the word *bloody* which she had picked up from Merlin. As a result of all his discoveries about himself and his wife, Lancelot sets out on a quest not for the Holy Grail but for evil. He rationalizes his becoming "The Knight of the Unholy Grail" as follows:

Suppose the Lowell Professor of Religion at Harvard should actually find the Holy Grail, dig it up in an Israeli wadi, properly authenticate it, carbon date it, and present it to the Metropolitan Museum. Millions of visitors! I would be as curious as the next person and would stand in line for hours to see it. But what difference would it make in the end? People would be interested for a while, yes. This is an age of interest.

But suppose you could show me one "sin," one pure act of malevolence. A different cup of tea! That would bring matters to a screeching halt. But we have plenty of evil around you say. What about Hitler, the gas ovens and so forth? What about them? As everyone knows and says,

Hitler was a madman. And it seems nobody else was responsible. Everyone was following orders. It is even possible that there was no such order, that it was all a bureaucratic mistake. (p. 138)

Lancelot believes that sin is somehow related to sexual behavior. Accordingly, he sets out to find it and, with the assistance of Elgin, a brilliant young black man whom he engages to spy on his wife's and daughter's relations with the movie makers in the local Holiday Inn, to film it. Lancelot intends not merely to discover evil at its source but to record it.

The "Andrewes" in Lancelot's name had been tacked on "to give it Episcopal sanction." What his father really had in mind "was that old nonexistent Catholic brawler and adulter, Lancelot du Lac . . . one of only two knights to see the Grail" (p. 116). Lancelot is confused about the legend of the Sangreal, but he does know that one of the knights who did see the Grail was Percival, the name of a boyhood friend, now a physician/priest to whom Lancelot speaks:

I cannot tolerate this age. And I will not. I might have tolerated you and your Catholic Church, and even joined it, if you had remained true to yourself. Now you're part of the age. You've the same fleas as the dogs you've lain down with. I would have felt at home at Mont-Saint-Michel, the Mount of the Archangel with the flaming sword, or with Richard Coeur de Lion at Acre. They believed in a God who said he came not to bring peace but the sword. Make love not war? I'll take war rather than what this age calls love. Which is a better world, this cocksucking cuntlapping assholelicking fornicating Happyland U.S.A. or a Roman legion under Marcus Aurelius Antoninus? Which is worse, to die with T. J. Jackson at Chancellorsville or live with Johnny Carson in Burbank? (pp. 157–58)

After finding Jacoby, the assistant film director, in bed with Margot, he engages him in a duel in the dark and cuts his throat with a Bowie knife, a family heirloom. While considering the possibility of going away and starting again, he lights the lamp that sets off the methane he had earlier released from the "Christmas tree" under the house. Like the original Lancelot after seeing the Holy Grail, he is "moved" by the explosion, literally blown through the wall and out into the yard. He is thrown off "the dead center of his life for the first time in thirty years."

In spite of his ordeal, in spite of all the buggery he has seen and committed, in spite of murder and revenge, Lancelot has not found a "sin." The fire and light of the explosion did not make a lasting impression as did the hot, bright radiation of the Grail on Lancelot du Lac. He still cannot believe in great historical moments because all the past is meaningless. "Violence does not signify," he tells his confessor (who is not really a confessor since Lancelot has not found sin). "Do you know what my memory records as the most unpleasant experience of that night?" he asks. "The damn fiberglass. Particles of it worked under my sleeve and collar. It makes my neck and arms itch just to think of it. Death's banal, but fiberglass in the neck is serious business" (p. 229). For Lancelot du Lac the hermit's hair that he wore next to his skin did far more than irritate. It "tormented."[32] In the view of Lancelot Lamar, the age of emotions has passed. Our own age is one of mere "interest."

Percival/Father John appears to accept Lancelot's evaluation of the times (the years of the Vietnam War and following) but not his solution. In his monosyllabic responses to Lancelot's questions at the end, he acknowledges Lancelot's argument that the age is awful. He does not approve of his means of salvation, a new beginning in the Shenandoah Valley with Anna, the girl in the room next door who had been sexually assaulted by three sailors. It is not, one infers, a new beginning in itself that Percival objects to, but the type of new beginning Lancelot proposes, one based more on Lee as a model than on Christ: "Then how shall we live if not with Christian love? One will work and take care of one's own, live and let live, and behave with a decent respect toward others. If there cannot be love—you call that love out there?—there will be a tight-lipped courtesy between men. And chivalry toward women. Women must be saved from the whoredom they've chosen. Women will once again be strong and modest. Children will be merry because they will know what they are to do" (pp. 158–59). It is not that Lancelot is opposed to Christian love so much as he is to what has been substituted for it. What, then, happened to Christian love? Lancelot's opinion is compelling; "Whatever came of it? I'll tell you what came of it. It got mouthed off on the radio and TV from the pulpit and that was the end of it. The Jews knew better. Billy Graham lay down with Nixon and got up with a different set of fleas, but the Jewish prophets lived in deserts and wildernesses and had no part with corrupt kings. I'll prophesy: This country is going to turn into a desert and it won't be a bad thing. Thirst and hunger are better than jungle rot" (p. 158).

It is difficult to tell who is fisher king and who is quester in *Lancelot*. Perhaps Lancelot and Percival both are fisher kings—according to Jessie L. Weston, the combination of two fisher kings does occur in medieval allegory—but there is no doubt as to who is the better man. It is Percival/Father John whom Lance in his swearing also ironically addresses as Christ ("Christ, what are we talking about? Oh yes, Percival, you wanted to know what happened? Jesus, what difference does it make?") and in doing so invokes the memory of the Grand Inquisitor scene from the *Brothers Karamazov*. As a young man Percival was also known as "pussy," one of several obscene nicknames in the DKE fraternity but a revealing one. The name, however, crudely implies the cup just as Lance's does the sword. Together, the two symbols form the ideal of God, the cup equating with beauty, the lance with strength. Lancelot has shown the futility of the life of the sword and believes that the quiet, tolerant life of Christian love of his friend is just as futile. Both their lives are wastelands in Lance's view, but he at least is finally beginning to look back and ask questions as any Grail quester must do. The last question Lancelot asks is even possibly the right one since it leads to an affirmative response that may in turn lead to Lance's salvation: "Is there anything you wish to tell me before you leave?" "*Yes,*" his friend answers.

Since this "Yes" is the last word in the novel, one must imagine what the physician/priest will say. Among his points, I believe, will be the following:

1. That Christ did bring a sword as well as love, but it was a sword of righteousness and not an instrument of revenge or of macho honor. Perhaps Lance's greatest sin was after the explosion when he tried to go back into the burning house not to save his wife, as the papers reported, but to retrieve the Bowie knife. He can never know the meaning of freedom unless he accepts

both the Christ of love and the Christ of the sword, the cup and the lance. Either may lead to excess and sin but both are essential for the awful burden of freedom.

2. That evil exists but cannot be defined any more than God can be defined and certainly cannot be put on film. Evil exists in the heart of man, which is where Hawthorne's Ethan Brand found it before he flung himself into the flames. Like Ethan Brand and the original Lancelot, he is "harder than stone, more bitter than wood, and more barren than a fig tree" (*Le Morte*, p. 377). Lancelot du Lac did not go away to brood, as Lancelot Lamar says, but to repent of his own evil ways and to meditate upon the words of the holy hermit which apply also to Lancelot Lamar: "for has He not given you strength, beauty, and seemliness in excess of any knight living? To God you owe your worldly fame, and yet you have presumed to enter His precincts and to discover His mysteries when you are in a state of mortal sin" (*Le Morte*, p. 378). All Lancelot Lamar had to do to find evil was, like Ethan Brand, to look within at the outset.

3. That the danger of being a gentleman, especially one with a sporting past in such violent games as football and boxing, is to see the world in either/or terms, to turn over the cup of human compassion and live by the sword. However civilized and genteel that life might appear, it is too harsh because it insists upon absolute categories. Good and evil may be absolutes, but man in his finiteness partakes of both. In her last words Margot was trying to tell him something extremely important: "with you I had to be either—or—but never a—uh—woman." The missing terms here Percival would say are *lady* and *whore*, as Lancelot well knows. Lancelot cannot tolerate combinations of extremes which is the condition of freedom. Manners that he wishes to reestablish are a charade unless there is also mystery, which Lancelot has, until now anyway, rejected.

4. That when as youths they had struck out for Jefferson's Island between Louisiana and Mississippi, it was a telling adventure of childhood, but still a childish act. There are really no new beginnings but only streams of various kinds. The stream that offers the greatest freedom, which Lance appears to cherish so much, is Christianity with its many paradoxes, its righteousness

and tolerance. The man for whom the island was named did not understand this with his talk of "my west" and a revolution each generation. Revolutions always fail because they succeed by the sword. Percival would say that we have had enough American Adams but not enough imitators of Christ. One of each, he would say, is enough, so follow the second, not because he came last, but because he promises redemption from the fall of the first.

In Mallory's *Le Morte D' Arthur,* "Sir Percival left the city, and adopting hermit's weeds, lived a holy life for a year and two months, and then died" (p. 431). Similarly, in Percy's novel, Percival is going to Alabama to carry on the work of the church, a mission quite different from the chivalric one planned by Lancelot. There is a chance, though, that Lance will have a change of heart and not go to Virginia after all. Just as he had often rescued Percival from stronger boys in their youth so now may Percival rescue him. This possibility is distinctly suggested by the author in the quotation from Dante's *Purgatorio:*

> He sank so low that all means
> for his salvation were gone,
> except showing him the lost people.
> For this I visited the region of the dead. . . .

If he doesn't change as a result of the words of the priest, Lancelot will remain merely another lost gentleman of another lost generation.

The Apotheosized WASP

"Aristocracy" means the rule of the best. If the all-important question is asked, "the best in what?" one answer can be found in Plato's *Republic.* The best, claims Socrates, is "he who mingles music with gymnastic in the fairest proportion and best attempers them to the soul. . . . [He] may be called the true musician and harmonist in a far higher sense than the tuner of the strings."[33]

Just as this union of opposites was the informing ideal of Greek education so it was of English education in the Victorian period and, to some degree, of American as well. In his inaugu-

ral address on October 19, 1869, at Harvard College, President
Charles William Eliot, almost as if he had Teddy Roosevelt in
mind, called for the education of "the aristocracy which excels
in manly sports, carries off the honors and prizes of the learned
professions, and bears itself with distinction in all fields of intellectual labor and combat; the aristocracy which in peace
stands for the public honor and renown, and in war rides first
into the murderous thicket."[34]

Excepting that he is a lost soul and failed gentry, Lancelot
Andrewes Lamar would qualify for this aristocracy. A much
more successful Episcopalian, at least one who has kept the faith,
is Frank Prescott, the rector of Justin in Louis Auchincloss's
novel by the same name. In many ways Frank too fails, but he
does not "go to seed" like Lancelot. In spite of self-
recriminations, he manages to uphold a spiritual tradition and
enters into a state of apotheosis in the memory of those who
attended his school.

A descendant of the Prescotts of Boston, Frank was born too
late to serve in the Civil War. This he regrets and, much like
Lancelot Lamar, "passionately believed that an age of heroes
had died with his father in the red clay of Virginia and that a
generation of jackals now gorged itself on the bloated carcass of
valor."[35] Frank, "the athlete and school leader," is also a Christian
and he uncompromisingly evaluates the character-shaping institutions he attends against the severe standard that the
Hellenic-Christian synthesis suggests. At Saint Andrews religion
had been shaped by the neglect of the body so that Frank found
it everything that a school should not be. The headmaster cared
only for the souls of his boys and reviled the human body as "an
unlovely thing" (p. 54). At Balliol religion suffered by neglect of
the faith, at least as seen in Frank's master, Dr. Benjamin Jowett,
the famous translator of Plato, in whose plump, soft figure
Frank also saw evidence of neglect of the body. Dr. Jowett is "full
of alternatives" and believes, somewhat like Emerson, that
"Christianity had been better stated by Plato than by Christ." To
Frank on the other hand, "Christ was all," the supreme position
in the trinity. Plato and the Greeks were important to the minister and educator-to-be, but the keystone of education at Justin
Martyr school would be Christ, in whom alone, Frank Prescott

believed, could body and mind be brought into harmony with the soul. It is necessary for an understanding of the meaning of the entire novel to keep in mind that the eponym of the school Frank made famous had tried to reconcile, much like Thomas Aquinas, "the thinking of the Greek philosopher with the doctrine of Christ" (p. 127). The priority here is significant; faith alone is not enough, but with Frank Prescott it is essential. Both the man and the institution reflect each other and the strength of both lies in the unity of mind, body, and soul. Herein lies the explanation of Jules Griscome's revenge upon the rector. What Jules desecrates is, quite obviously, music, gymnastics, and the soul, the Socratic-Christian trinity.

Frank Prescott, who believes in the integration of mind, body, and soul, must not be taken as a platitudinarian, for he is a complex and convincing character. The role of physical strength is decisive in his life, and his world view cannot be imagined without the playing fields of Justin. Hence clichés lurk just beneath the surface of his ministry and one student, according to Frank himself, had called the school "a pile of red brick, shrouded in the fog of its headmaster's platitudes" (p. 148). Frank is well aware of the ironic and perplexing kinship of clichés and ideals but this does not in any way make less certain for him the validity of ideals. What he is uncertain about is not idealism, but reality. Of heroic strain, he would rush eagerly into combat had he the chance. He has, in fact, longed for the test of battle to determine if he is a man, or "real." He dies, as he predicted, in his sleep, his mettle untested by combat and his recriminations for hating acknowledged. His consolation, if any, comes from having helped "a few boys."

The same dilemma between the ideal and the actual is illustrated in Charley Strong, the Golden Boy of Justin. While Frank had difficulty comprehending the "real," Charley, like Lancelot Lamar, has lost faith in the ideal, specifically the ideals he learned at Justin in the class of '09. At Frank Prescott's school, Charley was a kind of Rupert Brooke, as Frank's daughter Cordelia calls him, as well as "Billy Budd";[36] but the war changed all that, wounding him, like so many fictional American heroes, in body and soul, so much in fact that in postwar Paris he comes to wonder if the world of his youth had actually existed. Cordelia does nothing to alleviate his doubts. "The past," she tells him, "existed only in remembered emotions; therefore the retained horror of the trenches was more real than the vague, sweet pastoral idyll that had become Justin" (p. 142). Frank Prescott's mission is to rescue Charley from the effects of war and from Cordelia. To save Charley he must convince him, in spite of Cordelia, that all the past is real, including the ideals he learned at Justin. Frank must save Charley, in fact, to give meaning to his own life, to prove to himself that though he had not been tested, his most beloved protégé had been tested and had prevailed. Whether or not salvation is wrought in Charley before his death is left unanswered, but Auchincloss provides some hints with profound implications.

Though Frank does not experience the ravages of war firsthand, he does come face to face with the horror of evil as seen in Jules. This is for him the shock of recognition of a force his faith had been a guarantee against. He had always believed in evil as a force and not as the absence of good and had believed in innate depravity; what he had not been able to comprehend was that Jules, a blood brother of Iago and John Claggart, could remain unrectified throughout his days at Justin, that after the whole New England experience, one could remain perverse. He always knew, like Willie Stark, that good grows out of evil. What Frank Prescott did not realize until the end of his life is that evil flourished beautifully in the halls and fields of his beloved Justin. The corollary seems almost clear. If Frank "failed" with Jules, he might have helped Charley Strong "a bit." If evil can thrive in the sanctity of Justin, nobility of character might be redeemed from the ultimate degradation of war. If World War I was not the war to end all wars, then it might not be the war to end all idealism. From the ashes, perhaps, will come the Paraclete, and what Charley, like Frank his counselor, is left with at the end, one infers, is a more profound realization of Emerson's "Ole Double," the real and the ideal.

The role of Cordelia in the relationship between Frank Prescott and Charley Strong is important. Frank comes close to calling her a "bitch," but she is more to be pitied. She, rather than Frank, might be the one more sinned against than sinning.

Her complaint against Frank and his Hellenic idealism is that it
has excluded women and hence love, a charge that seems to be
substantiated by his life. Frank does love, certainly, but like all
idealists he is more deeply committed to duty, as he himself
admits, than to love. What children need, he says, "is devotion
not love." In this he of course is wrong, and his greatest fault is
not so much hating Jules at the end as not loving Cordelia more
from the beginning. Charley tells Cordelia while Frank is trying
to restore his soul that Frank will try to save her later; the irony
here is that Frank has already failed. Cordelia thus becomes a
sort of scapegoat, victimized, at least in part, by her father's
business, that is, perhaps too severely holding up to others an
eternal ideal.

In Brian Aspinwall's view, Frank understood himself completely and was so aware of his faults that he considered himself a
failure in the end. At his funeral, however, a "contrary view" is
overwhelmingly borne out as hundreds of graduates sing "the
son of God goes forth to war" and as the coffin, draped in the
school colors, is borne down the aisle of the chapel followed by
senators and judges and headmasters of every boy's school in
New England. Frank, the son of light, missed the great wars but
nevertheless did battle against the powers of darkness. In the
minds of the many he influenced the questions no doubt will
arise time and time again: how did he make distinctions between
good and bad so conveniently, and what was so tragic about "the
darkened stage" that he feared so much? But as everyone must
realize, there are no answers to mysteries—only reactions, and
Frank's reaction is marvelous indeed.

Like Charley Strong, Gordon Shaw of Eugene O'Neill's
Strange Interlude is a product of New England, a type of *ober-
mann,* and a victim of World War I. Like Frank Prescott and
Charley Strong, he is apotheosized but in a different way. While
Charley and Frank have passed on to the city of God, Gordon
Shaw takes his place in the American wing of Valhalla. While the
trials of Frank and Charley cannot be interpreted outside the
Christian tradition, O'Neill's concern, rightly or wrongly, is
much wider, for his hero is the central figure in the universal
human drama. The setting of the play is a New England college,

but the characters are universal. "Today," as Brian Aspinwall says at the end of *The Rector of Justin,* "we like heroes in shirt-sleeves, or, in other words, we don't like heroes. But things were not always that way, and today is not forever." Forever, in fact, can be glimpsed only in an "interlude" which invariably seems "strange" because we encounter it so seldom.

In an earlier play, *Abortion,* O'Neill had dealt briefly but savagely with the New England college hero in the form of the "Hero Jack Townsend," a Frank Merriwell on the surface but a hypocrite at heart. Jack is a "well-built handsome young fellow about twenty-two years old, with blond hair brushed back from his forehead, intelligent blue eyes, a good-natured, self-indulgent mouth, and ruddy tanned complexion."[37] Townsend also has the "easy confident air of one who has, through his prowess in athletics, become a figure of note in college circles and is accustomed to the deference of those around him." A star pitcher for his college team, he has also become accustomed to the deference of women. In one way or another every female in the play looks out for "hero Jack." His mother makes him promise not to play football so that he won't get hurt, sister Lucy whips up enthusiasm for parade in his honor, Nellie, who dies after an abortion, refuses to name him as her lover, and his fiancee Evelyn tells him what a great person he is.

Jack is adored and worshiped by everyone—"I'm black and blue all over from all their fond caresses this afternoon"—by everyone except Joe Murray, Nellie's brother, who accuses Jack of murdering Nellie while the parade in honor of Jack is approaching his dorm. In keeping with his romantic nature, Jack returns the gun he has just wrested from Joe and challenges him to use it. "It's too good for yuh," Murray says and leaves Jack to do the job himself just as a cheer goes up below his window: "For he's a jolly good fellow, which nobody can deny" (p. 34).

O'Neill did not dismiss the New England college hero with Townsend's suicide. That death has little or nothing to do with his extinction is a point well made in *Strange Interlude.* Gordon Shaw, the supreme athlete, the ideal lover of the Eternal Feminine Nina, has been killed in a plane crash in World War I before the play begins, and thereafter even the thought of him means more to Nina than the intellectuals who surround her. "It isn't Gordon," Professor Leeds, her father, tells Marsden, the writer. "It's his memory, his ghost, you might call it, haunting Nina, whose influence I have come to dread because of the terrible change in her attitude toward me."[38] Before dying, Professor Leeds confesses his hatred for Gordon, a hatred that comes to be shared in some degree by Marsden and Darrell, medical scientist and sire of Gordon Evans, carbon copy of Gordon Shaw.

If Professor Leeds, Marsden, and Darrell are different types of mind men, Sam is the hero-worshiping alumnus with the alumni intellect and spirit. He is proud that though he never made a college team, "he never stopped trying" and neither did he stop worshiping those who succeeded. When Marsden remarks that "the sport hero usually doesn't star after college," Sam replies, "Gordon did! . . . In the war! He was an ace! And he always fought just as cleanly as he'd played football! Even the huns respected him" (p. 30).

Because of the symbolic insanity in Sam the alumnus, Nina must call upon Darrell the "healthy male" and eternal rationalist to impregnate her with the seed that will produce the second Gordon. Thereafter she regards Darrell as one of the big happy family with Sam and Marsden, the family whose duty it is to look after and protect little Gordon. "You are my three men," she tells them. "This is your home with me! . . . Sssshh! I thought I heard the baby. You must all sit down and be very quiet. You must not wake our baby" (p. 133). To Nina all of these are necessary for the creation and care of little Gordon. Nina thinks, "My three men! . . . I feel their desires converge in me! to form one complete beautiful male desire which I absorb . . . and am whole . . . they dissolve in me, their life is my life . . . I am pregnant with the three! . . . husband! . . . lover! . . . father! . . . and the fourth man! . . . little man! . . . little Gordon! . . . he is mine too! . . . that makes it perfect!" (p. 135)

Yet there is never the unanimity of spirit among the men that Nina would like. There is in fact almost no unanimity at all. Marsden is thoroughly anti-Gordon, and Darrell wants his son to be anything but a "rah rah hero" like Gordon Shaw. Sam Evans,

however, is determined that he will become precisely that. When
little Gordon asks Sam if he is anything like Gordon Shaw, Evans
replied:

I hope you are. If when you go to college you can play football or row
like Gordon did, I'll—I'll give you anything you ask for! I mean that!
    GORDON. *(dreamily)* Tell me about him again, will you, Dad—about
the time he was stroking the crew and the fellow who was Number
Seven began to crack, and he couldn't see him but he felt him cracking
somehow, and he began talking back to him all the time and sort of gave
him his strength so that when the race was over and they'd won Gordon
fainted and the other fellow didn't.
    EVANS. *(with a fond laugh)* Why, you know it all by heart! What's the
use of my telling you? (pp. 153–54)

    Sam and Nina, then, mold Gordon Evans in the image of
Gordon Shaw; but when Nina sees that another woman, the
younger Madeline Arnold, is about to take him away from her,
she denies any similarity between the two whatsoever. When
Sam compared the two Gordons at the big crew race, Nina says,
"Don't be modest, Sam. Gordon *is* you. He may be a fine athlete
like Gordon Shaw, because you've held that out to him as your
ideal, but there the resemblance ceases. He isn't really like him at
all, not the slightest bit" (p. 163). Nina even intends to tell
Madeline that she cannot marry Gordon because of the insanity
in Sam's family, but Darrell intercedes to prevent her from ruin-
ing Madeline's life as she has his. "Pay no attention to anything
she may say to you. She's just passed through a crucial period in
a woman's life and she's morbidly jealous of you and subject to
queer delusions" (pp. 178–79). Nina having passed through the
change of life, Madeline then becomes the embodiment of
romantic love, leaving Nina still the role of wife and mother.
Madeline becomes the bride to be, as Nina was for Gordon
Shaw.
    At the crew race, Navy, the team to beat, becomes not only the
dragon but the symbol of the nonheroic and the rational. While
Sam and Madeline, the romantics, urge Gordon on, Marsden
and Darrell pull for Navy. "Gordon really should get beaten
today—for the good of his soul, Nina," Marsden says as all the
characters watch the race from Evans's motor cruiser. "That

Madeline is pretty, isn't she? Those Gordons are too infernally lucky—while we others—(*He almost starts to blubber*—*angrily*) we others have got to beat him today" (p. 175). So strongly is Darrell against Gordon that he openly shouts encouragement to the Middies, a slip that results in the best humor in the play.

DARRELL. (*exultantly*) Come on, Navy!

EVANS. (*who is standing next to Ned, whirls on him in a furious passion*) What's that? What the hell's the matter with you?

DARRELL. (*facing him—with a strange friendliness slaps him on the back*) We've got to beat these Gordons, Sam! We've got to beat—

EVANS. (*raging*) You—! (*He draws back his fist—then suddenly horrified at what he is doing but still angry, grabs Darrell by both shoulders and shakes him*) Wake up! What the hell's got into you? Have you gone crazy?

DARRELL. (mockingly) Probably! It runs in my family! All of my father's people were happy lunatics—not healthy, country folk like yours, Sam! Ha!

EVANS. (*staring at him*) Ned, old man, what's the trouble? You said "Navy."

DARRELL. (*ironically—with a bitter hopeless laugh*) Slip of the tongue! I meant Gordon! Meant Gordon, of course! Gordon is always meant—meant to win! Come on, Gordon! It's fate! (p. 181)

Gordon is indeed fated to win. With a superhuman effort he comes through at the very end and Madeline's response comes as no surprise: "Gordon! Gordon! He's won! Oh, he's fainted! Poor dear darling!" (p. 182) Neither does the response of Nina and Evans come as a surprise.

EVANS. (*bounding back to the deck, his face congested and purple with a frenzy of joy, dancing about*) He's won! By God, it was close! Greatest race in the history of rowing! He's the greatest oarsman God ever made! (*Embracing Nina and kissing her frantically*) Aren't you happy, Nina? Our Gordon! The greatest ever!

NINA. (*torturedly—trying incoherently to force out a last despairing protest*) No!—not yours!—mine!—and Gordon's—Gordon is Gordon's—he was my Gordon!—his Gordon is mine!

With these words the hero-worshiping Sam symbolically dies, freeing Nina for her final and most peaceful marriage with Marsden.

The concept of the hero is so vast and so complicated that the surface has scarcely been scratched. If the hero could be looked at alone, the matter could perhaps be simplified; but this is not the case. The hero cannot be regarded singly; he is not only an expression of the culture of the time and place in which he lives but also the figure in whom is manifested the age-old predilections. No American writer as far as I have been able to determine has examined this milieu and metier of the hero as thoroughly as has O'Neill in *Strange Interlude.* The play is indeed a "strange interlude" invoking race memories as old as the earliest myths and striking something deep inside us. Parallels between events in the play and those in the traditional life of the hero are striking as a comparison with the well-known pattern established by Lord Raglan will show:

(1) The hero's mother is a royal virgin; (2) his father is a king, and (3) often a near relative of his mother, but (4) the circumstances of his conception are unusual, and (5) he is also reputed to be the son of a god. (6) At birth an attempt is made, usually by his father or his maternal grandfather, to kill him, but (7) he is spirited away, and (8) reared by foster-parents in a far country. (9) We are told nothing of his childhood, but (10) on reaching manhood he returns or goes to his future kingdom. (11) After a victory over the king and/or a giant, dragon, or wild beast, (12) he marries a princess, often the daughter of his predecessor, and (13) becomes king. (14) For a time he reigns uneventfully, and (15) prescribes laws, but (16) later he loses favor with the gods and/or his subjects, and (17) is driven from the throne and city, after which (18) he meets with a mysterious death, (19) often at the top of a hill. (20) His children, if any, do not succeed him. (21) His body is not buried, but nevertheless (22) he has one or more holy sepulchres.[39] Applying the pattern to *Strange Interlude,* we can perhaps see why the play from the first seemed like a mythic rerun and why Gordon Shaw is so familiar.

Nina is (1) Gordon's "silly virgin," and while Darrell is not a king, he has about him (2) a decided royalty. In ability and appearance he is quite superior to others. While he serves the role of lover for Nina, he is also (3) a brother figure whom Nina would have little Gordon call "Uncle Ned." Certainly the circumstances of Gordon's birth are (4) unusual, for he is clearly (5) the

offspring of the "demigod" Gordon Shaw whose ghost visits
Nina at night like an incubus. (While Darrell is putting the horns
on Sam, Gordon is putting them on Darrell. Perhaps it would be
more accurate to say that Darrell becomes Gordon—in bed.)
Though not made at birth there is (6) an attempt on the part of
Darrell and Marsden, the father figure, to kill the ideal by which
Gordon Evans is being shaped. He is not "spirited away" but he
is (8) raised by Sam in the hero-worshiping country far from the
rational land of Darrell. Gordon is seen at the age of twenty-one
at which time he wins the greatest race in the history of rowing
(11) and (12) forthwith marries the beautiful Madeline. While he
does not prescribe laws or lose favor with the gods, he flies away
with Madeline and meets with a death that is (18) indeed mysterious. "Gordon is dead, Father," Nina tells Marsden. "I've just
had a cable. What I mean is, he flew away to another life—my
son, Gordon, Charlie. So we're alone again—just as we used to
be." Then "looking up at the sky—strangely she adds, 'My having a son was a failure wasn't it? He couldn't give me happiness.
Sons are always their fathers. They pass through their mother to
become the father again. The sons of the Father have all been
failures! Failing they died for us, they flew away to other lives,
they could not stay with us, they could not give us happiness'"
(p. 199). Like so many fictional athlete heroes, Gordon leaves no
children (20) and though "dead" is not (21) buried. Using the
Lord Raglan method of scoring, one can give twelve points to
Gordon which would place him in the same league with
Asclepios, Apollo, Joseph, Elijah, and Sigurd.

O'Neill looks at the hero archetypically and appears to conclude that the hero has his real being in woman for whom he
strives in all his undertakings, that the antipathy on the part of
mind man toward the hero is to some extent sour grapes, but
that the hero with all his systems of honor is rather inflexible,
hence quite superficial and, possibly, as Emerson decided, a bore
"at last." There is, for instance, no evidence whatever that the
Gordons, while intelligent, are in the least intellectual, a situation
that is not surprising considering all the praise, attention, and
favors that the Ninas, Sams, and Madelines bestow upon them
for not being intellectual. Yet O'Neill does not praise writing and
scholarship by any means. In many ways Marsden, "an old maid

who seduces himself in his novels," and Professor Leeds, with his old and rare editions, are sentimentalists who are beaten at their own game of romance by the Gordons. The character who best approximates the Greek ideal is the nonidealistic Darrell. Possessing a healthy body, he is at the same time highly intelligent and realistic. "Romantic imagination," he exclaims. "It has ruined more lives than all the diseases! Other diseases, I should say! It's a form of insanity!" Yet Darrell is not altogether sane either, for with his rejection of the "Gordon Myth" and "romantic imagination" he also abandons his own search for happiness, as he himself admits; and this is not at all an act of sanity.

Judging from our literature, one is tempted to conclude that probably no catastrophe in American history has had such a devastating effect upon idealism as World War I. In the case of fictional athlete heroes, Jim Randolph and Charley Strong, Golden Boys of the South and the East, become maimed in body and spirit. Tom Buchanan and Robert Cohn, the one attempting to embody Aryan supremacy and the other renaissance gentility, pathetically reveal themselves to be hopeless members of the lost generation. One seeks fulfillment of lust in the valley of ashes just inland from the green shores of the new world and the other a resurrection of romantic idealism in the moral ruins of the old. Gordon Shaw, like Princeton's Hobie Baker, dies in the holocaust, and like Frank Prescott, who to his regret never fought the rebel or the hun but only the devil, left a trail of glory in his apotheosis but also a vacuum in the faith in heroic vitalism. Indeed the question becomes: what happens to the "Gordon" and "Prescott" myths in a world that still needs to aspire but which is becoming more and more demythologized and perhaps disillusioned? We have already seen how Ring Lardner's fools rushed in to fill the eternal role of hero and all-round man, and in the muscular Christian, the booster alumnus, the model, and the brave new man, we will see other examples. Some form of transcendence is still sought or suggested but it is a shallow form of transcendence. The hero may bore "at last," as Emerson said, but the heroic never bores, else the attempt at heroism would cease altogether. This, as Ernest Becker has shown, can never happen.

The Muscular Christian

An observer of sports in America is apt to be struck by the platitudes that have developed around football. This game, supporters claim, develops character, the whole man, the full personality, leadership ability, "Americanism, Virtue, Godliness, Patriotism, and Charity."[40] Those who think in such a way are frequently called bromides who, according to Gelett Burgess, "are, intellectually, all peas in the same conventional pod, unenlightened, prosaic, living by rule and rote. . . . Their habits of thought are all ready made, proper, sober, befitting the average man. They worship dogma. The bromide conforms to everything sanctioned by the majority, and may be depended upon to be trite, banal, and arbitrary."[41] Being the game of the establishment, football produces many bromidic heroes, who are as much a caricature of the entire man as the dumb athlete, though in a different way. Such a one is *Elmer Gantry,* titular hero of Sinclair Lewis's novel.

Because of his physique and the glory he has won on the gridiron, Elmer Gantry feels that he is especially well equipped to inspire and lead others spiritually, just as Judson Roberts had inspired him. Judson had been a star football player and all-round man at the University of Chicago. "The praying fullback" had also played baseball, captained the debating team, "commanded" the YMCA, and reportedly had boxed with Jim Jeffries. These achievements along with his sermon in the school chapel at Terwillinger College remove any doubt that Elmer may have had.

Roberts' voice softened. He was pleading. He was not talking, he said, to weak men who needed coddling into the Kingdom, but to strong men, to rejoicing men, to men brave in armor. There was another sort of race more exhilarating than any game, and it led not merely to a score on a big board but to the making of a new world—it led not to newspaper paragraphs but to glory eternal. Dangerous-calling for strong men! Ecstatic—brimming with thrills! The team captained by Christ! No timid Jesus did he preach, but the adventurer who had joyed to associate with common men, with reckless fishermen, with captains and rulers, who dared to face the soldiers in the garden, who had dared the myrmidons of Rome and death itself! Come! Who are gallant?[42]

Elmer is gallant and he joins the team.

Until he becomes an established Methodist minister, Gantry uses essentially the same techniques of evangelism as Judson. He shows by example that a strong man can be a Christian; he uses his fist to knock out sinners and intersperses his sermons with metaphors from the gridiron. As a member of Sharon Falconer's evangelical crusade Gantry exhorts his listeners to get on "our team," to make "two yards for the savior," and he leads them in the "Hallelujah Yell," which he himself wrote and which is "the first one known in history."

But as Elmer rises in the world he uses football figures of speech less and less and "intellectual" methods more and more. He comes to realize that "if you're going to reach the greatest number and not merely satisfy their spiritual needs but give 'em a rich, full, joyous life, you gotta explain great literature to 'em." This realization is occasioned by his discovery of Longfellow who seems to him to contain "the best news to carry to this surprised and waiting world" (pp. 284–85). Gantry, however, does not abandon his old methods entirely. When on his way to preach in London as the Reverend Doctor Elmer Gantry, he admires fellow "athletic maniacs" on board the ship and is still so confident in his manly strength that he can indulge in a sort of self-effacing irony. When asked if he will have a "jolt," Elmer replies, "Well, of course, being a preacher, I'm not a big husky athalete like you boys, so all I can stand is just a ginger ale." He then asks the steward, "Do you keep anything like that buddy, or have you only got hootch for big strong men?" (p. 404) But while on ship Elmer decides to take an approach for his London appearance that will be different from either gallant athleticism or intellectualism. At this time Gantry looks upon himself as a "Sir Lancelot" and "the up-to-date John Wesley," but apparently realizing that the English have had all they want of both, he chooses instead to be a type of Natty Bumppo, a great natural, for whom the English had always had a weakness. "All the way over he had planned to be poetic in his first London sermon. He was going to say that he was the strong man, the knight in armor, who was most willing to humble himself before God; and to say also that Love was the bow on life's dark cloud, and the morning and evening star, both. But in a second of genius he cast it away, and reflected, 'No! What they want is a good, pioneering, roughneck American!'" (p. 406). And that he was splendidly.

The all-round man Robert Cohn aspired to be was the courtier of the Renaissance, but Gantry, being a modern Lancelot, harks back to the more religious days of the Middle Ages, though in the way he stays in shape and reads he does suggest more the Renaissance courtier than the earlier Christian knight. In literature Gantry prefers Tennyson to Browning, Elbert Hubbard to Carlyle. The *Saturday Evening Post* is a favorite as is Dickens. There are parallels, but Gantry's model is not so much Castiglione's secular courtier as the Christian Lancelot who, like Gantry, was a notorious adulterer. Gantry, unlike Lancelot, never feels any guilt for his sexual conquests.

Gantry shows clearly a much later influence, the Christ of Bruce Barton's *The Man Nobody Knows*, which, says Lewis in *Gideon Planish*, "inspired a generation and enriched an age." According to Lewis, Barton proved that "Christ Jesus was not a rebel or a peasant, but a society gent, a real sport, a press agent and the founder of modern business."[43] Barton did nothing less than to make Christ all things to all people, and *Elmer Gantry,* among other things, is a savage parody of Barton's Jesus. According to Barton, Jesus would have been in favor of athletics. Jesus, Barton shows, was a fighter, and so is Elmer Gantry. Christ was a businessman, an executive, and so is Gantry, who gets things done and who reassures his fellow bromides that were Christ living he "would be a Rotarian." I am not saying that Barton would have approved of Elmer Gantry, but I do assert that Lewis shows how easy it is for a bounder to be all-round in the same way that, according to Barton, Jesus was. It is no wonder that Lewis called the book an "Epistle to the Babbitts."

Contrasted sharply with the physical strength of Elmer Gantry is the intellect of Jim Lefferts and Frank Shallard. Neither is a mental giant, but both have an intellectual honesty and a curiosity which distinguish them from Elmer. Slightly pedantic and a little cynical, Jim reads to shore up his atheism rather than to satisfy a great desire for the truth; yet he has a natural perspicuity. He sees through "Old Jud" immediately, and at times he seems to speak for the author himself: "You bet I believe in the old bearded Jew God! Nobody but him could have made all the idiots there are in the world" (p. 41). He strongly opposes Elmer's conversion, and throughout the novel Gantry has the feeling that he has been "false to Jim." He lives in a waking nightmare of again seeing him; but when he does, it is not nearly so bad as Elmer had thought, for Jim, now a lawyer, looks stooped and broken. "And that," Elmer had thought, "is the poor fish that tried to keep me from going into the ministry" (p. 461).

By the time in his career of his London address Gantry had rid himself of an opponent more intelligent than Jim, Frank Shallard. Jim parts company with Elmer after his conversion at Terwillinger College, and Frank begins his association shortly thereafter when he meets Elmer at Mizpah Theological Seminary. The son of a Baptist minister and of a woman of a "main line family slightly run to seed," Frank has in him a good deal of the natural poet and "something of the reasoning and scientific mind." Instead of Ingersoll he reads such bootlegged works as Renan's *Jesus* and Nathaniel Schmidt's *The Prophet of Nazareth*. Though a good scholar, "he was a thorough failure. He lectured haltingly, he wrote obscurely, he could not talk to God as though he knew him personally, and he could not be friendly with numbskulls" (p. 118). In spite of all his doubts and disappointments "he clung to the church. It was his land, his patriotism. Nebulously and quite impractically and altogether miserably he planned to give his life to a project called 'liberalizing the church from within'" (p. 123). Frank stands for wisdom and common sense, but he is also a symbol of the devoted, civilized, scholarly clergymen who in this century have seen themselves too often rooted out by leather-headed Gantrys. After opposing prohibition—Elmer supported it—Frank is brutally beaten and eventually becomes blind. Thus while Elmer goes on to greater and greater things and eventually to the head of the National Association for Purification of Arts and Press (NAPAP), Frank Shallard is "to be read aloud to, the rest of his life" (p. 394).

In 1936 the editors of *Fortune* attempted to assess the changes that had taken place in the popularity of various heroes on the college campus. They found that the "muscular Christian"—a familiar figure in literature since the publication of Charles Kingsley's novels in Victorian England—still commanded "honor and respect." With this finding Lewis no doubt would have agreed. As late as 1943 in *Gideon Planish* the figure of Elmer Gantry is still going strong, is still a "handsome buck," still a "fine upstanding type of manly leader" (p. 374). Listed in *Who's Who*, Elmer Gantry is thought to be a graduate of Harvard and to come from one of the oldest Massachusetts families. Among the many organizations that he either heads or is a prominent member of are the NAPAP, the Modernistic Educational Bureau, the Society for the Rehabilitation of Erring Young Women, and the Dynamos of Democratic Direction.

Like Busher Keefe, Gantry is a caricature but, unlike Busher, a caricature that endures. The busher as a type of sports hero now belongs entirely to our past, but the Elmer Gantry figure never fades, not as long as there are profits in evangelism. It is never the loudly professed intentions of evangelists, muscular or otherwise, that remind us of Elmer but their method built upon the most fallacious of all assumptions, that physical strength and beauty are manifestations of inner grace.

The long and strange alliance between sport and religion has never received the extensive treatment it deserves, but it has been noted by several writers, especially by Veblen, who saw sport as a means of promoting religion: "It happens not infrequently that college sporting men devote themselves to religious propaganda, either as vocation or as a by-occupation; and it is observable that when this happens they are likely to become propagandists of some one of the more anthropomorphic cults. . . . They [sports] are apparently useful as a means of proselyting, and as a means of sustaining the devout attitude in converts once made."[44] This would seem to be true not only of Christianity but of other religions as well.

One wonders today, however, if the situation has not been reversed from that described by Veblen, that is, if religion, especially Christianity, is not used to promote sports by providing an aura of righteousness around certain practices that in a more civilized world would be condemned as outrageous. Though the sincerity and clean living of many great athletes devoted to the Christian cause cannot be denied, the Fellowship of Christian Athletes, through its implicit sanction of rampant commercialism in college sport, is guilty by association if not otherwise;

and the whole movement has been characterized by a booster-club consciousness and even a latent fascism as seen not only in Elmer Gantry but also in Ezra Pound's "Ballad of the Goodly Fere." Muscular religious models, whether Christian, Muslim, Jewish, or whatever, are always a little suspect for one basic reason—the simple equation of goodness with physical prowess. One purpose of religion is to help man to be good, but goodness and strength do not automatically correlate. In fact they are probably at odds more often than not. I have been moved a number of times by Pound's "Ballad of the Goodly Fere" since I first read it several years ago, but over the years I have become more and more suspicious of strength, even when that strength is moderated by the professed spirit of sacrifice. I believe in the combination of strength and beauty or strength and wisdom—the ideal of God as revealed throughout the Old and New Testaments—but I do not believe that this ideal can ever be fully articulated or captured in art, though it can be suggested and approximated. The danger, though, is always mistaking the shadow for the substance, the symbol for the thing symbolized, creeds and codes for the Unknown and the Unknowable. Hence beliefs should always be open-ended and tolerant. Herein lies the problem for muscular religionists with their implicit if not explicit expressions of self-righteousness, certainty, and take-it-or-leave-it dogmas. "Never to doubt, but always to trample forward," Thackeray once wrote, "is this not the way that dullness takes the lead in the world?" The answer is "yes."

The Booster Alumnus

An Apollo and bromide of another sort is the booster alumnus who begins to appear in literature in the second decade of the twentieth century, as for example in "Broad Shoulders" of Sherwood Anderson's *Windy McPherson's Son* (1917). With his brother "Narrow Face," Broad Shoulders heads the firm for which young Sam McPherson works in Chicago. Through these men with their Indian-sounding names Anderson seems to say that we cannot have even good half-men, much less whole men, for Broad Shoulders is a bromide while Narrow Face is a nut. "A tall, bald, narrow-shouldered man, with a long, narrow face," he moves "in and out of the office and warehouses and up and down the crowded street, sucking nervously at an unlighted cigar."⁴⁵ His advice to Sam is: "Spend your time with no one who hasn't money to help you." Broad Shoulders is "a much inferior man," if such is possible, who "had been a famous football player in his day and wore an iron brace on his leg."

He was a heavy, broad-shouldered, square-faced man of about thirty, who sat in the office dictating letters and who stayed out two or three hours to lunch. He sent out letters signed by him on the firm's stationery with the title of General Manager, and Narrow Face let him do it. Broad Shoulders had been educated in New England and even after several years away from his college seemed more interested in it than in the welfare of the business. For a month or more in the spring, he took most of the time of one of the two stenographers employed by the firm writing letters to graduates of Chicago high schools to induce them to go East to finish their education; and when a graduate of the college came to Chicago seeking employment, he closed his desk and spent entire days going from place to place, introducing, urging, recommending. (p. 127)

Though Anderson does not say so specifically, one can easily imagine that athletes are prominent among those whom Broad Shoulders seeks out for the old school. There would seem to be little doubt that he would stress the value of education, the role of football in building character, and the excellence of the alumni of his alma mater. Broad Shoulders is the familiar scout or bird dog. He is convinced that the worth and prestige of his school depend on recruiting and if asked would reply, in all probability, that success in recruitment is dependent to a large degree upon the fortunes of the athletic teams.

Anderson wrote about different types of sports and heroes, but his pattern was quite consistent. He disliked, rightly or wrongly, what were in his day the games of the upper class (football, golf) and favored instead the more earthy sports of the people (horse racing, baseball, boxing). Unlike the early Fitzgerald, who looked upon football as a tournament of knights in armor performed before glittering audiences of pretty girls, worshiping students, successful businessmen and their influential wives, Anderson saw football as a brutal game that crippled

young men for life and that was played for the entertainment of
"fat, middle-aged men" and "fat, well-dressed women, their
wives,"[46] that is, bromides of both sexes. If the football hero was
the idol of such overweight worshipers, he could not possibly
have been Anderson's hero too, unless like "Jim" of *Kit Brandon,*
he was an innocent rebel who played football because he was
daring and adventurous and not because he felt the game might
benefit him later in life.

Though Broad Shoulders takes a back seat to his brother
Narrow Face, he nevertheless foreshadows the all-conquering
ex-hero and business tycoon who takes a back seat to no one,
such as Charles McKelvey in Sinclair Lewis's *Babbitt.*

McKelvey had been the hero of the Class of '96; not only football captain and hammer-thrower but debater, and passable in what the State
University considered scholarship. He had gone on, had captured the
construction company once owned by the Dodsworths, best-known
pioneer family of Zenith. He built state capitols, skyscrapers, railway
terminals. He was a heavy-shouldered, big-chested man, but not slug-
gish. There was a quiet humor in his eyes, a syrup-smooth quickness in
his speech, which intimidated politicians and warned reporters; and in
his presence the most intelligent scientist or the most sensitive artist felt
thin-blooded, unworldly, and a little shabby. He was, particularly when
he was influencing legislatures or hiring labor-spies, very easy and lov-
able and gorgeous. He was baronial; he was a peer in the rapidly crystal-
lizing American aristocracy, inferior only to the haughty Old Families.
(In Zenith, an Old Family is one which came to town before 1840.) His
power was the greater because he was not hindered by scruples, by
either the vice or the virtue of the older Puritan tradition.[47]

In McKelvey and in George F. Babbitt, his admirer, Lewis tends
to confirm a significant aspect of Veblen's thesis, as did Anderson, that football is an "occupation" or manifestation of a predatory culture. It is not, to be sure, that Sinclair Lewis or Sherwood Anderson disliked sports; rather what they take issue with
is the significance that many Americans were coming to attach to
some sports, especially football. Indeed the impact of the game
on society was such that in his acceptance speech in 1930 for the
Nobel Prize, the first by an American, Lewis remarked upon the
prodigious emphasis upon football in American society: "Socially our universities are close to the mass of our citizens, and so

they are in the matter of athletics. A great college team is
passionately witnessed by eighty thousand people, who have
paid five dollars apiece and motored anywhere from ten to a
thousand miles for the ecstasy of watching twenty-two young
men chase one another up and down a curiously marked field.
During the football season a capable player ranks very nearly
with our greatest and most admired heroes—even with Henry
Ford, President Hoover, and Colonel Lindbergh."[48]

It might be expected that Lewis, an artist, would tend to deplore mass forms of popular entertainment but his disenchant-
ment went far beyond the stadium. Indeed he found as much
amiss in the classroom as on the playing field. "The paradox is
that in the arts our universities are as cloistered, as far from
reality and living creation, as socially and athletically and scienti-
fically they are close to us. To a true-blue professor of literature
in an American university, literature is not something that a
plain human being, living today, painfully sits down to produce.
No; it is something dead; it is something magically produced by
superhuman beings who must, if they are to be regarded as
artists at all, have died at least one hundred years before the
diabolical invention of the typewriter. To any authentic don,
there is something slightly repulsive in the thought that literature could be created by any ordinary human being, still to be
seen walking the streets, wearing quite commonplace trousers
and coat and looking not so unlike a chauffeur or a farmer. Our
American professors like their literature clear and cold and pure
and very dead" (p. 113).

Instead of merely venting his rage because he himself was not
as popular as the football hero with the masses on the one hand
or as revered as dead English writers by the professors on the
other, our first Nobel laureate could well have been identifying
for us the two old nemeses of the ancient world, identified by
Toynbee as the causes of the breakdown of civilizations:

The social havoc that is wrought on the one hand by esotericism on the
part of a creative minority and on the other hand by a spiritual defor-
mation of the souls of the rank-and-file of the uncreative mass is so
manifestly serious that, where and when it shows itself, there is apt to be
a powerful counter-movement to check it by adjustment or, failing that,
by revolution. And the more vigorous and vital the growth of a growing

civilization, the greater, as a rule, will be its members' sensitiveness to this particular social danger.[49]

Such sensitiveness, according to Toynbee was characteristic of the Hellenic civilization in the fifth century B.C., when it was moving toward its peak. The Greeks condemned both the *idiotai*, the "superior personality who committed the social offense of 'living to himself' instead of putting his personal gifts at the service of the common weal," and the *banausos*, the "person whose activity was specialized, through a concentration of his energies upon some particular technique, at the expense of his all-round development as a 'social animal.'"[50]

It is not surprising that the word *idiot* is so closely allied etymologically to the word *intellectual* nor that Toynbee fastens upon the athlete as the "horrifying example" in modern life of the specialist. If *Aretê* is to be achieved or maintained, then there must be in Toynbee's view some check upon polarizing trends. Lewis would seem to agree in his fiction, especially in his treatment of such a booster as George F. Babbitt and his hero, Charles McKelvey, until McKelvey's snub, that is. *Babbitt*, like most of Lewis's works, is in some degree caricature, but it nevertheless has the stamp of verity in its depiction of the shallowness of the hero worship of Americans. Lewis was, as Mark Schorer claims, "the first novelist to tell us explicitly into what stupid and finally devastating, social damnation we were drifting. Have we landed?"[51]

Another character from the same mold as that producing the has-beens of Anderson and Lewis is Joe Ferguson, football hero of "Midwestern University" in James Thurber's and Elliott Nugent's *The Male Animal*. An "all-time All American," who "made Red Grange look like a cripple," Joe is personality plus. His hail-fellow-well-met exuberance, dancing ability, business success, popularity both with men and women, his physique and devotion to the team, make him familiar indeed. Like all stereotypes, he is extremely shallow. When told by Ellen Turner that her husband, Tommy, a young associate professor, has had several articles in *Harper's* and the *Atlantic*, Joe responds, "No! Say, that's fine! But you'll have to boil them down to the *Reader's Digest* to reach me, Tommy. You know, that's a great little magazine."[52]

But if Joe Ferguson is a type, so is his rival, Professor Turner, who creates a disturbance on campus by his insistence on reading a letter by Bartolomeo Vanzetti because he believes it his duty "bring what light he can into this muddled world" (p. 179). In contrast to Joe, Turner is a sulphite, that is, "a person who does his own thinking ... who has surprises up his sleeve. He is explosive. One can never foresee what he will do except it will be a direct and spontaneous manifestation of his own personality."[53] Turner had wished to read his letter in peace, but his general instability throughout the play is sufficient to make one realize what Gelett Burgess means when he says that the division of humanity into bromides and sulphites is no classification of "desirable people."

It is difficult, however, to dislike either Joe Ferguson or Professor Turner for very long, and Irwin Shaw tells us why in *The Troubled Air,* a novel set in the "red scare" days, approximately a decade after publication of *The Male Animal.*

The play [*The Male Animal*] was all about the trouble the unpolitical English professor gets into by announcing that he is going to read as a model of English composition the last letter of Bartolomeo Vanzetti, written before his execution. It was a curious device to use as a basis for a farce, but, watching it from his seat ... Archer [the central character] realized how cleverly the authors had done it, avoiding tragedy yet not vulgarizing the document itself or the principles involved, comfortably assuring the audience by little deft strokes that all would in the end turn out well, that the ex-football player for all his bluster was a thoroughly good sort, that the Dean, when forced to a decision would behave admirably, however much he might sigh over his dilemma, that the wife would return to her husband and the young girl settle with the bright if somewhat radical young man, that all men were decent and susceptible to reason because the playwrights themselves were transparently decent and reasonable men. . . . Archer felt a nostalgia come over him for the lost, rueful academic world of the play, in which loud-mouthed trustee hundred-percent Americans and callow radical intellectuals could all be treated with the same gentle humor, with forgiveness and delight.[54]

The world of the play is gone, but the friction between academician and athlete is not. Thurber and Nugent deal only with the solution to their own plot and wisely make no attempt to resolve the larger problem on the place of sport in American

universities, though they do address the wider issue in some
gentle but effective satire.

DAMON. Mr. Keller, for forty-two years I have followed a policy of
appeasement. I might say I have been kicked around in this institution
by one Edward K. Keller after another. . . .

ED. There is only one Edward K. Keller.

DAMON. There has always been at least one. But there is an increasing
element in the faculty which resents your attitude toward any teacher
who raises his voice or so much as clears his throat. I warn you that if
you persist in persecuting Thomas Turner, you will have a fight on
your hands, my friend.

ED. Do you think that Bryson and Kressinger and I are afraid of a
few dissatisfied book-worms who work for twenty-five hundred dollars
a year?

DAMON. These men are not malcontents! Some of them are distinguished scholars who have made this university what it is!

ED. They've made it what it is! What about me? Who's getting this
new stadium? Who brought Coach Sprague here from Southern
Methodist?

JOE. He means this thing is bigger than stadiums and coaches, Ed.

ED. Nothing's bigger than the new stadium. (pp. 186–87)

Since the opening of *The Male Animal* some forty years ago,
the rise of stadiums, a sign of decadence in the eyes of Arnold
Toynbee, leads one to the unmistakable conclusion that even if
Toynbee is wrong, Dean Damon, head of the English Depart-
ment, is right with his assertion that there are many Edward K.
Kellers.

It is not as though Edward K. Keller and other boosters are vicious men. They are merely strange, when one really reflects on
the matter, far stranger than the relatively few who struggle
after truth through scholarship. There is nothing unusual, for
instance, about a person's wanting to become a scholar—men
have devoted themselves to study since the dawn of civilization—
but what can be said of those who devote a sizable portion
of their energies to supporting athletic teams? What lies behind such commitment? It may come as a shock, but the booster is a type of American Adam, though a jaded one to be sure.
Simple, practical, and usually good-natured, he finds less meaning in commencement than in reunion. The booster really has

no new beginnings, awakenings, or rites of passage. Neither has he ever fallen, for he is not conscious enough to be aware of a fall. His roots go back to the medieval burgher, and probably further, but he is truly a representative American. His influence upon our culture is absolutely astonishing and utterly incalculable, for it is he who has kept both the stadiums and the classrooms full. He is not especially selfish and is not as completely anti-intellectual as he may appear. With his money, he will dig a Pierian Spring on campus for those few who are thirsty, provided that a fountain of youth be erected nearby that he himself can drink from on homecoming weekends.

The booster alumnus is not necessarily a loud-mouthed college graduate. He may be and often is one who has graduated from high school and quietly returns periodically to the milieu, the high school practice field, that provided the only meaning he is ever to find. Such a pathetic one is Pat McGee, titular hero of a James T. Farrell short story.

Pat had been "all-Catholic-High-School football star," and in his own dreams "might have been an all-American." He is in fact more of "a might-have-been" than a has-been, though he is certainly not without marked ability in a number of sports, being "a natural-born athlete" and "the greatest ever turned out by M.O.M. [MARY OUR MOTHER]." After high school, Pat tries to continue pitching but throws his arm out in a semi-pro league. He keeps waiting for the arm to come back, but it never does. With no future in sports ahead, he begins more and more to look backward.

It is as much "the good old M.O.M. spirit" as a wish to be near the scene of his triumphs and failures (which in his dreams he converts to triumphs) that brings him back to watch the team practice. There at the edge of the field Pat, like Irwin Shaw's Christian Darling,[55] is transported back to another day: "He imagined himself as he used to run, going like a power house, knees hitting high, head low, his full hard body crashing and smashing forward. Running with the ball, smashing through a hole in the line and breaking out into the open, that had been his biggest football thrill. And he had gone sixty-five yards like that for a touchdown against St. Rose's in his junior year."[56]

Pat has a great deal in common with Christian Darling but he is different. He is a bromide but not a babe, and he returns to the past not merely to relive his own moments of glory but also to be reunited in the old school spirit. He is disappointed on both counts. The students do not notice him as he had thought, the coach "is nice but busy," and there is no longer any camaraderie among his old teammates who have also come out to watch the practice. Al, for "whom things weren't going right" and who is now smoking, has obviously had some disagreement with Tom, who had gone on to play for Knute Rockne and had "been a star in some games." To Pat, Tom had been a sort of hero which is why the following conversation is so sad:

"What are you doing?" Pat finally asked him.

Tom acted as if he hadn't heard. After about a minute of silence, he said: "I'm representing Stebbins and McCreary."

Tom handed Pat an engraved card with his name in the corner and the words *Sales Representative* after it.

"Are you selling bonds?" asked Pat.

The thud of a football being punted echoed across the field.

"Paint materials," Tom said.

Pat realized that it wasn't the same old Tom, and in his present mood this distressed him. He was ill at ease.

Tom said nothing for a moment, and then, with that same note of condescension in his voice, he asked: "Are you doing anything, Pat?"

"Oh, I'm selling cars, but I'll be back in baseball next year. I'm going to do some semi-pro playing with an eleven out in Pullman, too. I love the old game same as ever, Tom," Pat said, hoping this would restore their bond of high-school days.

"Oh," said Tom.

"Are you going to play any more football, Tom?" asked Pat, regretting now that he hadn't been able to go to N.D. as Tom had.

"No, I wouldn't be a professional athlete. It makes a bum of you," Tom said cuttingly. (p. 201)

This dialogue in a relatively obscure short story is one of the most telling in the literature of sports. In this brief exchange is clearly revealed all the deplorable consequences of a culture that cannot develop wider opportunities for personal heroism. Pat, who has graduated from high school, sells cars; Tom, who played for Notre Dame, sells paints. The implication is clear: what do ex-athletes in America do? They sell, and when possible they return to their alma mater to watch the next generation going through all the same old motions that will lead to the same old regrets and discontent. Pat, Al, and Tom on the sidelines of the practice field form in fact the most familiar group in America, the ex-high school players who come out year after year to watch the current edition of the varsity and by their presence give tacit support of an unending cycle that wins allegience but inhibits personal growth.

Farrell, himself a lover of baseball, treats the rather simple Pat McGee con amore as he does the equally simple Chris Terrett in "The Echo of Fame." Chris too is a booster alumnus but his school is the American league. Unlike Pat McGee, Chris had been a successful professional athlete, one of the "outstanding hurlers of his time," but like Pat he has a difficult time adjusting to life after the arm goes dead. Concealed beneath his games and amusements there is an unconscious despair.

Chris hunted and fished, played bridge, drank beer at the local Elks club, and sometimes saw old-time ball players. Every year at the time for spring training, he was both eager and depressed. Memories of his own great days would flood back upon him. He would visit the ball parks and watch the players working out or playing exhibition games. Seeing young prospects, full of hustle and wanting to play ball and to make it, he would think of his own youth. It was gone and nothing in his life, following his retirement from the game, was as rewarding as the gratifications, satisfactions, pleasures and the spotlight he had known when he had been one of the best pitchers in the American League.

Often he was bitter and surly. He knew nothing well but baseball. The fact that his income was sufficient for him to live comfortably did not ease or soften his bitterness. From the age of twenty-one he had made good money. He resented those who seemed more educated than he, and was ill at ease in their presence. Frequently, he was bored, and would freeze up in company, to sit frowning and silent. When he read the sports pages of the newspapers, *Sporting News* or the baseball magazines, and would see other old timers mentioned, he would become resentful. Once his name had been regularly printed in the scores of big-league games: now, he rarely saw his name in print.[57]

The story, however, ends happily for Chris. After participating in a baseball clinic for young boys in Florida, Chris realizes that he has the genuine respect and admiration of the boys—to them he wasn't a has-been"—and that he really does "love this damn game." Also with the other old-timers he experiences once again something of the atmosphere that had been part of the game. "He hadn't understood then how really important the fellowship of the game was, the jokes, the pranks, the rhubarbs and the talk. He missed this talk and the fellowship of baseball" (p. 25).

Then at the banquet following the old-timers' game Chris makes a sentimental speech calling for more get-togethers and good times. Afterward, Chris, like the others present, feels warm and friendly and "pleased with the whole affair." "Next year, he'd be back in there with the kids loving it." Thus what Pat McGee seeks, Chris Terrett finds and not only finds but also perpetuates. He will be a baseball booster until he dies. Old major leaguers never die—they don't even grow up.

Tom Buchanan, Boze Hertzlinger, Elmer Gantry, Joe Ferguson, and Broad Shoulders are all what the late Paul Gallico has called "the world's greatest bores—ex-football players."[58] Football, however, no more enhances philistinism or hinders maturation than the other highly commercialized collegiate sport—basketball. Though taller, fictional heroes of this game do not appear to be imbued with any more vision than the gridder. Certainly Ron Patimkin of Philip Roth's novelette *Goodbye, Columbus* is not.

The Patimkin family, with whom Neil Klugman visits in his suit of the daughter Brenda, is rich from the sale of "Patimkin Kitchen and Bathroom Sinks" and very sports-minded, so much so that Klugman, who majored in philosophy at "Newark College of Rutgers University," frequently finds himself engaged in various contests and exercises and sees all about him evidence of an "archaic disposition," to use Veblen's phrase, of members of the leisure class.

On the shelf back of the bar were two dozen bottles—twenty-three to be exact—of Jack Daniels, each with a little booklet tied to its collared neck informing patrons how patrician of them it was to drink the stuff. And over the Jack Daniels were more photos: there was a blown-up newspaper photo of Ron palming a basketball in one hand like a raisin; under the picture it said, "*Center*, Ronald Patimkin, Milburn High School, 6'4", 217 pounds." And there was another picture of Brenda on a horse, and next to that, a velvet mounting board with ribbons and medals clipped to it: Essex County Horse Show 1949, Union County Horse Show 1950, and so on—all for Brenda, for jumping and running or galloping or whatever else young girls receive ribbons for.[59]

Brenda disappoints her parents when evidence is found that she and Klugman have been making love in the Patimkin house, but Ron remains their pride and joy, mainly because he stresses the right things. "'We're going to have a boy,' he said, to his mother's delight, 'and when he's about six months old I'm going to sit him down with a basketball in front of him, and a football, and a baseball, and then whichever one he reaches for, that's the one we're going to concentrate on'" (p. 61).

Then in a letter that brings back memories of Lardner's Busher Keefe, Patimkin reassures his daughter of his love but at the same time reminds her of the fine example set by Ron. "Some people never turn out the way you hope and pray but I am willing to forgive and call Buy Gones, Buy Gones. You have always up till now been a good Buck and got good scholastic Grades and Ron has always been what we want a Good Boy, most important, and a Nice Boy" (p. 127).

While Ron may think of the future for his son, his look is mainly backward. Like so many stars he cannot escape the sentimental tug of the past, a fact he cannot conceal and probably does not even want to. Klugman had noticed that at night Ron would lock himself in the room with *Sports Illustrated* and Montovani, but Klugman heard Ron's "Columbus Record" the night before Ron's wedding.

"And here comes Ron Patimkin dribbling out. Ron, Number 11, from Short Hills, New Jersey. Big Ron's last game and it'll be some time before Buckeye fans forget him. . . ."

Big Ron tightened on his bed as the loudspeaker called his name; his ovation must have set the nets to trembling. Then the rest of the players were announced, and then basketball season was over, and it was Religious Emphasis Week, the Senior Prom (Billy May blaring at the gymnasium roof), Fraternity Skit Night, e.e. cummings reading to students (verse, silence, applause); and then, finally commencement:

"The campus is hushed this day of days. For several thousand young men and women it is a joyous yet a solemn occasion. And for their parents a day of laughter and a day of tears. It is a bright green day, it is June the seventh of the year one thousand nine hundred and fifty-seven and for these young Americans the most stirring day of their lives. For many this will be their last glimpse of the campus, of Columbus, for many many years. Life calls us, and anxiously if not nervously we walk out into the world and away from the pleasures of the ivied walls. But not from its memories. They will be the concomitant, if not the fundament, of our lives. We shall choose husbands and wives, we shall choose jobs and homes, we shall sire children and grandchildren, but we will not forget you, Ohio State. In the years ahead we will carry with us always memories of thee, Ohio State." (pp. 102–5)

The athleticism of Brenda herself figures in the breakup between her and Klugman. "If she had only been slightly *not* Brenda . . . but then would I have loved her?" Klugman asks. It is impossible to answer, of course, but perhaps worthwhile to speculate what Klugman meant by the phrase "slightly *not* Brenda." To have been "slightly not Brenda," Brenda would probably have been less concerned with appearances and with exhibitionism, both of which are symptoms of the sporting disposition. Brenda gives evidence of excessive concern for appearances by having her nose bobbed—of which Klugman disapproved—and of a certain degree of exhibitionism or carelessness (they are often indistinguishable) in leaving her diaphragm where her mother would find it. It is all enough to turn Klugman away and cause him to return to his job in the library. He himself is rather athletic; but after his sojourn with the Patimkins, his parting message seems to be not only "goodbye, Columbus" but also "farewell to sport."

Goodbye, Columbus provides insight into at least one Jewish family's view of sport, but *Portnoy's Complaint* contains perhaps a more typically Jewish attitude toward play and games. Baseball and softball the paranoid Portnoy loves—"Oh to be a center fielder, a center fielder—and nothing more!" he tells the doctor; and though he has a certain admiration for the brothers of the *shikses*, those "engaging, good-natured, confident, clean, swift, and powerful halfbacks for the college football teams called *Northwestern* and *Texas Christian* and *UCLA*"—it is clear that football is still for him a "thuggish" game of the gentiles. Even as a child he senses that it "is not exactly the ultimate catastrophe"

for the Jewish community for Weequahic High to go down in
defeat in this game, but there is a different feeling entirely
among the older men with whom the hero plays softball on
Sundays from nine to one, at about the time that good members
of the Fellowship of Christian Athletes would be in church. To
Portnoy they are an endearing lot to whom "losing and winning
is not a joke . . . and yet it is." And that, adds Portnoy, is "what
charms me most of all." These men seem to have found the
simple secret of play, now so long lost in the mad world of
acquisitiveness and unconscious conformity that, as Huizinga
puts it, "really to play, a man must play as a child."

Almost invariably the booster alumnus in literature is a comic
or pathetic character, but he raises deep questions: How loyal
should one be to institutions and for what reasons? If man is
either a hero or hero-worshiper as Ernest Becker and others
have claimed, then loyalty becomes almost synonymous with
quality, the third event in the universe. Loyalty is the bond between the form or idea, that is, a hero or institution, and energy
or admiration, the hero-worshipers or alumni. (Widespread
admiration is a form of energy.) For the booster, college has
become a symbol of transcendence and a way to a higher and
better life. In short, quality has been enhanced. Quality, though,
cannot be defined. It can be described or shown, which is why we
must finally turn to the artist to help us understand what is of
value in society and what is not. It is thus through the imagination of the artist that we "know," for example, that the al-
legiances of Joe Ferguson to Midwestern University, Broad
Shoulders to his New England college, George F. Babbitt and
Charles McKelvey to "The U.," Pat McGee to M.O.M. and Ron
Patimkin to Ohio State are pale and shallow loyalties compared
to the "consuming devotion" of F. Scott Fitzgerald to the Princeton football team or his awe of Hobie Baker. Loyalty, a type of
consciousness, can at times be marvelous. The only other parallel in the literary world that comes immediately to mind is the
homage and allegiance rendered by Frederick Exley to Frank
Gifford and the New York Giants as described in *A Fan's Notes.*
Clearly one form of excellence can inspire another. There are
many paths to quality and personal heroism, but the booster,
unfortunately, sees only one.

The Model or the Hollow Apollo

If God, the highest Good, is a synthesis of opposites, then it should not be surprising that the athlete has often been given divine or semidivine status or held up as some sort of social model of the good life. In the mastery of his body he reveals to us not only strength but beauty or cosmos and virtually demands our attention. If the athlete is the paragon of wholeness, the true priests of our time are the advertising men, the promoters of the good life and the body beautiful.

To look good, however, is not to be either whole or holy. That appearances are often deceiving is perhaps the major theme in all American literature. The frequently anthologized short story of Henry James, "The Real Thing," is illustrative in the case of the model, as are several other stories by James. Heroes must announce themselves in symbols and hero worshipers must imitate, and everywhere we are surrounded by walking eidólons. No one has summarized this aspect of the modern condition more succinctly than Saul Bellow in *Mr. Sammler's Planet*:

Art increased, and a sort of chaos. More possibility, more actors, apes, copycats, more invention, more fiction, illusion, more fantasy, more despair. Life looting Art of its wealth, destroying Art as well by its desire to become the thing itself. Pressing itself into pictures. Reality forcing itself into all these shapes. Just look (Sammler looked) at this imitative anarchy of the streets—these Chinese revolutionary tunics, these babes in unisex toyland, these surrealist warchiefs, Western stagecoach drivers—Ph.D.s in philosophy.... They sought originality. They were obviously derivative. And of what—of Paiutes, of Fidel Castro? No, of Hollywood extras. Acting mythic. Casting themselves into chaos, hoping to adhere to higher consciousness, to be washed up on the shores of truth. Better, thought Sammler, to accept the inevitability of imitation and then to imitate good things. The ancients had this right. Greatness without models? Inconceivable. One could not be the thing itself— Reality. One must be satisfied with the symbols. Make it the object of imitation to reach and release the high qualities. Make peace therefore with intermediacy and representation. But choose higher representations. Otherwise the individual must be the failure he now sees and knows himself to be. Mr. Sammler, sorry for all, and sore at heart.[60]

But what are the "higher representations," the positive exempla? It is impossible to say. One proceeds by "faint clues and indirections," to borrow Whitman's phrase, in determining the best modes to live by, to say nothing of the models. The literary artist can help us choose by revealing the consequences of particular forms of hero worship, especially that based on physical appearances alone, as William Inge has done so devastatingly in two famous plays, *Come Back, Little Sheba* and *Picnic*.

Turk in *Come Back, Little Sheba*, Inge tells us, has "the openness, the generosity, vigor and health of youth." Of these only generosity is always a virtue; but if Turk has any generosity, it is not apparent. His "openness" can easily be confused with arrogance and braggadocio as his vigor can be identified as rudeness. "I guess I'm a man of action, baby," he tells Marie, and again he says, "Honey, I know I talk awful rough around you at times; I never was a very gentlemanly bastard."[61] He is certainly not "very gentlemanly" though he seems to do all right as a "bastard." "He always enters unannounced," purposely teases Lola, and does not know the meaning of modesty. "I won the state championship," he tells Lola, and when he and Marie are discussing a tryst, he says, "Bring her [Lola] along. I'll take care of her too." Moreover, Turk's "youth" should not be taken for innocence. When Lola tells him that he should be in Hollywood making Tarzan movies—a line that Lola also uses on the milkman—Turk replies, "I had enough of that place in the Navy." Hollywood and the Navy. Turk thus becomes a young man with a past, a young man who has all the qualifications of a rogue.

Still he has everything that Doc does not have: Youth, health, good looks, athletic ability, and the affection of Marie. Doc hates his guts and not without reason. The fact that a young, egotistical athlete is posing half naked in his house and at the same time becoming the idol of his wife and the sweetheart of a girl for whom he has affection would be enough to unsettle a more stable man than Doc. Marie and Turk in fact are creatures of the romantic American dream stuck right under Doc's nose: Marie the beautiful young artist and Turk the handsome young stud. By having Turk pose with the javelin, Inge intended no doubt to suggest the ephebus of ancient Greece, usually depicted on emblems, according to Gardiner, with a spear; but if "big," "beautiful" Turk has strength and physical beauty, he does not have the moral qualities that must accompany them, and all goes for naught. One must sympathize with the warm-hearted Lola for being taken in by the posing but also with Doc when he screams: "Tell the world I'm drunk. Tell the whole damn world. Scream your head off, you fat slut. . . . I oughta hack off all that fat, and then wait for Marie to chop off those pretty ankles she's always dancing around on. . . . then start lookin' for Turk and fix him too" (p. 57).

Early in the play, before Turk appears, Doc says that he is not going to be in "any competition with a football player." This statement is ironic. For throughout Doc is in competition with him, and much of the meaning of the play centers around Doc's athletic victory in Lola's dream at the end.

Oh, it was about everyone and everything . . . Marie and I were going to the Olympics back in our old high school stadium. There were thousands of people there. There was Turk out in the center of the field throwing the javelin. Every time he threw it, the crowd would roar . . . and you know who the man in charge was? It was my father. Isn't that funny? . . . But Turk kept changing into someone else all the time. And then my father disqualified him. So he had to sit on the sidelines . . . and guess who took his place, Daddy? You! You came trotting out there on the field just as big as you please. . . .

DOC. (*Smilingly*) How did I do, Baby?

LOLA. Fine. You picked the javelin up real careful, like it was awful heavy. But you threw it, Daddy, *clear,* clear up into the sky. And it never came down again. (Doc *looks very pleased with himself.*) . . . Then it started to rain. (p. 68)

Lola goes on to tell how she saw little Sheba dead in the mud, "that sweet little puppy . . . her curly white fur all smeared with mud, and no one to stop and take care of her." Thus in the same dream in which she drives Turk from her mind she comes to accept the loss of Sheba. If she could never again have Sheba, neither could she harbor a superficial ideal like Turk. She comes to accept both reality and Doc, who in her dreams becomes her own Olympian.

Hal Carter in *Picnic* is simply another Turk. He is not only an ungentlemanly "bastard" like Turk but also "a poor bastard," "a bum," by his own admission. "I'm a *bum!*" he tells Madge.

"There's just no place in the world for a guy like me."[62] One reason why there is no place for him is that Hal wants everything for nothing. When Alan asks him what kind of job he wants, Hal replies, "Oh, something in a nice office where I can wear a tie ... and have a sweet little secretary ... and talk over the telephone about enterprises and ... things ... I've always had the feeling, if I just had the chance, I could set the whole world on fire" (p. 25). Football had done nothing to arrest his paranoia, had in fact even aggravated it, as he himself comes to realize. "A guy gets spoiled if he's a good football player or something. He thinks he can expect his whole life to be bigtime" (p. 61). Hal thus tries to make Madge think that he can be happy "working on a pipeline" or a "job like that," but the reader has no doubt that he, like Boze Hertzlinger and others, will go on "chasing the rainbow," hoping for a windfall and eternal youth.

While Hal accuses others of being phony, he himself is the biggest phony of all. The decadent romantic personality he wears is as much for show as the physical poses he is always striking. He has been so warped by his megalomania, however, that he cannot really identify any one basic personality within him, and all he says somehow sounds insincere and suspicious. When he thinks that Alan is going to press for the hundred dollars he owes, he tells about two girls raping and robbing him after picking him up on the highway in a yellow convertible—the police had called it wishful thinking—and all the talk about the tough time he had as a kid has the sound of a line. The truth is that he has dreamed of Big Deals and stardom so often, has posed so much, has allowed his dreams to go so unchecked that he no longer knows what is true about him and what is not. Hal obviously has many characteristics that would go well in Hollywood, but like all heroes, he too has a flaw that he reveals to Alan.

HAL. Then they put me in a pair of tights—those pants that fit you down here like a glove—(*Runs his hands down his legs to show, then jumps up on the stump.*) and they gave me a big hat with a plume, (*Pantomines putting on the hat.*) and had me poking at things with swords. (*He gets into duelling position, leaps off stump to right, parries, lunges, withdraws, wipes blood off blade.*) Touché, mug! (*Sheaths his sword with a smack, turns and*

enjoying the memory of it immensely he crosses to stump, speaking as he crosses.)
It was real crazy.

ALAN. Did they give you any lines to read?

HAL. Yah, that part went okay. It was my teeth.

ALAN. Your teeth?

HAL. Yah! Out there, you gotta have a certain kind of teeth or they can't use you. Don't ask me why. *(Foot down off stump, turns to Alan.)* This babe said they'd have to pull all my teeth and give me new ones, so naturally—(p. 22).

Hal is anti-intellectual, unceasingly. His study habits are the same as Turk's. He cuts classes, pays no attention to lectures, and eventually flunks out without cultivating mental discipline or acquiring any real desire to achieve. If Joe Ferguson is impressed by the *Reader's Digest* and Elmer Gantry by the *Saturday Evening Post,* Hal is impressed and even intimidated by the Book of the Month. "I used to go with a girl once who read books. She joined the book-of-the-month club and they had her readin' books all the time!" (p. 45)

Hal, then, is a bromide too but one without any direction or loyalty. For whatever number of causes, all of which are expressed by a loss of manners, he is a piece of matter in motion. He has been, as he says, "rolling around like a pin ball," exhibiting a congeries of attitudes and poses that characterize the male version of the bitch goddess. Totally self-centered, idle, irresponsible, wild, and contemptuous of others, he has arrogance but not hubris, which suggests a certain nobility of character before the fall. Hal does not fall; he is rotten from beginning to end. A poser of all show and no substance, he has great success with women, a fact that might cause a cynic or misogynist to agree in part with Jack Burden in Robert Penn Warren's *All the King's Men*: "There is nothing women love so much as the drunkard, the hellion, the roarer, the reprobate. They love him because they—women, I mean—are like the bees in Samson's parable in the Bible; they like to build their honeycombs in the carcass of a dead lion."[63] Out of the strong shall come forth a sweetness. Also out of the strong shall come forth rottenness when not accompanied by the queen of virtues, *sapientia.*

Brave New Man

The most recent Apollonian symbol in literature is the brave new man, a product of behavioral thought, the dream of fascists, and the nightmare of those who read history. Edward Albee's *Who's Afraid of Virginia Woolf?* is a masterful depiction of this struggle between old and new, and the protagonists, not surprisingly, are that old familiar pair, professor and athlete, in this case George and Nick, avatars of the great American archetypes, Ichabod Crane and Brom Bones. To understand the significance of this war in one of its most recent and complicated forms, however, it is necessary to look briefly at all the characters in *Who's Afraid*, especially as conscious beings, and their relationships.

The lowest order of consciousness is seen in Honey. Sweet, cute, and decorous, she embodies all the saccharin superficialities of the day. "A wifey little type," she throws up often, sucks her thumb, and sleeps curled up on the floor like a fetus. She can be hurt but there is little evidence that she experiences suffering. She is "fragile" but strong enough to bear the misfortunes of others, which, according to La Rochefoucauld, is true for most.

Basically the *Weltansicht* of Nick is as blighted as that of his wife. Though a teacher, he is nevertheless a Thing-man, a member of what Phillip Wylie, speaking of scientists, called "brilliant legions of the half-conscious." Says Martha in a trite but funny observation,

Oh, little boy, you got yourself hunched over that microphone of yours. . . .
    NICK. Microscope. . . .
    MARTHA. . . . yes . . . but you don't see anything do you? You see everything but the goddamn mind; you see all the little specs and crap, but you don't see what goes on.[64]

Since Nick does not look for the mind, it is worthwhile to consider why he, a promising scientist and former star athlete—one without "any scars"—became a teacher. When George ("of or pertaining to a farmer") asks him, Nick ("victorious among the people") replies,

Oh . . . well, the same things that . . . uh . . . motivated you, I imagine.
GEORGE. What were they?
NICK. Pardon?
GEORGE. I said, what were they? What were the things that motivated me?
NICK. (*Laughing uneasily*) Well . . . I'm sure I don't know.
GEORGE. You just finished saying that the things that motivated you were the same things that motivated me.
NICK. (*With a little pique*) I said I *imagined* they were.
GEORGE. Oh. (*Off-hand*) Did you? (*Pause*) Well . . . (*Pause*) You like it here? (p. 31)

Obviously Nick and George were not motivated by the same things. Nick is an ambitious young man on the move up the academic ladder, while George is a failure because he had been no good at either trustees' dinners or fund raising, had no personality, and had played with the muses. Nick, by contrast, has no interest in the muses whatever, of either the arts or sciences, does not understand about drinking at Parnassus—a private joke between George and Martha—has no head for heights, has never experienced the terror, absurdity, and wonder of awareness, and cannot, George leads one to believe, be initiated—only punished, as Martha too senses: "Look boy," she says to him. "Once you stick your nose in it, you're not going to pull out just whenever you feel like it. You're in for a while."

But he is only *in* for a while. When George begins to tell Martha about the death of their imaginary son, a "little all-American something-or-other" George associates with Nick—another reason perhaps why George wants to kill his "son"—Nick is struck "with the beginnings of a knowledge he cannot face." In all fairness to him one must admit the possibility that he does see, if only briefly, that he too becomes "afraid of Virginia Woolf." Earlier Martha, obviously referring to more than their bedroom episode, has said that his potential was better than his performance, and his impassioned "JESUS CHRIST I THINK I UNDERSTAND THIS" seems rather convincing. But somehow one feels that if Nick does understand, it is not for long and that recidivism will follow exorcism, if in his case it ever occurs. That he is sobered to some degree is undeniable, but that he is exorcised along with Martha does not seem likely, especially when

one considers the earth-shattering consequences of the transformation: "Before encountering the absurd, the everyday man
lives with aims, a concern for the future or for justifica-
tion. . . . He still thinks that something in his life can be directed.
In truth he acts as if he were free, even if all the facts make a
point of contradicting that liberty. But after the absurd everything is upset."[65] Clearly Nick is not so affected by his confronta-
tion with absurdity.

Nick is only threatened with consciousness and manages, in
all probability, to withstand it. Martha, for whom everything has
long been "upset," tries to make do but fails. Deprived of the life
that Honey suppressed, she attempts to mitigate her misery by
creating an unnatural world with its pathetic poses: shrew,
temptress, tough babe, and "Earth Mother." Venting her frustration on George, the one she loves most, she turns to Nick,
athletic champion and romantic lover. By such actions Martha
tries to live for sensation, to become unconscious, but this
George will not allow. As magician, he casts out her illusions,
making her what she naturally is, a warm and sentient woman.

If Nick does not see the mind at all, George perhaps sees too
much of it, and with Mephistopheles he and Martha as much as
say, "Now we're back . . . on our wit's end—the point where
human intelligence snaps,"[66] where thought and language dis-
sociate. But for George there is no retreat or compromise. To do
so would sanction the brave new world he sees symbolized by
Nick: "A civilization of men, smooth, blond, and right at the
middleweight limit . . . a race of scientists and mathematicians,
each dedicated to and working toward the greater glory of the
super-civilization." There is a certain humorous ambivalence in
practically everything George says, but his sincerity in the wish
for the preservation of "the surprise, the multiplexity, the sea-
changing rhythm of history" can scarcely be doubted. What he
fears is a world without fear, a world in which sick puns are
made about a great artist who cared enough to take her life.
What George fears is a surfeited world of Nick and Honey. He
rescues Martha from this world not through revenge but
through love. George, in fact, is a type of saviour figure, the
curse being a godlike consciousness. For Martha he finally becomes Jung's animus in its most developed form: "the wise guide

to spiritual truth." George will not allow her to ignore what Eliade calls "the terror of history" by taking comfort in a primitive archetype represented by Nick, for Nick, though a brave new man indeed, is also archaic man who in health, beauty, and youth tempts us into the belief in the myth of eternal return and in the insignificance of historical events. For George, neither the history of the world nor his own, real or imagined, can be ignored. Nick's plans for aggrandizement do not seem to be altered permanently by his night with the history professor and his wife.

There are, then, four recognizable states of consciousness in *Who's Afraid of Virginia Woolf?*: the almost nauseous insensateness of Honey; the potential but repressed pathos of Nick; the futile, desperate escapism of Martha; and the wide-ranging, freewheeling historical consciousness of George. Looking at them all one might be inclined to think that the extended consciousness of George and Martha, George in particular, should be avoided at all cost, that blessed are they who either cannot see (Honey) or will not see (Nick), but Camus says that this is not so, that the disturbed man can, like Sisyphus, face the blackness and in the very effort to see—and be—take heart. Repugnant as he often is, George is nonetheless an ethical being; suffering, he obeys at length and in his own way calls for "a revaluation of all values."

Enough conflict between intellectual and athlete has now been seen to cause one to ask what possibly can be done to bring about some tolerable understanding between the intellectual and the muscular. Very little can be done, it seems, and one reason (among many) is that today the bromide (Nick) cannot understand the *revolté* (George). The opposite cannot work: The *revolté* cannot accept the bromide. To do so is to admit that Nick is a fine example of *mens sana,* which he is not. Perhaps the greatest irony is that George, the professor, paunch and all, is the last hope for the reawakening of the concept of the entire man. In any event George is a Dionysian figure and, in his rebellion, a blood brother of those alienated athletes I have called the Adonic. The warring roles are always the same, conformity and conscious revolt, and athletes and intellectuals qualify for either.

3. Dionysus

The Darling

Just as there are many masks for Apollo, so are there many for Dionysus. The sacrificial Dionysus or Adonis gains one's admiration or pity, but that Dionysus whose forms are the lovely youth with curled hair or the wild bull and burning flame is the unconscious apostle of chaos and death. I have designated these Dionysian athletes the "darling," the beloved pet of the witnessing woman, and the "naked beast," a sadist who cannot transcend a perverted nature.

Other terms that might apply in discussion of the darling are "golden boy," "pretty boy," "lover boy," and "sonny boy," but none of these seems to apply quite as well as "darling." As a general type the darling dates back to antiquity, but he appears to have gained in popularity since the rise of courtly love in the twelfth century. He is not a dandy or fop but he has a babyishness or boyishness which sometimes borders on effeminacy. To be sure he is quite a scrapper, but his success in sports depends more upon finesse and skill than upon strength. Generally not big physically, he is handsome and frequently has blond hair. Often the darling is a sad young man whose personal sorrow helps attract the female to him. Knowing nothing of camaraderie, his whole being is tied up with women who pursue, protect, and applaud him. As a boxer, the darling is the modern male Cinderella who usually beats the big guy but cannot give direction to his own life.

Probably no American writer worshiped strength and beauty more than Jack London, and attempts to embody this ideal in some degree are apparent in Pat Glendon of *The Abysmal Brute*, Sandel of "A Piece of Steak," and Joe Fleming of *The Game*. Pat

Glendon will be considered in detail later on, and Sandel, from the little that is seen of him, has possibilities for approximating that severe synthesis of the ancient world. Tom King in fact saw in him "glorious youth, rising exultant and invincible, supple of muscle and silken of skin, with heart and lungs that had never been tired and torn and that laughed at limitation of effort."[1] In the case of Fleming, however, London overemphasized Fleming's beauty, which is too pretty to be the ideal of a Myron, "the perfection of line and strength and development" notwithstanding. Part of the difficulty, however, lies in the fact that aside from the illustrations of the 1905 edition the reader must look at Joe through the eyes of his sweetheart, Genevieve, who disguises herself as a man in order to gain admittance to the fight in which Joe is one of the participants. This could be the chief reason why the image of Fleming is replete with feminine metaphors and why, therefore, Joe is a darling instead of the ideal of strength and beauty that London obviously intended him to be: "When she thought of Joe, the Joe instantly visualized on her mind was a clothed Joe—girl-cheeked, blue-eyed, curly-headed, but clothed.... His skin was fair as a woman's, far more satiny, and no rudimentary hair growth marred its white lustre. This she perceived, but all the rest, the perfection of line and strength and development, gave pleasure without her knowing why. There was a cleanness and grace about it. His face was like a cameo, and his lips, parted in a smile, made it very boyish."[2]

If London through Genevieve's eyes stresses Fleming's beauty to a fault, he inartistically but significantly from a philosophical point of view overemphasizes the lack of grace of his opponent, John Ponta.

Here was the fighter—the beast with a streak for a forehead, with beady eyes under lowering and bushy brows, flat-nosed, thick-lipped, sullen-mouthed. He was heavy-jawed, bull-necked, and the short, straight hair of the head seemed to her frightened eyes the stiff bristles on a hog's back. Here were coarseness and bruteness—a thing savage, primordial, ferocious. He was swarthy to blackness, and his body was covered with a hairy growth that matted like a dog's on his chest and shoulders. He was deep-chested, thick-legged, large-muscled, but unshapely. His muscles were knots, and he was gnarled and knobby, twisted out of beauty by excess of strength. (pp. 117–18)

Here then is the familiar battle, not only strength and beauty versus ugliness, but also the little guy against the big guy ("Joe Fleming fights at one hundred and twenty-eight . . . John Ponta at one hundred and forty"), the fair-haired boy against the villain, David against Goliath, Beowulf against Grendel, Cosmos against Chaos. Here there is a difference, however, for while Joe wins for a time, he is struck down and killed by a "lucky punch" by the bigger Ponta.

London is clearly reflecting the belief that there is "no place for strength and beauty among men," especially in the world of professional boxing. "The Game had played him false," London says, just as it does the heroes in his other boxing stories. Were the milieu of boxing the best imaginable, one would still wonder about the chances of Joe's success in any contest where the agon is heightened. He is too delicate to win in any agonistic encounter. He is pretty for the female to gaze upon, but too brittle and precious for a world that first and foremost requires prowess and action. Too much beauty and grace in athletes is by definition a luxury but also, according to coaches, a handicap. Joe Fleming needed to be stronger, and the defeat of this "girl-cheeked," "blue-eyed" piece of Dresden china at the hands of a "bull-necked" beast is a piece of romantic *Weltschmerz*.

If London knew that one of his heroes had been called a darling, he would probably be shocked, and yet the charge is not necessarily as serious as one might suppose. Just as there are degrees of brutality, so are there degrees of darlingness to which writers have at one time or another fallen prey. Some darlingness, then, is understandable, but that of Joe Bonaparte, Golden Boy, in Clifford Odets's play by the same name is a perversion closely related to hubris and cruelty.

It should first be understood that *Golden Boy* is, in the words of the narrator of Budd Schulberg's *The Harder They Fall*, "a nine dollar bill" and that the hero is "a peculiar duck." Perhaps in no other play are the animus and anima levels of characters so thoroughly confused. Tokio, the trainer, calls Joe a "real sweetheart" and says that "if you want the goods delivered you have to treat him delicate, gentle—like a girl."[3] Roxy apparently takes the advice, for he addresses Joe as "My Boy! My darling boy!" and Fuseli is simply, in the view of Moody, "a queer." In many ways Lorna is the most masculine character in the play. Certainly her language is at times that of a man: "My father's an old drunk son-of-a-bitch.... Twice a week he kicked my mother's face in. If I let myself go I'd be a drunkard in a year" (p. 269). While she regrets that Joe became a killer, it was she who helped to make him just that by encouraging him like a tough promoter and tutelary male: "Be a fighter! Show the world! If you made your fame and fortune—and you can— you'd be anything you want. Do it! Bang your way to the light- weight crown. Get a bank account. Hire a great doctor with a beard" (p. 264).

This is the second speech in which Lorna uses the word *beard* in a particular way. The other occurs early in Act 1 when she asks Moody who is desperate for boxers how he would like "a nice lady fighter with a beard." This phrase tells us not only much about Lorna but also a great deal about the androgynous nature of the other principal characters. Eight lines after Lorna mentions "a nice lady fighter," Joe Bonaparte enters.

If through her parentage Lorna is a type of warrior woman, a tough babe, an "old lady" who has seen the world but who can still slug it out—"I'm not afraid of you" she says to Fuseli—she is also the moon-eyed young girl, the female witness to the deed of the hero. "Joe, I think you're it! I don't know why, I think you're it! Take me home with you" (p. 285). She becomes the bride to be won and the object of all the striving for the hero as lover. She is the maiden described by Joseph Campbell.

The hegemony wrested from the enemy, the freedom won from the malice of the monster, the life energy released from the toils of the tyrant Holdfast—is symbolized as a woman. She is the maiden of the innumerable dragon slayings, the bride abducted from the jealous father, the virgin rescued from the unholy lover. She is the "other portion" of the hero himself—for "each is both": if his stature is that of world monarch she is the world, and if he is a warrior she is fame. She is the image of his destiny which he is to release from the prison of enveloping circumstance.[4]

Lorna, then, is both warrior woman and bride-to-be, the god- dess of love and war, and both roles are continually in conflict. If as guide she helps to make Joe a killer by spurring him to the crown, as bride-to-be she also laments the fact; for like all young maidens, she too likes the finer things of life and all the romantic ideas.

> LORNA. . . . go back to your music—
> JOE. But my hands are ruined. I'll never play again! What's left, Lorna? Half a man, nothing, useless. . . .
> LORNA. No, *we're* left! Two together! We have each other! Somewhere there must be happy boys and girls who can teach us the way of life! We'll find some city where poverty's no shame—where music is no crime!—where there's no war in the streets—where a man is glad to be himself, to live and make his woman herself! (pp. 315–16)

Lorna is a paradox, as peculiar as the young man she plans to marry. Like the women in the life of Roy Hobbs in *The Natural,* she is forever changing; and had she lived, one might guess that within a year she would have had her darling husband back in the ring.

It is probably not surprising that the problem of sadism appears to emerge most frequently in sports literature in stories of boxing, but it might be surprising to learn that the punishment is usually delivered by the boxing darling in the presence of the witnessing female. Examples are plentiful, though a few will suffice. In Frank Harris's "The Great Game" Kate, the girl friend of the corrupt Dick Donovan, is "flooded" with a "delicious triumph" as she observes the speed and strength of her victorious lover in the ring,[5] Genevieve of London's "The Game" experiences primitive feelings when she sees Joe Fleming hammering away at the grisly Ponta: "She, too, was out of herself; softness and tenderness had vanished; she exulted in each crushing blow her lover delivered" (p. 140); and Schulberg's Buddy Stein of *The Harder They Fall,* a decadent darling, slaughters the Andes giant Toro Molina while a beautiful blond in the third row begs "in a shrill, unpleasant voice, 'Kill im, Buddy.'"

Stein leaped in with a powerful right to the body that made Toro bend over. Then he straightened him up with a paralyzing left to the jaw. Toro toppled over. He fell so awkwardly that his ankle twisted under him. With horrible concentration, he lifted himself to his knees. He crawled forward on his knees, slipping in his own blood, like a dying beast. His mouth was open and the lower part of his jaw hung hideously loose. "Jaw's busted," I heard someone say. The big orange mouthpiece flopped out of his mouth and rolled a few feet ahead of him. For some reason he did not understand, he crawled painfully toward it and tried to stuff it back into his mouth in a slow-motion gesture of futility. He was still fumbling with his mouthpiece when the referee finished his count and raised Stein's hand. Buddy danced around happily, mitting his gloves over his head to acknowledge the ovation of the crowd.[6]

This contest is more like a bullfight than a boxing match, and in a bullfight it is again the little guy versus the big guy, the toro, the darling versus the big dark villain. In the *corrida* too sadism is always latent. In *The Sun Also Rises* Brett denies being a sadist, but the chances are that she sees in Romero's humiliation of the "big guy" something other than art. "She saw how Romero avoided every brusque movement and saved his bulls for the last when he wanted them, not winded and discomposed but smoothly worn down" (p. 67). It is perhaps this expertise in movement and method, an expertise shared by the skillful fighter that is so essential to sadism; the kicks come more with the adept toying and torturing than with the kill. Actually the anima arrangement in the boxing darling does not differ greatly from the animus of the female tough babe and super-woman so popular today on television, the movies, and sub-literature; and if in her expert use of swords, firearms, and judo superwoman falls into the lowest animus level of mere physical and detective expertise, the boxing darling reflects a negative anima through his prettiness and moodiness. Both he and the tough babe—the boxing darling is a tough babe—are negative types, appealing to the perverse in human nature, as well as to the ridiculous.

It is impossible to estimate the influence that Joe Bonaparte as a frustrated scholar and musician has had upon attitudes toward heroes in America. A number of popular books deal with the theme, but the chances are that the myth of the musician-intellectual forced to turn pro owes more to *Golden Boy* than to any other single American work. In his discussion of the myth in relation to him, Sandy Koufax seemed to have Joe Bonaparte specifically in mind.

Although I have not pored over the works of Huxley and Wolfe, I have read enough books to know that there are themes that appeal to writers. None of them is much better than the one about the sensitive man, longing to lead the monkish, contemplative life for which he is best suited by nature—enjoying good music, reading the masters and writing an occasional monograph in illuminated script. And doomed by a freakish physical ability to suffer through life as a national hero amidst the howling mobs, winning a success that he despises but cannot somehow give up. Because, where else, after all, could he earn that kind of money?

Just between you and me, I think I'd enjoy being a doomed, tragic figure as much as anybody. The only trouble with this tale of one man's struggle against his inner nature is that none of it is true. I wish my reading tastes were classier, but they happen to run to the best-seller lists and the book-club selections.[7]

Koufax is to be commended for setting the record straight; so is Budd Schulberg who wished to write about real boxers and not about "violinists with brittle hands," and so is Damon Runyon, who in "Bred for Battle" incisively satirizes the whole notion of the musician-boxer.

Having received a free pass for a fight at Madison Square Garden from Bill Corum, the narrator of "Bred for Battle" is approached by Spider McCoy, who tells him about the ideas of selective breeding of a Professor D who had quit teaching in an Ohio college "to handicap the horses." Spider thinks that if selective breeding works for horses and dogs it should also work for heavyweights and that he has found just the right combination of bloodlines in Shamus Mulrooney and Bridget O'Shea who, says Spider, "herself can lick half the heavyweights I see around nowadays if she is half as good as she is the last time I see her." The issue of Shamus and Bridget whom Spider has such great hopes for, however, appears to the narrator to be anything but bred for battle.

I am personally somewhat disappointed when I see Thunderbolt Mulrooney, and especially when I find out his first name is Raymond and not Thunderbolt at all, because I am expecting to see a big, fierce guy with red hair and a chest like a barrel, such as Shamus Mulrooney has when he is in his prime. But who do I see but a tall, pale looking young guy with blond hair and thin legs.

Furthermore, he has pale blue eyes, and a far-away look in them, and he speaks in a low voice, which is nothing like the voice of Shamus Mulrooney.[8]

Nevertheless, Spider maintains that here is the next heavyweight champion of the world if his fighting nature can only be aroused.

"Why," he says, "the guy is nothing but a baby, and you must give him time to fill out. He may grow to be bigger than his papa. But you know," Spider says, getting indignant as he thinks about it, "Bridget Mulrooney does not wish to let this guy be the next heavyweight champion of the world. In fact," Spider says, "she kicks up an awful row when I go to get him, and Shamus finally has to speak to her severely. Shamus says he does not know if I can ever make a fighter of this guy because Bridget coddles him until he is nothing but a mushhead, and Shamus says he is sick and tired of seeing the guy sitting around the house doing nothing but reading and playing the zither."
    "Does he play the zither yet?" I ask Spider McCoy.
    "No," Spider says, "I do not allow my fighters to play zithers. I figure it softens them up. This guy does not play anything at present. He seems to be in a daze most of the time, but of course everything is new to him." (pp. 214–15)

Understandably Spider is disconsolate when in the first fight, which is fixed so that Thunderbolt's opponent, Bubbles Browning, is to take a dive the first time he is hit, Thunderbolt goes to a neutral corner, puts his head into his gloves, and begins to cry. Spider and the narrator take Thunderbolt home where Spider asks Bridget the name of the hollow-chested, soft-voiced, music-loving guy she dated before marrying Shamus. While talking with Bridget, Spider discovers that he has been working with the wrong offspring of Bridget, that it is Terence, her youngest and the real son of Shamus who is the potential heavyweight, and not Raymond, who, Spider discovers, was sired by Cedric Tilbury, a floorwalker in Hamburgher's Department Store. As a light-weight "Tearing Terry Mulrooney" becomes "the new sensation," one reason being that unlike his half-brother, he was never torn between music and boxing.
    Yet behind the absurdity of *Golden Boy* and the superb humor of "Bred for Battle" is the same old problem, the splintering of

the ideal of the perfect man. In a sense Odets and Runyon are only footnoting Plato, who long ago arrived at the opinion that excessive concentration upon either "music" or "gymnastic" will lead to some kind of maladjustment of spirit and, conversely, that the balanced combination will lead to wholeness in body and mind.

By becoming a professional, Joe Bonaparte waives all chances of achieving a happy combination between "music" and "gymnastic," for in boxing there is no significant place for the civilizing effect of music. (Spider McCoy would not let his fighters play the zither.) Since winning is the only thing with the professional, he must concentrate upon the sport itself and forget about music. This basically is why professionals are more apt to be misologists than the philosopher-athletes in the Greek tradition. The concern in American sport, however, is not that the professional cannot be the gymnast-musician but that all too often the collegian cannot be one, especially those in the major sports simply because of the emphasis on winning and the horrendous and senseless demands upon the athlete's time. Rome taxed the brothels to keep the Colosseum going; today we tax the college athlete by depriving him of the opportunity of an education. Thus, early in life far too many young athletes must decide between "music" and "gymnastic" for they cannot have both any more than could Joe Bonaparte or Raymond Mulrooney.

Notwithstanding the many faults of all the athletes studied thus far, they frequently have redeeming characteristics. Their vices, quite often, are excess of virtue and almost all make an attempt, however pathetic in some cases, to use the mind. Tom Stark, of Robert Penn Warren's *All the King's Men,* by contrast has no positive qualities. He has conceit but not concern, arrogance but not ambition to achieve, to know, or even to save. Instead of pride being a fatal flaw in him it is only one among many shortcomings in a flawed character.

It is no accident that each of the major southern writers, Faulkner, Wolfe, Warren, and Williams, have written about football heroes, for in the South, especially the Deep South, football and not cotton is king. One reason for this perhaps is that football is a survival of a form of chivalry which found its most fertile soil in the Gulf states; and if Sir Walter Scott caused

the Civil War by filling the southern mind with "sham gran-
deurs," as Mark Twain asserted, he may also, as the following
poem suggests, have something to do with the hoopla with which
football is invested in the South.

> Then strip, lads, and to it, though sharp be the weather,
>   And if, by mischance, you should happen to fall,
> There are worse things in life than a tumble on heather,
>   And life is itself but a game at football.
>
> And when it is over, we'll drink a blithe measure
>   To each Laird and each Lady that witnessed our fun,
> And to every blithe heart that took part in our pleasure.
>   To the lads that have lost and the lads that have won.
>
>   Chorus [Alumni?]
>
> Then up with the Banner, let forest winds fan her,
>   She has blazed over Ettrick eight ages and more;
> In sport we'll attend her, in battle defend her,
>   With heart and with hand, like our fathers before.[9]

Scott was writing for and about amateurs and one is certain
that he would no more encourage the commercialism of today's
college football by writing fanfarish jingles than would southern
authors, who, however, do not appear to dislike the game itself.
It can even be said that on the whole they find in it a certain
fascination much like that other writers have found in boxing.
Moreover, fictional rebel gridiron heroes by southern and non-
southern writers are, in spite of numerous faults, generally
treated sympathetically, for example, Faulkner's Labove,
Williams's Brick Pollitt, Anderson's Jim of *Kit Brandon,* and
Mark Harris's Bruce Pearson (more famous as a catcher). One
notable exception, however, is Warren's Tom Stark, who in Jack
Burden's view is "a son-of-a-bitch."

At least, if he wasn't a son-of-a-bitch yet, he had shown some very
convincing talent in that line. You couldn't much blame Lucy for wanting to stop the football—his name always on the sporting page—the
pictures—the Freshman Whiz—the Sophomore Thunderbolt—the
cheers—the big fat hands always slapping his shoulder—Tiny Duffy's
hand on his shoulder—yeah, Boss he's a chip off the old block—the
roadhouses—the thin-legged, tightbreasted little girls squealing. Oh,

Tom, oh, Tom—the bottles and the tourist cabins—the sea-roar of the
crowd and always the single woman-scream spangling the sudden silence like damnation.[10]

   A chip off the old block. That Tom is, but he is more than that
too. He has inherited all Willie's bad qualities and none of his
good. And Willie does have good points. One can even sympathize with him to an extent. In many ways he is a classic figure,
a backwoods Henry IV, but Tom is no Prince Hal. Those con-
frontations in Willie's office in which Tom's whoring and hell-
raising are discussed do not lead on the part of Tom to an "I
know you all." Tom is intelligent and perhaps has possibilities
but he is anything but a royal hero and a far cry from his father.

The big difference was this: Back in those days the Boss had been
blundering and groping his unwitting way toward the discovery of himself, of his great gift, wearing his overalls that bagged down about the
seat, or the blue serge suit with the tight, shiny pants, nursing some
blind and undefined compulsion in him like fate or a disease. Now Tom
wasn't blundering and groping toward anything, and certainly not toward a discovery of himself. For he knew that he was the damnedest,
hottest thing there was. (p. 365)

Tom is so bad that Lucy will not name his illegitimate son after
him but after Willie instead; yet it is Willie, in Lucy's view, who
destroys Tom by allowing him to play football. In her objection
to the macho of Willie and his son Lucy can be taken as a representative of the dissenters whose arguments, invariably, have
come to sound like a woman's as probably they always have in
both North and South: "Southerners [in the Old South] tended
to associate male effectiveness not only with horsemanship and
other soldierly and outdoor qualities but also, as Northerners
did, with financial success. Again like Northerners, they also
tended to associate such qualities as moral consciousness, senti-
mentality, introspection and benevolence with femininity."[11]
"Lucy did not have a chance," Burden says. "For he was going to
be all American. All American quarterback on anybody's team.
If bottle and bed didn't manage to slow down too soon something inside that one hundred and eighty pounds of split-
second, hair-trigger, Swiss-watch beautiful mechanism which

was Tom Stark, the Boss's boy, the handsome Sophomore Thunderbolt. Daddy's Darling" (p. 204).

Daddy's Darling believes like Daddy that he is different and exempt from the ways of others. Breaking training rules and becoming involved in a brawl with some yokels at a roadhouse for trying to birddog their girls, he is suspended from the team but allowed to play after Willie intercedes. Then playing out of shape and playing for the stands in the [Georgia] Tech game, Thunderbolt breaks his neck and later dies of pneumonia. Thus Tom lies dead at his mother's feet, and the murderer, as Lucy recognized, is the common overweening of father and son, the overweening that Willie had instilled by precept and example and that which cannot tolerate defeat even in a game. For the most chilling words in American literature, I nominate Willie's explanation to Burden why he put the heat on the coach to let Tom play after he had broken training: "It's not Tom, it's the championship by God.... If it weren't anything but Tom, I wouldn't say a word." If this sounds unrealistic I simply invite comparison with the following: "Winning may not be the most important thing, but it beats whatever comes second." Wherein lies the difference?

Early in Eugene O'Neill's *Strange Interlude,* Professor Leeds, echoing Aristotle, says, "College heroes rarely shine brilliantly in afterlife. Unfortunately the tendency to spoil them in the university is a poor training...." What Professor Leeds had obviously intended to say was that the tendency to spoil the hero in college is poor training for later life. It is perhaps this tendency to pamper the hero which creates in him darlingness and which frequently prevents him from facing life with the same inspiration and enthusiasm with which he met opponents on the field. Not equipped to face the awesome realities of the later years, a number of heroes try to reenact the past, to come back for a repeat performance, as does Irwin Shaw's Christian Darling, hero of "The Eighty-Yard Run."

In many ways, however, Darling is not at all representative of the type. He would never miss a career in music as would Joe Bonaparte (or Raymond Mulrooney), and he would never be caught in the same honky-tonk with Tom Stark. Neither does his athletic grace and handsomeness spill over into preciousness, as in the case of the blue-eyed, "girl-cheeked" Joe Fleming. Yet Darling has two traits in common with all of these: his dependency upon the female and his regression to youth.

Louise Tucker begins to mother Darling in college, watching him faithfully in the games, showering him with presents, driving him around in her convertible with the top down to let everyone know that she is his girl, and smothering him with love after his heroic deed of the eighty-yard run.[12]

If Louise is aggressive and protective before marriage, she is even more so after. Presumably through her influence, her father sets Darling up in business in New York where they go to all the shows and speakeasies and spend fifteen thousand dollars a year provided by Louise's father. After the stock market crash and the suicide of her father in 1929, Louise begins to make the living while Darling sits at home and drinks, and as she grows stronger, he becomes more petulant and resentful. He abhors the new world she moves in as an editor of a woman's magazine but lacks background and backbone to become independent of it. The stylish hat she wears on one occasion becomes all that is repulsive to him and also all that eighty-yard runs had not prepared him to deal with.

It was nothing, a scrap of straw, a red flower, a veil, meaningless on his big hand, but on his wife's head a signal of something. . . . big city, smart and knowing women drinking and dining with men other than their husbands, conversations about things a normal man wouldn't know much about, Frenchmen who painted as though they used their elbows instead of brushes, composers who wrote whole symphonies without a single melody in them, writers who knew all about politics and women who knew all about writers, the movement of the proletariat, Marx, somehow mixed up with five-dollar dinners and the best-looking women in America and fairies who made them laugh and half-sentences immediately understood and secretly hilarious and wives who called their husbands "Baby." (p. 22)

It is this epithet that he understandably detests most, mainly because it hits the mark perfectly. "I wish you wouldn't call me 'Baby,'" he tells her. She begins to call him "Baby" after she begins to make the living, and noting his juvenescence, she continues to do so. Even Darling realized that while she was maturing and moving ahead he was regressing, trying to star again in a boy's game that had not, as its supporters maintain, taught him how to play "the game of life."

Thus in Darling can be seen the consequences that result from the pampering of the hero by students, alumni, and especially the witnessing female. Such uncalled-for attention instills in the athlete a ridiculously false sense of accomplishment, leaving him what Hemingway called in "The Short Happy Life of Francis McComber" "the great American boy-man." But while Francis's life was short and happy after his heroic deed, Christian Darling's is long and sad. For the eternal boy-man, joy in life varies inversely with the time elapsed from the single moment of victory.

Christian Darling is a babe, and so is Victor Herres in Irwin Shaw's novel of the fifties, *The Troubled Air*. Whereas Christian Darling can find no greater glory than that provided by football, Victor Herres disdains the game and strikes out in other endeavors. Both end up as failures and, for the same reason, with selfish pride.

Clement Archer first notices Victor Herres in his history class on the back row in the midwestern university in the mid-thirties. Upon seeing his "dashing and mocking" appearance, Archer thinks "flunking material" and upon observing the quality of the suit he is wearing, "a wealthy rowdy." Then when he sees the name and hears the clipped "here," Archer recognizes him as the quarterback on the football team and immediately surmises: "Probably there'd be a hearty, embarrassed visit from Samson, the coach, in a month or two, with the plea to keep the boy eligible . . . even though he cut half his classes."[13] But Archer's first impressions turn out to be wrong, at least temporarily, for Victor "cut no classes, listened carefully, whispered very seldom to the pretty girl at his side while others were talking, seemed to take no notes, but answered swiftly and easily in his cool confident voice, was witty on occasion without being a clown, and obviously had read a great deal more on the subject than anyone else in class. Archer was first surprised, then suspicious, and finally grateful to have someone like that in his class" (p. 36).

Later Archer finds himself accepting two tickets to a game, even though "he had been religiously devoting Saturdays and Sundays to writing a play on Napoleon III."

At the game Archer becomes even more fascinated with Victor. He notes that Victor plays with "cold recklessness," that he never congratulates anyone else on making a play, that he remains outside the huddle during time-outs, and that when Samson the coach talks into his ear, Herres acts "as though he had heard everything the coach had to say and was bored by it." From Nancy, Victor's girl friend and later wife, Archer learns that Victor the quarterback once knocked out the center for standing in his way, and that Victor will not be elected captain even though he is the best player on the team.

Herres is indeed rare, so rare that he quits football to devote all his spare time to the Dramatic Society. "Poor Samson, who had had his troubles in years of coaching, who had had boys flunk out on him and turn up drunk at practice and contract gonorrhea on road trips, had never heard anything like this before" (p. 49). Samson sums up his feelings about Herres when he calls upon Archer to intercede. "He's ungrateful. . . . He's a boy without spirit. He has no team feelings. He's a God-damn intellectual." It is also Archer who hears Victor's side.

"Aside from everything else, I got bored with playing football. The games're all right, but the practice is a nuisance. And if the team loses a game or two because of me, what the hell do I care? Or for that matter, finally, what the hell does anyone care? There's one boy, Sam Ross, a tackle, who cries in the locker room every time we lose a game. Twenty-three years old, weight two hundred and seven, blubbering away for fifteen minutes at a time. He ought to be put away. In a home for expectant mothers. Once he wanted to fight me because he heard me whistling in the shower after we lost by two touchdowns. Character building! You know what aspects of my character I built up playing football?"

"What?" Archer asked curiously.

"Cruelty, sadism, duplicity, pleasure in destruction," Herres said slowly. "I figured it out before I quit. The reason I enjoyed playing was because I like to knock people down. I broke a man's leg in a game last year and I walked alongside the stretcher pretending I was upset, but I was pleased with myself all the time. Looking down at him, yelling on the stretcher. Clean-cut American boy, building a sane mind in a sound body every Saturday afternoon." (pp. 51-52)

Archer no doubt can appreciate some of Herres' reasons for quitting, but Archer cannot appreciate the way he has gone about it or the hubris that Archer apparently notes for the first time.

I'm speaking as a teacher and friend. There's a certain minimum of decency you owe whatever society you find yourself in. When you do something that seems strange or harmful or unfriendly to the people you've been working with and who depend on you for one thing or another, it seems to me you owe them some kind of explanation. You have to live with them and they have to live with you, and they have a right to be able to locate you in a general sort of way." (p. 52)

For the next fifteen years Herres virtually controls the professor's life. After bringing Archer to New York to write for and later direct a radio show, Victor, who in the war had won a Silver Star in Italy but who later turns communist, resorts to all sorts of underhanded tactics to implicate him, including forging Archer's name to a nominating petition for a communist candidate to the New York State Legislature. Just as Victor quit football so he quits "the American way of life," and again it is Archer who must hear the reasons, that is, that everybody in the country hates everyone else and that "nobody who ever accomplished anything ever behaved like a boy scout on Sunday." Again Archer tells Victor that he is suffering from the sin of pride and pleads with him to try to save his soul. Victor, however, is beyond all help, and he and Archer part as sworn enemies. "And in the end, if it comes to it," says Archer, "I swear to God I'll pick up a gun and kill you" (p. 415).

Why would Shaw allow a hero of the All-American game and winner of the Silver Star to turn communist? Why did he make of the footballer a "God-damn intellectual" and a radical? One guess is that Shaw wanted to show how topsy-turvy everything had become during the "red scarce" days of the early fifties. Another reason perhaps was to provide a means of indicting our whole shallow and wretched manner of worshiping heroes. Not only does Victor have firsthand knowledge of the hubris-

creating environment he has been subjected to, but he also has
the ability and detachment to describe it.

"Ever since I was a kid America's flopped on the bed and spread its legs
and said, 'Do it again, baby, do it just the same way to me again.' Do you
think I want revenge for that?" He chuckled harshly. "So you're down
to the bedrock horror about me. The one thing you can't bear to believe. That I'm doing all this not for myself, because I got mine, but for
the hundred million poor, tortured, screaming, beat-up, shot-up,
scared, bomb-happy slobs out there...." He made a stiff, awkward
flinging gesture toward the city, toward the dark, stretching country
outside the hospital. "I despise them, but I feel responsible for them
and I want them to live a little happier and die a little later." (p. 414)

In his self-appointed role of martyr and savior, Victor illustrates the validity of Joseph Campbell's observation: "The hero
of yesterday becomes the tyrant of tomorrow unless he crucifies
himself today." In taking up the communist cause, Victor, like
many reformers, is not so sincerely interested in changing society as in feeding some insatiable and infantile urge within the
self. When he says that America called him "baby," he uses precisely the right word, the same term Louise uses in addressing
Christian Darling. Victor is victor over nothing, not even the
narcissism of childhood. Instead of trying to be a Victor, Shaw
suggests, it is much better to be an Archer, a "merciful" Archer,
one, that is, who shoots high but always turns to others for
evaluation of target, accuracy, and method of shooting.

Victor of John Steinbeck's play-novelette *Burning Bright* has
more in common with Victor Herres than name. Both are
athletes—Steinbeck's Victor had played football, run the half
mile, vaulted, and tumbled—both are attractive to women—
"They always wanted me again," says Steinbeck's Victor, and
both are egotistical to a fault. Says Steinbeck, "Victor's unfortunate choice it was always to mis-hear, to misjudge.... His was the
self-centered chaos of childhood. All looks and thoughts, loves
and hatreds, were directed at him. Softness was softness toward
him, weakness was weakness in the face of his strength. He pre-
heard answers and listened not. He was full colored and brilliant
—all outside of him was pale."[14]

A newcomer to the circus high bar act, Victor, who is "large

and powerful, dark and young," falls in love with the beautiful
Mordeen, wife of Joe Saul, veteran performer and Victor's part-
ner, who dislikes Victor from the start. Reprimanding him for
playing touch football and spraining his wrist, he says, "If you
were a musician, you'd bat a tennis ball with your violin. If you
were a surgeon, you'd sharpen pencils with a scapel. . . . You're
stronger, quicker, younger, even more sure than Cousin Will
[who missed the net] but now I know what it is. Whatever you do
is an accident of youth and muscle. You have not the infinite
respect for your tools and your profession—Profession! You
have made it a trade" (p. 38). Joe hates Victor, Victor loves
Mordeen, but Mordeen loves her husband, so much so that she
allows Victor to sire a son for him. Thereafter Victor's fate is to
be near the woman he loves (in the circus, on the farm, and on
the sea) to know that she carries his child within her but still to be
rejected. This he cannot believe nor accept, that one he loves
loves another more. Neither will he consider compromise. When
before the birth of the child Mordeen tells him that though she
must remain the wife of Joe, she will try "to open the family . . .
and take" him in, he exclaims, "Then I say no. . . . No!" On the
symbolic level this is the "no" directed at the condition, a kind
of everlasting nay. Hearing it, Friend Ed, the Clown, enters,
takes Victor on deck, murders him, and dumps his body into the
sea. Friend Ed neither hates Victor nor forgives him; he simply
accepts him. He agrees with Mordeen when she says that Victor
is "not evil," but he also says, "There are many Victors. There
will always be a Victor."

But Victor is not the only character confronted with a choice.
Possessed with the sin of family pride, Joe regards as the supreme catastrophe the fact that he is impotent: "My line, my
blood, all the procession of the ages is dead. And I am only
waiting a little while and then I die." Not knowing that Friend
Ed has murdered Victor and realizing that the child cannot be
his own, Joe feels that he must hunt Victor down and kill him.
"There is no place in the whole world for him to live, knowing
and sneering, maybe never telling but always knowing. I cannot
have his mind living in the same world with me" (p. 145). Once
again the action of the clown is crucial. Seeing Joe consumed by
revenge and self-pity, he slaps him with contempt—an incident

paralleling Joe's slapping Victor in Act I. Moved by the words of
the clown, Joe subdues his hate and envy and comes to realize
that all men are fathers of all children, or ought to be, and that
"with all our horrors and our faults" there is in us "a shining."
"That is the most important of all facts," he adds. *"There is a
shining."* In Joe there finally is a shining, but in Victor it is difficult to detect because of his "full-colored" brilliance of youth. A
shining suggests a glow which in turn suggests wisdom that
Victor never acquired.

How can the familiar phenomenon of immaturity of the
American male be explained? Partially by the widespread passion for eternal youth, for the new Eden in the New World, and
partially by the infectious anti-intellectualism immediately obvious in national addiction to television and especially to television
sports. Here on weekends, Monday nights, and Super Sundays
"has beens," "never weres," and "never will be's" by the tens of
millions confirm Thoreau's opinion that "a quiet desperation
lurks beneath the games and amusements of mankind." In our
very unconsciousness we silently admit to higher needs so well
articulated by our epic bard, Walt Whitman, who announced a
nation of glorious athletic youth, including "athletic mothers,"
but who also announced "a race of splendid and *savage* old
men." In these parlous times it is such old men we are lacking
and the wisdom that grows not out of strength but out of age.

The Naked Beast

Whereas the darling reverts to babyhood, or never grows beyond it, there is a kindred type who never rises above a natural
bestiality and abhorrent sadism. In the eyes of the authors who
create him he is the neurotic, devoid even of the veneer of civilization, one who mindlessly indulges the blood lust within. He is
Dionysian like the babe or darling in that he has no other world
toward which he moves; or if he does have another world, it is so
absurdly shallow as to be nothing more than a sentimental
dream.

The question of heroics posed by Hemingway in *The Sun Also
Rises* was taken up again eight years later by Robert Sherwood in
The Petrified Forest and the same conclusion was reached, that

ideals bequeathed by the past are no longer applicable. "It's a graveyard of civilization that's been shot from under us," the writer-hero Squier tells Duke the glorified gangster. "It's a world of out-moded ideas. Platonism—patriotism—Christianity—romance—the economics of Adam Smith—they're all so many dead stumps in the desert."[15] To the list of outmoded ideas Squier might have added *sapientia et fortitudo,* strength and beauty, and *mens sana in corpore sano,* for these ideals seem as much like relics as the others do, particularly when applied to Boze Hertzlinger.

Once a star dressed in resplendent colors, Boze finds himself an attendant at the Black Mesa filling station where he wears "dirty white canvas pants and a filthy football jersey, on the back of which is a patch with the number 42." Around his neck he wears a chain on which hangs a gold football he once won "for intercepting a pass and running sixty-eight yards for a touchdown." Another reminder of Boze's days of glory is the newspaper clipping he carries in his wallet and which he shows to the customers at every opportunity. The article by Sid Ziff of the *Los Angeles Herald* reads: "Tip to the pigskin fraternity: When pondering your All-American selections for this current Anno Domini, just mull over the name Boze Hertzlinger of Nevada Tech. Playing with an admittedly minor league club, and protected by interference of cellophane strength, Hertzlinger managed to remind some of us observers of the Illini Phantom himself" (p. 918). Of all the "outdated romantics" in the Bar-B Q lunchroom none is so effective in reliving the past as Boze.

Boze, however, is not the least depressed by his present circumstances. He has that supreme confidence which ironically is common to both the great genius and the incurable romantic. "I could be making good money in a lot of ways right now," he tells Gabby, "engineering, coaching, the insurance game—lots of ways. But—I just can't be tied down—not yet. I've got an itch inside here that keeps me on the move—chasing the rainbow" (p. 918). The very term "lots of ways" defines Boze's impression of his versatility.

Not only in Boze himself is seen the fracture of strength and intelligence but also in the rivalry between him and Alan Squier, the writer-intellectual. The flawed combination of the writer-athlete has been seen in Busher Keefe, Danny Warner, and Robert Cohn and the utter lack of communication between intellectual and athlete in Bolenciecwcz and Mr. Possum and in Tom Buchanan and the "rather literary" Carraway. In these cases the fragmentation of strength and intelligence has been more or less implicit, but with Boze and Squier there is an open war in which much more is at stake than the love of Gabby. Squier tells her:

It's nature hitting back. Not with the old weapons—floods, plagues, holocausts. We can neutralize them. She's fighting back with strange instruments called neuroses. She's deliberately afflicting mankind with the jitters. Nature is proving that she can't be beaten—not by the likes of us. She's taking the world away from the intellectuals and giving it back to the apes. . . . You can easily be one of Nature's own children, and therefore able to understand her, and laugh at her—or enjoy her—depending on how you feel. You're the only one who can say whether or not you should yield to the ardors of number 42 out there. (p. 926)

Since Sherwood is clearly on his side, Alan wins the love of Gabby and also achieves the greater heroism, for which he had also been in competition with Boze.

"Of course I'm showing off," he says after asking Duke to kill him so that Gabby can be beneficiary to his insurance policy. "But is there anything unnatural in that? Boze was ready to sacrifice his life to become an All-American star" (p. 940). Alan's death wish is fulfilled when Duke carries out his request and shoots him; and since Alan commits suicide—Duke had merely pulled the trigger—he does not really sacrifice anything for Gabby. His wish for a better world, though, seems genuine. In any event he comes out much better than Boze, his rival, whose last words seem guaranteed not to leave one admirer for the former star of Nevada Tech: "Boy—it did me good to see that Jackie in a pool of blood."

But Boze is not the only hero to fall in the play; in fact *The Petrified Forest* is probably the best American version of Ragnarok (death of the gods). Our Aesir (pioneer, patriot, writer-intellectual, athlete, and businessman) are set upon by Loki (gangster but quondam Aesir member) and the host of Hel (bandits) at Vigrid (The Black Mesa Filling Station). Though there is "quite some shooting," only Alan and some of the lesser deities are slain physically; but allegorically all our heroic models are destroyed. Squier, the writer, is well aware of his failure to "say something of enduring importance" and of the debility of intellectuals generally—the symbolism of his walking stick is obvious—Jason the patriot and Mr. Chisholm are abominable, and Gramps, the pioneer, the most traditional of American heroes, admires Duke more than he does Alan. The gangster, who "if he hadn't elected to take up banditry, might have been a fine left-fielder," reminds Gramps of Billy the Kid whose skill and individualism Gramps admired. Alan, on the other hand, reminds him of Mark Twain, concerning whom Gramps says, "He was the best goddam liar I ever seed, and I've seed plenty. He used to say he did his writing on the principle that his readers wanted everything but the truth, so that's what he give 'em." There are three versions of Billy the Kid[16] and at least three Mark Twains; and by associating Duke with one and Alan with the other and by having our most honored hero, the pioneer, choose the bandit, Sherwood shows how incredibly confused our concepts of heroes have become.[17] That the only genuinely heroic figure is one who never strove to be heroic at all constitutes the essential irony of the play. "She [Gabby] has heroic stuff in her," Squier says, a fact that she herself is forced to realize. At the end she is seen standing beside the dead body of Squier making a vow for the generation of life. Gabby is *Lif* (woman survivor of Ragnarok) but the tragedy of the play is that there is no *Lifthrasir* (male survivor of Ragnarok).

Quite obviously Robert Sherwood has used the athlete to reveal the bloodthirsty savagery that lurks immediately beneath the surface of society. Ring Lardner too was concerned with deceptive appearances as is evident in perhaps his only iconoclastic story, "Champion," a chilling commentary on professional boxing and the fans who follow it.

Midge Kelly scores his first knockout by flooring his crippled brother. When his mother reproaches him for the act, he knocks her down, and later on his honeymoon he punches his bride in the face. After he is a big success, his mother and wife write for money—his baby is dying of malnutrition—but he rejects their pleas. He gives money to his mistress until he leaves her and takes up with the wife of a new manager. He also hits a couple of managers and throws a fight, but the story and the "picture lay-out" in the Sunday edition of the New York *News* attribute to him all the virtues of the Spenserian knight and the All-American boy. Had the reporter Joe Morgan interviewed people other than Midge's latest manager he could have "written more accurately," but such a version would not have gotten by the sporting editor. "Suppose you can prove it," that gentleman would have said, "it wouldn't get us anything but abuse to print it. The people don't want to see him knocked. He's champion."[18] The story is obviously an exaggeration but an exaggeration that results from a love of truth.

"Champion" is unique among Lardner's athletes. While his ball players are frequently boastful, arrogant, and hotheaded, they are, excluding managers, first and foremost boobs, simps, and saps and, unlike Midge Kelly, generally more comic than mean. Midge Kelly, on the other hand, is not only mean but vicious as well. Admittedly a similar case might be made for Elliott of "My Roomy" who at one point smears the narrator's face with blood and attacks his fiancee and her new boyfriend with a baseball bat—his specialty is hitting. But Elliott is simply a maniac and an exception to the bushers in the other stories.

Comic characters can be deceptively cruel. Such is the case with Damon Runyon's Haystack Duggeler of "Baseball Hattie."

[Haystack] comes to the big league with more bad habits than anybody in the history of the world is able to acquire in such a short time. He is especially a great rumpot, and after he gets going good in the league, he is just as apt to appear for a game all mulled up as not. He is fond of all forms of gambling, such as playing cards and shooting craps, but after they catch him with a deck of readers in a poker game and a pair of tops in a crap game, none of the Giants will play with him any more, except of course when there is nobody else to play with. He is ignorant about many little things, such as reading and writing and geography and mathematics . . . but he is so wise when it comes to larceny that I always figure they must have great tutors back in Haystack's old home town of Booneville, Mo.[19]

Baseball Hattie saves Duggeler from a "posse of . . . infuriated
Philadelphia fans" on Haystack's second day with the Giants
both by her language and by her adept use of a brickbat; and
after their marriage, she protects him from the gamblers. When
she learns that Haystack plans to accept payment from Armand
Fibleman for throwing a game, she says, "Haystack, I know you
are a liar and a drunkard and a cheat and no account generally,
but nobody can tell me you will sink so low as to purposely toss
off a ball game. Why, Haystack, baseball is always on the level. It
is the most honest game in all the world. I guess you are just
ribbing me, because you know how much I love it!" (p. 335)
When Hattie realizes that Haystack is not ribbing, she shoots his
left arm off with a long-nosed .38. Presumably Hattie, a watch-
dog committee of one, had been shooting at Armand Fibleman,
the briber, and sports writers make of her "a great heroine and
Haystack . . . a great hero, though nobody thinks to ask Haystack
how he stands on the bribe proposition, and he never brings it
up himself." Years later, however, before Haystack dies a "respectable grocer" in Los Angeles, he tells the narrator the truth.

"Look," Haystack says. "Hattie does not miss Fibleman. It is a great
newspaper story and saves my name, but the truth is she hits just where
she aims. When she calls me into the kitchen before I start out with
Fibleman, she shows me a revolver I never before know she has, and
says to me, 'Haystack,' she says, 'if you leave with this weasel on the
errand you mention, I am going to fix you so you will never make
another wrong move with your pitching arm. I am going to shoot it
off for you.'"
    "I laugh heartily," Haystack says. "I think she is kidding me, but I
find out different. By the way," Haystack says, "I afterwards learn that
long before I meet her, Hattie works for three years in a shooting
gallery at Coney Island. She is really a remarkable broad," Haystack
says. (p. 338)

    It is frequently difficult to distinguish between comic charac-
ters and brutes, and admittedly Haystack would not be suspended from a league of Lardner's saps. But there are differences, the most significance being the "pastings" Haystack
administers to Hattie; and sports writers, Runyon suggests, simply lie when they imply that the churlish Haystack is essentially

harmless. "The baseball writers speak of Haystack as eccentric, which is a polite way of saying he is a screwball, but they consider him a most unique character and are always writing humorous stories about him, though any one of them will lay you plenty of nine to five that Haystack winds up an umbay" (p. 330). Haystack winds up "respectable," but this is because Hattie deprives him of his most profitable means of sinning, his left arm.

The athlete as beast is a thoroughly repulsive figure. Without exception all examples are bad or rotten; but if there were some way to graduate the hideousness of athletes falling in this category, the champion monster would be Joe Lon Mackey of Harry Crews's *A Feast of Snakes*. "Boss Snake" of the Mystic Georgia Rattlers high school team, Joe Lon had been an All-American and highly sought by colleges, even though he had never learned to read, at least in the opinion of several of his teachers who passed him anyway and liked him for his "exceptional quietness" which they called "courtesy." "He had the name of being the most courteous boy in all of Lebeau County, although it was commonly known that he had done several pretty bad things, one of which was taking a traveling salesman out to July Creek and drowning him while nearly the entire first string watched from high up on the bank where they were sipping beer."[20]

Just as deceptive as Joe Lon's courteousness is his intelligence. He is anything but dumb and is in fact highly conscious, reflecting on his own condition throughout the novel. "He was stronger and faster and meaner than other boys his age and for that he had been rewarded. He had even suspected that he was smarter, too. For whatever reason, though, the idea of *studying*, of sitting down and deliberately committing facts and relationships to memory was deeply repugnant to him. And always had been. Unless it had to do with violence. He liked violence. He liked blood and bruises, even when they were his own" (pp. 45–46).

Little is gained in cataloging Joe Lon's outrages. Whatever is repugnant to civilized people, Joe Lon has done. He beats his wife and sister, drinks constantly, and "screws" at every opportunity. *Screws* is the proper word since Joe Lon never makes love. The whole idea of love in fact is to him a crippling mystery.

Eventually, as might be expected, he goes on a shooting spree, killing a snake-handling minister, who is also a Christ figure, and his own high-school sweetheart Berenice. He is finally overcome by an angry crowd and tossed into a pit of boiling snakes. "For the briefest instant, he gained his feet. Snakes hung from his face" (p. 165).

The question is not what all Joe Lon did or did not do, but what does such unrelieved bizarre behavior mean? What is Crews saying in such a ghastly story and what exactly do sports, football in particular, have to do with the message? The answers are simple and infinitely complex. From one point of view there is no answer. *A Feast of Snakes* is a story of evil, an eternal mystery. Again there are no answers to mysteries, but only responses. The only thing that can be said with certainty is that Joe Lon's response is one to be avoided.

Falling into the genre of southern Gothic, *A Feast of Snakes* is a highly symbolic novel. The characters, while realistic to a degree, are for the most part representative, and what Joe Lon represents is raw, untamed energy, however platitudinous that may sound. He is All-American but also All-Id. Prowess does come first in any endeavor, as Robert Frost had said, but in Joe Lon's world prowess is the only thing, courage and knowledge and nobility of character being beneath contempt. He rejects study—"the very idea of anyone studying French threw Joe Lon in a rage"—love, which in his view has messed up his life, and religion, the most outrageous lie of all. But it is not just intellectual and abstract endeavors that Joe Lon despises. He also hates debaters and those who play soccer.

Joe Lon seems literally hell-bent in making a lie out of every human endeavor, from marriage to cheerleading. Looking at his wife through the window of his house trailer and listening to the screaming of his babies, he engages Berenice in the congress of animals while Berenice, who is engaged to Shep, a debater, speaks or babbles on the significance of one of her second worlds, competing in the Dixie National Baton Twirling Institute: "see, it's beginning solo, intermediate solo, advanced solo, strutting—beginning and military (I was always good at strutting)—two batons, fire baton, duet, trio and team." At the same time he reflects on the tragedy of his own life, revealing finally the bitterest (to him) pill of all:

And the bitterest, most painful thing Joe Lon ever had to do was admit to himself that his mother had been fucking the little shoe salesman for reasons of love when she had a house and a husband and children and a flower garden and friends and a hometown and a son famous through the whole South and meals to cook and clothes to wash, a woman like that—no, not a woman, his *mother*—lying down on her back with a little man who walked always leaning slightly to the right from carrying a heavy suitcase full of shoe samples. (p. 112)

As if in repudiation of his mother's love for a shoe salesman, he leads Berenice into fellatio, concluding that such an act, especially following anal entry, is the only "*true* love" there is.

Joe Lon's perversion and hatred are set against the backdrop of the Mystic Annual Rattlesnake Roundup, an orgiastic festival of blood lust and macho violence. Everything in the novel is snaky. The name of the football team is the Rattlers, the band makes serpentine formations, and for noisemakers at the games the fans bring huge gourds "shaped like crooked-neck squash, and full of dried seed so that when they were shaken they vibrated the air with the genuine sound of a snake." Then there is the snake-condomed penis of sheriff Buddy Matlow, a former star at Georgia Tech, that Lottie Mae cuts off with a razor for having been abused by him. Though it is not identified as such, the rage inside Joe Lon is a type of blind devouring reminiscent of the "bosom serpent" in Roderick Elliston in Hawthorne's "Egotism; or, the Bosom Serpent." In Hawthorne's story the main character finally learns the secret of getting rid of the gnawing creature within—merely to think of someone else. This solution seems far beyond the pale of possibility for Joe Lon.

Still another snaky symbol pervades the novel and underscores the horror. This is the feces. Crews clearly has no sympathy for the Lawrentian philosophy that sees the snake as a misunderstood and mistreated relative to man. Man is kin to the snake all right but only because he is a low-down, fallen creature himself, a brother to dragons. Crews apparently does not think too highly of either snakes or people. To him life feeds on life, and the result of this blind devouring is a snake, the feces. The theme of defecation—indeed the stench of it—is everywhere in the novel. Portable privies are brought in for the roundup and are themselves reservoirs where the final product of all the snake-eating and hard-drinking will be deposited. Characters never let one another (or the reader) forget that man is a creature who defecates, and, upon discovery of her mother's suicide, Beeder, Joe Lon's sister, becomes so mentally deranged that she places dung in her hair. Obviously, Harry Crews is in complete agreement with Ernest Becker: "The great enemy of mankind is the turd."

The feces is part of nature, and nature equates, in Becker's view, with death. Hence both nature and the feces must be transcended in some degree if life is to have meaning. Pleasure can be had by merging and indulgence, but pleasure is not meaning. The mode of living that seeks only satiation Otto Rank called the Dionysian, the injunction of which is "*be thyself.*" Says Rank:

This mode, in contrast to adaptation . . . leads to ecstatic-orgiastic destruction, as seen in Greek mythology and also as Ibsen shows in Peer Gynt, who on the basis of the same principle landed in a madhouse. The true self, if it is unchained in Dionysian fashion, is not only anti-social but also unethical, and therefore the human being goes to pieces on it. Seen in this sense, the longing of the neurotic to be himself is a form of the affirmation of his neurosis, perhaps the only form in which he can affirm himself. He is, as it were, already himself, at any rate far more than the others, and has only a step to take in order to become wholly himself, that is, insane.[21]

This is Joe Lon Mackey to the letter. He goes to pieces in the unchaining of his "true" self which knows no check by any illusions that sustain others and make life bearable and, on occasion, even meaningful.

4. Adonis

Thus far the image of the athlete has not been particularly flattering, but as a "natural" he is seen in an altogether different light. While he is now an admirable Adonic figure, he is ironically unappreciated or rejected by his society. To one degree or another he is a rebel, and in his refusal to come to terms with the establishment he illustrates what has been a major theme in American literature since the second quarter of the nineteenth century: the plight and flight of the natural person. Natty Bumppo one step ahead of "all the inventions and deviltries of man," Thoreau at Walden, Whitman on the road, and Huck Finn striking out for the territory are some of the more famous examples.

While all the naturals share certain qualities: innocence, an innate moral sense, and love of life and independence, the folk hero seems to have certain characteristics that set him apart. Following the general pattern of the earliest folk heroes, he seems to spring from the soil—appears to have been sired by an oak and issued from the earth—and comes to the city in hope of winning prestige and a princess. With his prodigious strength and purity of soul—though from the country he is the antithesis of the busher—he rises from the hills in the West or the boondocks of the South to recall those values that commercialism tends to destroy. Illustrative of this type of hero is Pat Glendon of Jack London's *The Abysmal Brute*.

Having passed through the alembic of both Sinclair Lewis and Jack London, Pat is a highly contrived "folk hero," by which term he is described. Perhaps, however, Lewis and London had no idea how well they succeeded, for Pat fills the bill perfectly.

"There is . . . a type of folk-tale in which the hero (or heroine) though of obscure origin, obtains a royal spouse and a throne, but this type of tale is probably derived from romances based on the central part of the myth [see page 60] in which . . . the hero, though really of royal birth appears . . . out of the blue. In these tales we are never told of the hero's death, but merely that he "lived happily ever afterwards."[1] Now let us separate incidents in this pattern and see how they apply to Pat.

1. Obscure origin: When Pat Glendon Senior, ex-ring hero, was last seen over twenty years ago, his wife had just died, and he, carrying a baby in his arms, was headed toward the woods of California.

2. Appearing out of the blue: One day Sam Stubener, a manager, receives a letter from Pat Senior telling him about his son who "at two hundred and twenty pounds fighting weight," "can hit and kick twice as hard as the best ever" and who is "the hope of the white race."[2] Skeptically Sam goes to the wilds of Northern California and seeks out old Pat who tells him,

He's a giant, and he's lived natural all his days. Wait till he takes you out after deer. He'll break your heart travelin' light, him carryin' the outfit and a big buck deer belike. He's a child of the open air, an' winter nor summer has he slept under a roof. The open for him, as I taught him. The one thing that worries me is how he'll take to sleepin' in houses, an' how he'll stand the tobacco smoke in the ring. 'Tis a terrible thing, that smoke, when you're fighting hard an' gaspin' for air. (p. 14)

Later with the young giant before him, Pat adds: "See the softness of him. . . . 'T is the true stuff. Look at the slope of the shoulders, an' the lungs of him. You're lookin' at a man, Sam, the like of which was never seen before. Not a muscle of him bound. No weight-lifter or Sandow exercise artist there. See the fat snakes of muscles a-crawlin' soft an' lazy-like. Wait till you see them flashin' like a strikin' rattler. He's good for forty rounds this blessed instant, or a hundred" (pp. 25–26). Then in a brief sparring session Sam, ex-fighter himself, finds that neither Old Pat's praise nor young Pat's appearance has been deceiving.

3. Obtaining the royal spouse: Through his looks, manners, and character Pat wins the heart of Maud Sangster, a millionaire's daughter who has all the qualities of a princess:

wealth, beauty, intelligence, poetic and athletic ability, love of learning and adventure, courage, and honesty. Previously Pat had been afraid of women, but he has not known Maud for long before he says, "God! . . . You were made for me." Indeed she is. If he is superman, then she is superwoman; and while they are not married in the novel, there is no doubt that they will be.

4. Obtaining the throne: Pat never loses a fight, and that he will become heavyweight champion of the world is a foregone conclusion; but since boxing is so rotten, he chooses to retire though not before he exposes all. Prior to the fight that will give him a shot at the championship he inveighs against all the corruption associated with the game. When he denounces the heavyweight champion who is at the ringside, the champion steps through the rope to challenge but is knocked unconscious by a single blow. Thus Pat does obtain the championship and throne, but not officially.

5. Living happily ever after: There is every indication that Pat and Maud will live together for the rest of their days in complete peace and contentment in the California mountains. "In his hugeness he seemed a fit dweller among the forest giants, while for her, as a dweller with him, there were no signs of aught else but happiness."[3]

As a fit dweller among forest giants, as a champion of the good, simple, and natural, Pat is indeed a folktale hero; but he is also an all-round man in the manner of the Greeks. He is perhaps London's best example of strength and beauty, though not in the least convincing. Intellectually curious, he reads Shakespeare and Longfellow and attends Browning lectures because "Browning is the sort of writer you need assistance with" (p. 54). All this strikes one today as absurd and farfetched, but if the heavyweight who reads poetry sounds ridiculously unreal, I offer a look at Gene Tunney, who probably read *The Abysmal Brute* and who was himself a folk hero.

Dempsey had been a mauler at the beginning of the decade; he was an ex-mauler at its end. Not so Tunney. From the pinnacle of his fame he stepped neatly off on to those upper levels of literary and fashionable society in which heavyweight champions, haloed by publicity, were newly welcome. Having received $1,742,282 in three years for his prowess in the ring, Tunney lectured on Shakespeare before Professor

Phelps's class at Yale, went for a walking trip in Europe with Thornton Wilder (author of the best-selling novel of the year, *The Bridge of San Luis Rey*), married a young gentlewoman of Greenwich, Connecticut, and after an extensive stay abroad returned to the United States with his bride, giving out on his arrival a prepared statement which, if not quite Shakespearian or Wilderesque in its style, at least gave evidence of effort.[4]

While there is always the faint suggestion of poetasterism about the famous athlete turned critic or writer, he has come off perhaps as well as the intellectual turned athlete, George Plimpton, for instance. Aristocratic, intelligent, athletic, and handsome, Plimpton somehow seems bent upon showing how inferior he is to the "person whose activity [is] specialized, through a concentration of his energies upon some particular technique, at the expense of his all-round development as a 'social animal.'"[5] While Lardner's Busher Keefe is the buffoon trying to take on the role of the royal hero, Plimpton in a sense is the royal hero playing the role of the buffoon, a modern-day Don Quixote tilting at modern wildmills, professional basketball players.

Between Lardner's "Champion" and *The Abysmal Brute* one can see the distortion of which sportswriters, in the eyes of sports writers themselves, are capable. Midge Kelly, a savage, is made an idol, while Pat, a Baldur, is presented to the public as a brute.

Because he had little to say to those he encountered, he was called sullen and unsocial, and out of this a newspaper reputation took form that was not an exaggeration so much as it was an entire misconception. Boiled down, his character in print was that of an ox-muscled and dumbly stupid brute, and one callow sporting writer dubbed him the "abysmal brute." The name stuck. The rest of the fraternity hailed it with delight, and thereafter Glendon's name never appeared in print unconnected with it. Often, in a headline or under a photograph, "The Abysmal Brute," capitalized and without quotation marks, appeared alone. All the world knew who was this brute. (pp. 66–67)

While both stories themselves are obvious distortions or at least overreactions, it is common knowledge that sports writers are especially careless in their reports. Frequently they have lost sight of what is admirable in heroes and what is not. This is unfortunate, for the influence the sports writer has upon the shaping of ideals is enormous, since it is now he and not the poet who records the deed. The enthusiasm of Pindar has remained, but quality and mode of expression have changed considerably.

It is in the realm of myth, however, that *The Abysmal Brute* most directly engages our attention. From any other point of view it is a silly story unworthy of the time required to read it. But as a reflection of our cultural history and search for a national hero it is significant, as the description of Pat Glendon, "the hope of the white race," would indicate. *The Abysmal Brute* was published in 1913 during the reign (1908–1915) of black heavyweight champion Jack Johnson, the hero of Howard Sackler's celebrated play, *The Great White Hope.* In his excellent book, *White Hopes and Other Tigers,* John Lardner states that those who worked the term "most busily" were commercial boxing men and that one talent scout, Walter (Good Time Charlie) Friedman, went "to China to look for a white hope among the Chinese peasants." According to Lardner, "the last publicist to invoke the idea—or rather to paraphrase it—was Dr. J. P. Goebbels, when he billed Max Smelling's second fight with Louis, in 1938, as a mission to restore the championship to aryan control."[6]

According to Dick Schapp, it was London himself who as much as any other person sparked the search for a White Hope. It was London who, in covering the Burns-Johnson fight, concluded his story as follows: "Jeffries must emerge from his alfalfa farm and remove the golden smile from Johnson's face. Jeff, it's up to you!"[7] Thus, it is no accident that Jack London (and Sinclair Lewis) in his novel exploiting this contemporary theme equated a white hope with a "natural." Indeed this has been a major endeavor in American literature, to create an epic hero of old-world virtues who is also at home in the forest, a formula that explains why Natty Bumppo was a Christian knight and woodsman, why Walt Whitman, in D. H. Lawrence's phrase, was "the first white aborigine," why Pat Glendon reads Shakespeare in the open air of Northern California, and why Thomas Wolfe made his home-run king part Cherokee Indian.

The Indian has long been identified as a natural but so has

another American, the black man, and for most of the American experience neither, unfortunately, has had even the slightest chance of becoming an exemplary model of wholeness in the minds of the white majority, until perhaps only recently. How can this situation be explained? Why have whites been so determined to find their cultural heroes within their own race? Nothing is known with any certainty, but within limits it can be generally said, I think, that in the past the Indo-European has been Apollonian, the black and the North American Indian, Dionysian or Adonic, the one committed to doing, the other to being, the one to thought, the other to feeling, the one to creating a Leviathan, the other trying to escape it! The Indo-European has always had a degree of reverence for naturalness, as a look at his myths will abundantly illustrate, but never so much naturalness as that of the original African slave or the native American. (It is not just a myth that blacks and Indians like to dance.) So why did Jack Johnson outrage the white establishment and create a call for a white hope? He was too natural, too Dionysian. Says Dick Schapp in the introduction to Johnson's autobiography: "Jack Johnson was a swinger before the term was known. He lived high, surrounded by his retinue, enjoying and apparently satisfying women by the dozens, driving fast cars, drinking good liquor, dressing royally, playing the champion to the core" (p. 16). A different type of natural was wanted. Hence the call for a challenger and the perpetuation in fiction of the myth of the young white god raised in the boonies but who nevertheless was led to Shakespeare and who did not smoke, drink, or consort with wild women, who was so pure in fact that he could not abide the corruption surrounding boxing, as could, by implication, the naturally debauched heavyweight champion. Poor Jack London! He sought the Holy Grail all his life and had no more success than Monty Python.

An interesting phenomenon needs to be noted here—the relative paucity of black athletes in our literature by both white and black authors, an anomaly considering both the number of black athletes and their towering success. Literture dealing with blacks has generally been concerned with the matter of simple justice rather than philosophic examination of subtle mind-body relationships. The black athlete in life has so frequently reminded us of what all men have long admired in sport and out, power, energy, grace, courage, and soul, but it remains to be seen if he can teach us anything new about the integration of body and mind as more and more recognition, long overdue, is paid him by a society that is becoming more and more tolerant and fair-minded. What a tragedy it will be if the black athlete, in the extension of his success off the field, simply apes all the old, threadbare Apollonian conventions that American white authors have shown were never worthy of adoption—the leisure-class gentleman, the booster babbitt, the true believer in an anthropomorphic cult, the Hollywood model, the self-anointed specimens of the body beautiful, in short the empty vessels and insufferable bromides. If we are truly honest with ourselves, though, we can already see in some instances the same old pattern emerging among black athletes, the black athlete turned movie star, religious prophet, and TV celebrity. The same fear obtains in the case of women, black and white, as more opportunities are opened up under Title IX of the Education Amendments Act of 1972. Will readers of the future have to suffer through female equivalents of Tom Buchanan, Robert Cohn, Tom Stark, Hal Carter, Boze Hertzlinger, and all the others, or will the fiction and drama in the years ahead move in exciting new ways? Let us hope with George Leonard that Title IX will not "simply encourage women to mimic the old male model, splitting the athletic departments from physical education . . ., going all-out for scholarships in female competitive sports, and ending up with cries of 'Winning isn't everything. It's the only thing! Already there are some rumblings of this nature from the direction of the women's gym but, in the words of a female AAHPER official, 'Women have too much good sense to take that path.'"[8] Perhaps this is so, but we remember too the words of Schopenhauer, the arch pessimist of all time, in his exasperating motto of history: *eadem sed aliter,* the same but otherwise.

In *The Abysmal Brute* London went to some length to decry the morally lamentable milieu with which the folk hero in boxing would have to contend; but if there are similar problems in major league baseball, none ever seems to weigh heavily upon Nebraska Crane of Thomas Wolfe's *The Web and the Rock* and

You Can't Go Home Again. "Hell, I ain't kicking," Bras says, "I had ten years of it already and that's more than most."[9] Through baseball Nebraska earns enough money to help his wife's folks and to buy a three-hundred-acre farm on which he can retire and live happily ever after, which is what folk heroes want most to do.

Nebraska is a superb creation, at once an archetypal figure and an individual so real that one suspects that Wolfe knew someone like him. In a letter to sports writer Arthur Mann, dated February 16, 1938, expressing Wolfe's appreciation for Mann's having arranged for him to be present at a New York Baseball Writers' Dinner at which big league players were guests, Wolfe wrote:

One of the characters in the book [*The Web and the Rock*] I am writing is a baseball player. . . . One reason I have always loved baseball so much is that it has been not merely "the great national game," but really a part of the whole weather of our lives, of the thing that is our own, of the whole fabric, the million memories of America. . . . One of the characters is out of this weather, from this setting; he becomes a Big League player, but it is of this kind of man, strong, simple, full of earth and sun, and his life in relation to other lives that I want to write: I have got the man, I knew him as a child—he never made the Big League, but he could have. I mean, he would have looked real in a Big League uniform because, as I saw at the dinner, it was from just such fellows that the Big League players come. And I am not making the mistake of trying to write about him too professionally—too technically in relation to his merits as a player—I am simply trying to write about him as a living man.[10]

Whether or not Nebraska was fashioned after a real-life figure, what makes him so fascinating is that Wolfe has altered the folktale pattern sufficiently to give the life of Nebraska verisimilitude. The early chapters of *The Web and the Rock* dispel any mystery about the background of Nebraska but at the same time show him to be "the best boy in town" and a hero in the making, particularly in the way he saves Monk Webber from the "West Side gang." He does not come out of the blue, but he does "crash" into the big leagues and become a home-run king. Myrtle cannot be classified as royalty but she is exactly the type of wife that Nebraska needs. "She was simple and natural in her talk and bearing and George liked her at once" (p. 60). After years of success as a slugger Nebraska plans to go to the farm and live in paradise with Myrtle and his child. When Monk asks him how he will "get used" to farming in Zebulon after being in the spotlight so long, Nebraska replies, "Git used to it? . . . Why what are you talkin' about? That's the greatest life in the world!"

While Nebraska seems real, he is too good to be true. He is an ideal husband, father, and friend, behaving always with "spontaneous warmth and kindliness." Through him Monk is able "to get back in his blood once more the honest tang of America" (p. 57). So strong in character is Bras that one feels he is never tempted like Roy Hobbs of *The Natural* by the American dream. He is not the least interested in the excited talk on the train about the opportunities for economic advancement in Libya Hill nor the least impressed with arguments by the members of the Establishment of Libya Hill that he invest his money in property in town. He is courteous to them but has nothing in common with them whatsoever. "He was completely detached from the fever of the times—from the fever of the boom-mad town as well as from the larger fever of the nation. The others talked incessantly about land, but George saw that Nebraska Crane was the only one who still conceived of the land as a place on which to live, and of living on the land as a way of life" (p. 80).

Nebraska breaks into the big leagues in 1919, baseball's darkest year, and, as in the case of Jim Randolph, the date appears to be significant. Realizing that Jim Randolph, the southern knight, was dead along with other gods, Wolfe perhaps tried to revive not just the southern folk hero but one whose name suggests the very heart of America and whose Cherokee ancestry hints at family ties with all the flora and fauna on the North American continent.[11] Wolfe not only made of Nebraska the friend that he always wanted but never had, as Aswell says, but he also made of him the hero who could do what Wolfe could not do—"remain detached from the fever of the times" and, indeed, go home again. "I believe that we are lost in America," Wolfe wrote, "but I believe we shall be found." In Nebraska Crane this great, misunderstood American genius pointed the way back to our roots, and possibly to wisdom and salvation.

Roy Hobbs of *The Natural* by Bernard Malamud is a folk hero
par excellence who in his obscure origin and natural ability re-
calls actual folk heroes: the home-run king who grew up in an
orphanage, the bragging busher from Arkansas, and one of the
greatest natural hitters (the greatest according to Ty Cobb) coming out of the South Carolina hills to be victimized by big city
sharpers. Roy also calls to mind Odysseus, Achilles, Paul Bun-
yan, and the Grail hero. He is a larger-than-life figure in whom
is found all that is good and natural but also that which is vendible.
In Roy one sees not only the problems facing the mythic hero in
a nonmythopoeic age but also one's own problems as an attempt
is made to reach some understanding with a society characterized by an ever-decreasing relationship with the soil, the
forest, and natural objects. In addition to all his other heroic
roles, Roy is an American Everyman.

In folk-hero fashion Roy comes out of the blue, wins a
throne—he becomes the "King of Klouters"—but fails to marry
a princess, loses his throne—"he coulda been a king," one fan
says after he strikes out—and he does not live happily every
afterward. Instead of finding love, success, and fulfillment Roy
(the name "Roy" means "king"; "Hobbs," perhaps, rustic clown)
loses his manhood, a common tragedy for American naturals,
Faulkner's Benjy, "the natural," and Ralph Ellison's invisible
man, for example. Roy's moral ruination is occasioned by a
complete psychological and sexual disintegration which can best
be understood, perhaps, by a brief examination of one small
part of the novel's abundant symbolism, that of the birds.

While the trees in the novel stand for fulfillment, the birds,
often associated with transcendence, here represent all the false
dreams that Roy is led to pursue; while the trees stand for potency and masculinity, the birds suggest all the castrating forces
of modern society. Each of the women who influence Roy is in
one way or another associated with birds. His mother, a whore, is
"that bird"; Harriet Bird wears a black-feathered hat when she
shoots him; and Memo reminds him of "a little lost bird." Nothing is said specifically about Iris Lemon being a bird, but that
she, Harriet, and Memo are different images of the same woman
is obvious, Iris representing the positive anima or the eternal
feminine and Harriet and Memo the negative anima or *femme*

fatale, along with Lola the shamaness and Roy's whore of a mother. In Roy's mind each of these is in some way associated with the others and finally indistinguishable. Roy is pulled apart by woman as guide and woman as bitch, both of whom in his dreamlike life are the same person who will talk about "values" without the least shame or sense of irony.

Just as the women are associated with birds, so are the unsavory male characters. Fowler's conscience is not troubled at all in selling out, and Vogleman (Birdman) wants primarily to win because he believes it will inspire his wife to make love to him. Ever and anon the bird is a threat to masculinity. When Olson spots a woman in the stands wearing a brown-feathered hat, he spits between his fingers; and whenever a bird flies over his head, Flores reassures himself by secretly touching his genitals. Even the baseballs appear to change into birds and birds are mistaken for balls.

Until it is too late Roy is unable to distinguish between the *femme fatale* and the eternal feminine, between balls and strikes, but Malamud never leaves any doubt in the reader's mind about which characters are good and which are bad. The conflict between good and evil is archetypal and suggestive of a morality play. Judge Goodwill Banner (Polyphemus) is the personification of evil, and Roy, in spite of his failure, is the "good person," as is Sam Simpson and Pop Fisher, both of whom are father figures (note the names) and both of whom in one way or another try to get Roy to stay straight. While the love of money characterizes the villains and villainesses, the good men are characterized by a certain earthiness and love of the soil. Roy feels at home in the forest and dreams of mountains and idyllic scenes in the country. Pop wishes that he had been a farmer, and so does Herman Youngberry, the young man who strikes out Roy and who, when he pitched, sometimes "saw fields of golden wheat gleaming in the sun." Youngberry's victory is the fourth instance of the soil man beating the man who has sold himself to the birds, of the victory of innocence over experience, of the little guy over the big guy (Youngberry weighs one fifty-eight; Roy is a giant). In the duel with Whammer, the competition with Bump, and even in his display of magic in the night club, Roy has been the little guy, the underdog battling against heavy odds; but by the time he comes to face Youngberry, Wonderboy has split.

Again the contests between the Champion and the smaller challenger are waged before the female and again, in the case of Harriet Bird, sadism is aroused. At the duel with Whammer she had been "a girl on horseback—reviewing the inspiring sight (she said it was) of David jawboning the Goliath-Whammer, or was it Sir Percy lancing Sir Maldemer, or the first son (with a rock in his paw) ranged against the primitive papa?"[12] Harriet loves "contests of skill" and also winners, but what she (like Circe) really loves most is collecting scalps of heroes.

Once more the sportswriter is seen as a detractor, one who blinks the good in the hero and scrapes around in his past for dirt. For Roy Hobbs, Max Mercy has minimum mercy. Motivated no doubt by jealousy, Mercy tries to do Roy in by the surest way of wrecking heroes and nonheroes alike: by revealing their past. Max's interest in Roy is aroused after he sees him dethrone the Whammer, but it is an interest which bodes only ill, a fact that Roy senses: "I don't want his dirty eyes peeking into my past" (p. 81). But Max was made to pry, to give all the inside dope, the latest scoop. He tries to find what Roy's salary is, casts suspicion upon the legality of Wonderboy, publishes a picture of Roy as a clown, tagging it with "Roy Hobbs, Clown Prince of Baseball," and, after Roy's fall, comes out with what he had long been looking for: "'Suspicion of Hobb's Sellout—Max Mercy.' Under this was a photo Mercy had triumphantly discovered, showing Roy on his back, an obscene bullet imbedded in his gut. Around him danced a naked lady: 'Hobbs at nineteen'" (p. 190).

The folk hero and the natural flat on his back at the feet of a pistol-packing naked *femme fatale* is itself a telling comment on degeneracy and emasculation of society. The picture is perhaps even slightly out of place on the sports page; it would be more appropriate as an ad for a movie.

Damon Runyon in his own inimical way has something worthwhile to say about the athlete hero. His observations on the busher-brute and the musician-boxer have already been noted; now let us see how he feels about the natural.

Again the author runs into Spider McCoy, who is still looking for heavyweights but who now feels sure that he has found a

champion in a good-looking young man with blond hair, pink
cheeks, and shoulders like the back of a truck.[13] "Here is without
a doubt the next heavyweight champion of the whole world,"
Spider tells the narrator. "It is the best natural right hand I ever
see. He reminds me of Jack Dempsey . . . also Gene Tunney" (p.
214). When Spider is asked who the man is, he replies,

What difference does it make who a guy is who can punch like he
can? . . . All I know is that he is the next heavyweight champion of the
world if he gets in the proper hands, such as mine. The broads will go
crazy bout his looks and the way he dresses. He will be a wonderful
card. . . . You can see by the way he carries himself that he is a natural
fighter. He is loose and light on his feet. . . . Chances are there is plenty
of animal in him. I like my fighters to have plenty of animal in them,
especially . . . my heavyweights. (p. 215)

As it turns out this boxer has no more of the animal in him than
does Raymond Mulrooney. He is an ex-king by the name of
Jonas who would "never think of striking anybody without serious provocation." The blow that Spider had seen him administer
to a taxi driver was simply an accident. Even after hearing all this
Spider refuses to accept the fact that he has not finally found a
genuine champion. "Spider McCoy cannot look at six feet two
and 190 pounds of anybody under thirty without becoming most
avaricious, and so after a couple of more Scotches, he begins
feeling the ex-king's muscles, which cause the ex-king to laugh
quite heartily, as it seems he is a little ticklish in spots, and finally
Spider says: 'Well . . . there is undoubtedly great natural strength
here, and all it needs is to be properly developed'" (p. 216).

In spite of his niece's accusations that Jonas is another big
umbrella like his other fighters and despite Spider's misgivings
when he sees "a certain look" in Jonas's eyes which reminds him
of other failures, he proceeds with the training of Jonas who
becomes quite a sensation in the way he flattens "the sure-footed
watermen, who plunge in swiftly and smoothly when Jonas
waves at them" (p. 220). Then one day Jonas gets word that the
dictator who has run him off wants him to return. Leaving the
ring Jonas goes back to his country in Europe, gets into a ruckus
with the dictator, and gaining confidence from Spider's niece
gives the big tyrant a good licking and regains the throne. Spider

regrets having lost another heavyweight but takes consolation in having won a wife for himself, the sister of the dictator.

What then can one say about the natural in Runyon? Parallels must not be pushed too far but perhaps it can be said that even in Runyon the natural is a folktale hero. The royal hero (in disguise) appears out of the blue, gains a throne (in this case regains), marries a "swell looking Judy," Spider's niece, and lives happily ever after, the troublemaker Poltafuss having learned his lesson. "Jonas and Poltafuss get along very nicely indeed together afterward, except once in a cabinet meeting when King Jonas has to flatten Poltafuss again to make him agree to some unemployment measure" (p. 225).

The Country Boy from the City

Another type of natural person might be called "the country boy from the city," a term that Mark Harris uses in his fiction for both fun and meaning. Henry Wiggen, the splendid hero of his baseball novels is such a one, and so is Biff Loman of Arthur Miller's *Death of a Salesman*.

It should be said at the outset that Biff's theft of the basketballs, suits, and pens perhaps ought to be acknowledged, but such actions in the overall context of the play are little more than peccadilloes. What is far more telling is his reaction to Willy's adultery and to all the pretenses that, as a result, were made evident to him. Willy in the room with another woman is Biff's great eye-opener, his first contact with deception. From that moment his hegira and his quest begin.

In refusing to come to terms with Willy and his world—he does forgive Willy—by refusing to go to summer school so that he can go to college and continue to be a surface hero, Biff becomes a bum; but there is a great difference between him and Hal Carter of *Picnic*. While Hal is a poser and an All-American heel, Biff is a natural who refuses to compromise. He can no more be the gray-flannel success that Willy wants him to be than he can accept with equanimity Willy's unfaithfulness. He must be himself and this involves for him either one of two choices: returning to sport or going West and working near the soil. Biff chooses the latter. The idea of selling sporting goods by staging exhibitions does not work out because Oliver, the man who would sponsor the Loman brothers, has forgotten that Biff was a hero and Biff realizes that it would simply be tortuous and not at all like "out playin' ball again." Reporting to Willy on his interview with Oliver and his swiping of Oliver's pen, Biff says,

"I ran down eleven flights with a pen in my hand today. And suddenly I stopped, you hear me? And in the middle of that office building, do you hear this? I stopped in the middle of that building and I saw—the sky. I saw the things that I love in this world. The work and the food and time to sit and smoke. And I looked at the pen and said to myself, what the hell am I grabbing this for? Why am I trying to become what I don't want to be? What am I doing in an office, making a contemptuous, begging fool of myself, when all I want is out there, waiting for me the minute I say I know who I am? Why can't I say that, Willy?[14]

After Willy's death he does say it: "I know who I am, kid" (to Happy).

Through the discovery of himself Biff becomes the play's hero. While nobody "dast blame Willy" he is an exponent of the philosophy of defeat. The very thought of him causes a hemorrhaging of depressing emotions. Biff, by contrast, has no idea of taking his life. When Willy tells him to hang himself for spite, he replies, "No! Nobody's hanging himself, Willy." Happy, the playboy, is the complete jerk and almost the anti-hero. Like Tom Stark he inherits the bad from his father but none of the good. At Willy's grave he says, "I'm gonna show you and everybody else that Willy Loman did not die in vain. He had a dream. It's the only dream that one can have—to come out number one man. He fought it out here, and this is where I'm gonna win it for him" (p. 139). This speech is simply an echo of Willy's answer to Ben after Ben tells him about the opportunities in timber in Alaska: "We'll do it here, Ben! You hear me? We're gonna do it here!" (Uncle Ben is a symbol of the law of the jungle, of dog-eat-dog, of get-rich-quick philosophy, of the Big Deal.) Of all the Loman men, only Biff comes to see things clearly. He rejects all the bad in Willy while manifesting all that is good: the love of out-of-doors and of working with one's hands. "You know something, Charley," he says at Willy's funeral, "There's more of him in that front stoop than in all the sales he ever made. . . . He had the wrong dreams. All, all, wrong." Biff wins out over the birds. He realizes that it is much better to try to be *a* man than *top* man.

A word should be said about Bernard. As an intelligent being, he is the familiar figure for whom the athlete serves as a foil, but as the socially prominent lawyer he is representative of a changing trend in the type of character contrasted with the athlete. There are exceptions to be sure but somewhere around World War II the athlete began to be contrasted less with the intellectual, writer, and professor and more with other types: sports writers, businessmen, lawyers, and ministers. The American intellectual, as his counterparts in England had already done, seems for the most part to have abdicated in the ancient feud and allowed the athlete to compete with other members of the establishment, with whom he generally compares favorably. In fact as Adonis the athlete assumes the role of the forever-alienated intellectual. This is essentially the case in *Salesman*. Bernard becomes the successful lawyer while Biff remains a misunderstood outcast. But being a member of the establishment is not necessarily bad. While Biff through his failures and eventual triumph has much to tell us, so does Bernard, who sums up the tragedies of many ex-heroes when in reference to Biff he says: "He never trained himself for anything." But Bernard does not say this in an "I told you so" manner. He was never envious of Biff but "loved him" instead and, like Frank Merriwell, cheated in order to help him pass. Then after his own success he has no wish to create envy or animosity in the Lomans. Bernard seems to be a combination of Happy and Biff. In his last conversation with Willy he says, "If at first you don't succeed" (Happy's philosophy) but then reverses himself and adds, "But sometimes, Willy, it's best for a man just to walk away" (Biff's philosophy). Perhaps it is the tenacity of one of these views coupled with the wisdom of the other that allows Bernard to do so well professionally and socially without the least suggestion of compromise or Big Dealism. Bernard, incidentally, is a tennis player, the implication being that tennis is more conducive to later success and a well-rounded life than football. "Someday," says Willy in the saddest line in the play, "they'll all [Biff, Happy, and Barnard] play tennis together"— and hunt golden disks in the sunlit grass.

The works of Arthur Miller have frequently reflected a knowledge and love of sport, but when in a 1968 interview he was asked his opinion on modern sports, he replied, "I play tennis as much as I can, but on a purely amateur basis. I have almost no interest in the big spectator sports any more.... There doesn't seem to be any humanity left in big-time sports.... People go to watch a machine operate. They admire the efficiency with which it was put together. That wipes out the connection between spectator and team. The human side is out."[15] Miller does not tell us anything new here about the American sporting scene, but what is remarkable is that he is telling us something old, that which has been implied throughout twentieth-century literature and explicitly stated even to the use of identical metaphors. Over a quarter of a century earlier Thomas Wolfe had described alumni and fans in the following manner:

They fill great towns at night before the big game. They go to night clubs and to bars. They dance, they get drunk, they carouse. They take their girls to games, they wear fur coats, they wear expensive clothing. They are drunk by game time. They do not really see the game and they do not care. They hope their machine runs better than the other machine, scores more points, wins a victory. They hope their own hired men come out ahead, but they really do not care. They don't know what it is to care. They have become too smart, too wise, too knowing, too absurd, to care. They are not youthful and backwoodsy and naive enough to care. They are too slick to care. It's hard to feel a passion from just looking at machinery. It's hard to get excited at the efforts of the hired men.[16]

What Miller and Wolfe both deplore is not sport or even team sport but the sad and all too often indisputable fact that *homo ludens* has become *animal laborns,* the laboring animal.

Whereas *The Natural* in literary parlance is a romance, Mark Harris's baseball stories, *The Southpaw, Bang the Drum Slowly,* and *Ticket for a Seamstitch,* are novels. There is no mystery about the hero Henry Wiggen as he goes into detail about his background and many of the games; and though events in his life have little in common with those of the traditional folktale, Henry springs from folk, people who have remained people through all the

dehumanization of the twentieth century. His Pop, Holly, and
Aaron are in fact incorruptible, but they unfortunately seem
now more like museum pieces than flesh and blood characters.
So do many of the Mammoths appear real but also as archaic in a
sense as the eight-team league in which they compete. Archaic or
not, they are alive, much more so than many who breathe. There
is much about some of them that is unsavory, but most have a
sense of life, especially Henry Wiggen. "Life is good," he says.
Long live Thoreau!

Unlike Roy Hobbs, Henry breaks into the big time early and
has great success; but he too is tempted, and in a small degree
succumbs—his throwing the spitter, for instance. This is really a
humanizing flaw (as is his finger sign to the crowd) without
which Henry would be almost saintly. Perhaps he is a saint;
certainly he is, like Roy Hobbs, a "good person." Henry is also
tempted by the *femme fatale*, Patricia Moors, but he is rescued by
Holly, the positive anima, the woman as guide, who tells him,

"It is not a matter of me marrying either you or a gas pumper. It is a
matter of marrying a man. I do not much care what he does, so long as
he is a man. You are 21," she said, "and under the law you are a man,
and your height and weight is that of a man. In the bed you are a man,"
and she smiled a little. "But you are losing your manhood faster than
hell. Pretty soon in bed will be the *only* place you are a man. But that is
not manhood. Dogs and bulls and tomcats do the same. Yes, you are
losing your manhood and becoming simply an island in the empire of
Moors."[17]

Holly reads him Durocher's ideas on winning and concludes her
little lecture with some Platonic ideas.

"You are a lefthander, Henry. You always was. And the world needs all
the lefthanders it can get, for it is a righthanded world. You are a
southpaw in a starboarded atmosphere. . . ."
    "I hold your hand . . . and your hand is hard, solid like a board. That
is all right, for it must be hard against the need of your job. On a job
such as yours your hand grows hard to protect itself. But you have not
yet growed calluses on your heart. It is not yet hard against the need of
your job. It must never become hard like your hand. It must stay soft."
(pp. 307–8)

At the time of Holly's intervention Henry is apparently considering measuring everybody by the amount of money he has and
adopting the view that winning is all that matters, but later he is
unashamedly subscribing to the wisdom of Grantland Rice's
once-famous quatrain which the seamstitch sends to one of the
Mammoth players "sewed in the Mammoth's home colors, one
word red and the next word blue and the background white."

FOR WHEN THE ONE GREAT SCORER COMES TO MARK
AGAINST YOUR NAME,
HE WRITES—NOT THAT YOU WON OR LOST—BUT HOW
YOU PLAYED THE GAME.[18]

Henry praises Rice—"He was a very fine man, the best"—and
calls the poem "beautiful." The poem is the biggest joke on
campus—and off—but Henry, though tempted, lives by its
"beautiful thought." He does not talk about the "one great
scorer" but neither does he allow his values to be distorted. He
retains his independence of spirit, his hatred of sham and snob-
bery, his almost passionate love for baseball, and his capacity for
friendship, which is clearly revealed in his loyalty to Bruce Pearson in *Bang the Drum Slowly*.

Bruce, third-string Mammoth catcher, is "not a natural,"
Henry says, but here one must disagree; for Bruce is a natural,
perhaps not a natural baseball player—he can only hit to left
field—but a natural person as Henry implicitly admits in his
attempt to build Bruce's confidence.

"You been dumb on one count only. You left somebody tell you you
were dumb. But you are not. You know which way the river run, which
I myself do not know. Even Holly does not know, and I doubt that Red
Traphagen [a Harvard graduate] himself can look at a river and tell
you which way it runs without throwing a stick in it. All the way down
from Minnesota I never knew."

"I thought you knew," he said.

"Because I bullshit you," I said. "You know what is planted in the
fields and you know the make of cows. Who in hell on this whole club
knows one cow from the other? I could be stranded in the desert with
412 cows and die of thirst and hunger for all I know about a cow."[19]

Not only does Bruce have a knowledge of natural objects but like Pat Glendon, Nebraska Crane, Pop Fisher, and Roy Hobbs, he, having been raised on a farm in Mill, Georgia, has a natural love of the land, rivers, and solitude. He "would of give almost anything to settle down forever on a farm near Bainbridge, never mind the fame and glory, only give him time to live."[20] He likes to hear farm talk, to fish, to sing, to play golf with Henry, to wash his car, to reminisce quietly about his boyhood, "to watch the sun go down and up"; and the knowledge that he is to die from Hodgkins disease only makes all these things somehow more dear. "The world is all rosy," he says. "It never looked better. The bad things never looked so little, and the good never looked so big. Food tastes better. Things do not matter too much any more!" (p. 41)

The bad things never looked so little. The reader who can be unashamedly sentimental is apt to leave Bang the Drum with the same feeling, for the transcendent knowledge of Bruce and the friendship between him and Henry somehow dwarf all that is wrong in the Mammoth organization. Somehow the reader does not feel depressed that no one except Henry goes to the funeral in Georgia—certainly he is not surprised, for no one had visited Ugly Jones, the team captain, while he was in the hospital in The Southpaw. It has long been known that professionalism can cause athletes to do worse; what reassures one is that humanity is retained. Leslie Fiedler perhaps carries his "No! In Thunder" thesis too far by knocking this novel. Says Fiedler, "Reading, say, All the King's Men, one need only to think of The Last Hurrah or Advise and Consent—or picking up The Natural, one only to recall Mark Harris's Bang the Drum Slowly to realize how we inordinately lust to being lied to, and how seldom we are granted the privilege of hearing the truth." Earlier Fiedler says, "What life refuses, the anti-artist grants: the dying catcher hits a three bagger and everyone loves him." James T. Farrell takes an opposite view, praising Harris as a novelist, and while admitting that Malamud can write, calls The Natural "highflying banality."[21] Neither Fiedler nor Farrell, it seems, has granted either Harris or Malamud his subject. Further, if Harris is not a dyed-in-the-wool "naysayer," he is nevertheless a fine "lefthander."

Bruce lacks the extra something to be a first-team major

leaguer—he is not consistent and cannot play well under
pressure—but he is an excellent all-round athlete, a fact that
allows Henry to come up with some superb satire of the athletic
policies of bowl-minded southern universities. In high school
Bruce had played all sports and "Southern States U" had been
anxious to land him. When Bruce dropped out of high school
after football season in his senior year to help on the farm, SSU
bought his father an experimental tractor so that Bruce could
stay in school and get his diploma. Later they send college boys
to help (experimental labor) and finally even come across with
some "experimental money." In college as a passer and
linebacker Bruce is instrumental in helping SSU compile outstanding records and a bowl victory, as is his roommate, Hut Sut
Sutter, later a star with Green Bay. Concerning Hut Sut, Henry
says, "I run across him 2 winters ago on the banquet circuit at a
Youth Jamboree in Baltimore where we both spoke, the only
time I ever laid eyes on him, a short, wide fellow, and he told me
he would show me some fine whorehouses in Baltimore. But I
had a train to catch and anyhow was never interested in
whorehouses to begin with" (p. 23). But Hut Sut, Henry says,
had long been interested in them, had even minored in them.
"All winter they [Bruce and Hut Sut] horsed around the gymnasium [at SSU] shooting baskets and swinging on the ropes and
swimming in the pool, and once a month they took off in a
college car and hunted up whorehouses, Sutter a regular expert
in the matter" (p. 23).

Bruce at SSU raises the question of the role of college in the
life of the natural and the folk hero. As a rule folk heroes have
shunned formal education; and since Bruce played football he is
no exception, since it is utterly impossible to play football for
SSU and gain even the semblance of an education. Like Natty
Bumppo and Huck Finn he has a natural knowledge of natural
things but apparently no great desire to learn from books,
though he asks Henry an endless train of questions. It is safe to
say that higher education simply goes against the grain of "the
folk" and tends to make the natural person into an Organization
Man and perhaps something of a bird.

To the growing list of abominable fictional sportswriters
should be added Krazy Kress. In Henry's view he is the villain of

baseball who, through distortions and Big Deals, not the least of which is the promotion of the sports–war metaphor, has changed baseball from a game of the people into one for the birds. "You have mixed it all up," I said. "I do not know how. I know only 1 thing. I know only that from here on in I play baseball for the kicks and the cash only, for I got to eat like you do, but as for the rest—Japan and Korea and society bastards like the Moorses, writers and fans and spontaneous demonstrations cooked up by drunks like Bill Duffy, fancy celebrations and the wars and the politics of it—all this I leave to them that glories in it."[22] Henry's attitude toward the Korean War has drawn fire from others besides Krazy Kress and not altogether unjustifiably. After his rookie year Henry is perhaps a bit too rebellious, has yet to learn that if he will not be "an island in the empire of the Moors," neither can he be an island completely unto himself or that the right to be an island completely unto himself has been provided by others who had no choice but to join hands against raging seas of trouble. Yet who is to say, for who would long deny Henry's tremendous worth? In the long run he is right and the joiners wrong. He is a great American in the tradition of Thoreau. "You are part of the organization," Patricia tells him. "I am part of nothing," he responds.

In a *Time* Essay, "The Difficult Art of Losing" (November 15, 1968), there appears this statement: "Whole libraries could be filled with American novels whose villain is success, or a misunderstanding of what success means." Among these novels would be the works of Mark Harris. Henry Wiggen comes to look sensibly upon success, but too many of us in America have not. Much of the misunderstanding is reflected in our attitudes toward winning in sport, attitudes that seem to have changed drastically—and for the worse—within the last quarter of a century. Undoubtedly there have always been those who regard Rice's poem as "classic corn," as *Time* calls it, but it is interesting to speculate why there arose in the fifties such an unabashed emphasis on winning and cynical views on losing in such persons as Leo Durocher, Paul Bryant, and the late Vince Lombardi and Jim Tatum. Possibly the popularity of the philosophies of these and others was determined to some extent by the national frustration that resulted when the United States painfully discovered in the Korean War and later in Vietnam that MacArthur's "There is no substitute for victory" was not exactly applicable and would never be again in a nuclear age and that a tie—"like kissing your sister," claimed coach Jim Owens—was all that could be hoped for.[23]

But what feeling must one try to cultivate? Willie Stark's "It's the championship by God" is clearly not the answer nor is the practice of the British who, says David English in *Divided They Stand,* "often prefer a good loser to a good winner" and who in sport because of "this built-in reflex" succeed in "losing in the nick of time." Again, the Jewish men in the Weequahic section in *Portnoy's Complaint* come close to the answer in their paradoxical view of victory: it is important and it is not. The sense of personal and even ethnic pride demands one's best and most honorable efforts, but race memories of a thousand defeats by fanatic bullies quietly hint at the possibility of the truth of Charles Lawrence's dictum in *The Huge Season:* "Nobody wins at any game." But Rice's advice and Henry Wiggen's practice of it must still serve. Perhaps finally no one wins, but one still might take some satisfaction in imagining what the great Scorer might have said.

The Cripple

Since the days of the earliest myths, a physical injury, especially to the foot or leg, has indicated a spiritual wound, the foot, according to Jung, being a symbol of the soul. In the case of the myth of the wounded Adonis much more than soul is symbolized: his condition becomes inextricably related to that of the land, a situation paralleled in *Cat on a Hot Tin Roof* by Tennessee Williams. The future and fertility of "twenty-eight thousand acres of the richest land this side of the valley Nile"—roughly a thousand acres for each year of Brick Pollitt's life; he is twenty-seven—depend upon his recovery. The former Ole Miss star who cripples himself on the hurdles of the "Glorious Hill High School" athletic field becomes an analogue not only of the fisher king but also of Adonis. That one of his age can be the fisher king would not appear to be out of keeping with the legend. "Sometimes while still comparatively young he [the fisher king]

is incapacitated by the effects of a wound, and is known also by
the title of *Roi Mehaigne*, or Maimed King."[24] Further, as with
the fisher king, Brick's injury is related to his emasculation in
which, in turn, lies the threat to the land. Only in Brick is there
hope, for regardless of his weaknesses, he has a certain modesty
and honesty or at least he does not evince that mendacity which
the potent Gooper and the fertile Mae would wreak on the plantation.

Understandably, Brick's condition leads to the consideration
of suicide, but this he dismisses, though the stated alternative,
according to him, is a poor one. "Then why don't you kill yourself, man?" Big Daddy asks. "I like to drink" is his reply. Again
he says, "My head don't work any more and it's hard for me to
understand how anybody could care if he lived or died or was
dying or cared about anything but whether or not there was
liquor left in the bottle. . . . In some ways I'm no better than the
others, in some ways worse because I'm alive. Maybe it's being
alive that makes them lie, and being almost not alive makes me
sort of accidentally truthful."[25] But Brick does not do himself
justice. He is more self-effacing than fair. He is truthful not
because he feels close to death but because he is, in the words of
Maggie, "an ass-aching puritan." Brick chooses to live, one feels,
not because he likes to drink or because he prefers not to die but
because he wishes with his presence to continue to reject the
"mendacity" around him; in doing so he becomes something of a
sedentary saint.

This admittedly is only one view. That there is the possibility
that Brick did do an "unnatural thing" with Skipper and that he
is lying to himself and others Williams wants to be kept in mind.

The thing they're discussing, timidly and painfully on the side of Big
Daddy, fiercely, violently on Brick's side, is the inadmissible thing that
Skipper died to disavow between them. The fact that if it existed it had
to be disavowed to "keep face" in the world they lived in, may be at the
heart of the "mendacity" that Brick drinks to kill his disgust with. It may
be the root of his collapse. Or maybe it is only a single manifestation of
it, not even the most important. . . . Some mystery should be left in the
revelation of character in a play, just as a great deal of mystery is always
left in the revelation of character in life, even in one's own character to
himself. (pp. 98–99)

There is a mystery about Brick but if there is doubt about his relationship with Skipper he should be given the benefit of it. Says Norman Mailer,

The accusation of homosexuality arouses a major passion in many men; they spend their lives resisting it with a biological force. There is a kind of man who spends every night of his life getting drunk in a bar, he rants, he brawls, he ends in a small rubble on the street; women say, "For God's sakes, he's homosexual. Why doesn't he just turn queer and get his suffering over with." Yet men protect him. It is because he is choosing not to become homosexual. It was put best by Sartre who said that a homosexual is a man who practices homosexuality. A man who does not, is not homosexual—he is entitled to the dignity of his choice. He is entitled to the fact that he chose not to become homosexual, and is paying presumably his price.[26]

For one to accuse Brick of homosexuality is not only an ill-founded charge but one that is mean and unfair. One should conclude that there are between him and Skipper camaraderie and friendship, that he is truthful with himself, and that the disgust he feels stems from the mendacity of others.

It must be granted, then, that the problem facing Brick is not homosexuality but mendacity of others. The problem for Big Daddy, who becomes a sort of quester figure, is to ask Brick the question that will get to the heart of the matter, so Brick can become "young" and potent, get Maggie with child and heir and save the land from desolation, "bring life to this place that death has come unto." But Big Daddy fails. His questions lead only to the discovery of his own malignant condition; and when he leaves Brick at the end of Act 2 he, Big Daddy, "*looks back as if he has some desperate question he couldn't put into words.*"

But what Big Daddy cannot do, Maggie possibly can do, not through questions but through lies and perseverence. It is not certain, however, that she succeeds. As a castrator of Skipper, she is also a threat to Brick, indeed one of the causes of his infirmity. In her attempt to take care of Brick, to make him love her again, she takes on the role of Omphale and Cleopatra: "Brick, I've laid out your beautiful silk shirts. I'll put your cufflinks on it, those lovely star sapphires I get you to wear so rarely." Brick recognizes the threat, and his reply constitutes perhaps the most heroic utterance of an athlete in our literature: "I'm not going to get dressed Maggie." Brick tries to avoid becoming a toy darling, to remain in his natural state, but it should be noted that he puts on "*white silk* pajamas" (italics added). Not only does Brick compromise, but he also reveals that Maggie can to some extent get him to do what she wants him to. Brick's malleability is thus evident, even during his resentment toward Maggie. That she will seduce him after throwing away the crutch and liquor, Skipper's nemesis, seems not only possible but probable.

The hope is that if Brick does throw away his crutch he will not, after long travail, throw away his soul as well. For with the crutch Brick takes on the traditional qualities of the radical intellectual typified by Squier in *The Petrified Forest:* lameness, consciousness, shame, and guilt. Yet he himself is not "intellectual." Perhaps it would be more correct to say that he becomes the proxy for the intellectuals or even their *ami damnée.* In any event he continues to slug it out with the ancient foe, the member of the Establishment, "Brother Man." Like Bernard in *Salesman* "Brother Man" (Gooper) is a lawyer but one with considerably different scruples.

Even with his crutch, Brick is a superb example of strength and beauty; it is remarkable how mythological Williams has made him while at the same time making him real. Both as an ex-star for Ole Miss and as Adonis Brick is successful. He is, as Maggie realizes, something extraordinary. "You see, you son of a bitch, you asked too much of people, of me, of him, of all the unlucky poor damned sons of bitches that happen to love you . . . you asked too goddam much of people that loved you, you—superior creature!—you god like being!" (pp. 39-40) What it is exactly that makes Brick so godlike is difficult to say, but perhaps it is the same quality of Biff, in *Salesman,* the blessing (or damnation) of *aidos,* that which Pindar says makes a man a "straight fighter" and all too often, the modern might add, a cripple.

Another famous athlete hero who maims himself in attempting to regain the glory of former years is Cash Bentley of John Cheever's "O Youth and Beauty!" Like Brick, Cash tries to be young again by running and jumping, not while drunk and

alone on a high school track field but while drunk with an audience in a "suburb of Shady Hill."

Trace and Cash moved the tables and the chairs, the sofas and the fire
screen, the woodbox and the footstool; and when they had finished, you
wouldn't know the place. Then if the host had a revolver, he would be
asked to produce it. Cash would take off his shoes and assume a starting
crouch behind a sofa. Trace would fire the weapon out of an open
window, and if you were new to the community and had not understood what the preparations were about, you would then realize that
you were watching a hurdle race. Over the sofa went Cash, over the
tables, over the fire screen and the woodbox. It was not exactly a race,
since Cash ran it alone, but it was extraordinary to see this man of forty
surmount so many obstacles so gracefully. There was not a piece of
furniture in Shady Hill that Cash could not take in his stride. The race
ended with cheers, and presently the party would break up.[27]

At such a party Cash breaks his leg, a piece of carving on a
chest having brought him down. The points of contact between
this story and the nature cults and the Grail legend are not so
evident as in *Cat on a Hit Tin Roof*, but certain overtones are
discernible. That Cash is to be taken as symbol of the fisher king
seems strongly implied after he sustains the injury, and the
young doctor who comes to him appears to be the questing hero
but one who does not know the right question to ask. "Yerkes
was a young man—he did not seem old enough to be a doctor—
and he looked around at the disordered room and the anxious
company as if there was something weird about the scene. He
got off on the wrong foot with Cash. "What seems to be the
matter, old-timer?" he asked (p. 22).

Thereafter the symptoms in Cash are also those of his society.
The gloom and discontent he feels for having lost his youth and
athletic prowess are reflected in all that he sees and does.

A few nights later, he was walking down a New York side street in the
rain and saw an old whore standing in a doorway. She was so sluttish
and ugly that she looked like a cartoon of Death, but before he could
appraise her—the instant his eyes took an impression of her crooked
figure—his lips swelled, his breath quickened, and he experienced all
the other symptoms of erotic excitement. A few nights later, while he
was reading *Time* in the living room, he noticed that the faded roses

Louise had brought in from the garden smelled more of earth than of
anything else. It was a putrid, compelling smell. He dropped the roses
into a watebasket, but not before they had reminded him of the spoiled
meat, the whore, and the spider web. (pp. 22–23)

If those on the Delta are ailing, so are the semi-campy of
eastern suburbia, especially those in Shady Hill after Cash's fall.
For him, a has-been, conditions go from bad to worse. Then one
night in his own home Cash wants to try hurdling the furniture
again; becoming impatient with his wife for not giving him the
starting shot with the pistol, he begins the course anyway. When
Louise, who had never fired the pistol before, finally removes
the safety and shoots, she catches him "in mid air," shooting him
dead. *Le Roi est mort.*

With "Gee-Gee" of "The Scarlet Moving Van" the king lives
again (*Vive le Roi*) but he is still ailing in a "stuffy" environment,
an unincorporated township in the eastern United States. Like
Cash, "Gee-Gee" ("Greek God," a nickname from college) had
been a great athlete, an all-American twice in football, but he
had been much more, having had the quality of *aidos*. "He was
never a money player" ("*aidos* is stolen away by secret gain") and
"he always played straight out of his heart" (*aidos* is that which
makes a man a "straight fighter"). He had been an "Adonis," and
he had been loved by all, especially by Peaches, who is "blonde
and warm" and who laments the transformation in her husband.

"Now it's all gone, but I tell myself that I once had the love of a good
man. I don't think many women have known that kind of love. Oh, I
wish he'd come back. I wish he'd be the way he was. The night before
last, when we were packing up the dishes in the old house, he got drunk
and I slapped him in the face, and I shouted at him, 'Come back! Come
Back! Come back to me Gee-Gee!' But he didn't listen. He didn't hear
me. He doesn't hear anyone anymore—not even the voices of his children. I ask myself every day what I have done to be punished so
cruelly."[28]

What has happened to Gee-Gee is difficult to say. While sober
he is personable and basically he has retained the innocence that
he had in college, but at a party he becomes a holy terror. At the
social initiation for him and Peaches in the town, Gee-Gee be-

comes the center of attention midway through the dessert.
"'What a God-damned bunch of stuffed shirts!' he said. 'Let's
put a little vitality into the conversation, shall we?' He sprang
onto the center of the table and began to sing a dirty song and
dance a jig. Women screamed. Dishes were upset and broken.
Dresses were ruined. Peaches pled to her wayward husband"
(p. 45).

Gee-Gee indulges in such practices because he says he has "to
teach them." "I've got to teach them," he says desperately (*aidos*
is "a sense of duty" to "an eternal ideal"), but when his neighbor,
Charlie Folkestone, asks him what he is trying to teach them,
Gee-Gee replies, "You'll never know. You're too God-damned
stuffy."

Gee-Gee cripples himself while playing football and, like
Cash, has to wear a cast, but he is not, like Cash, so much a fisher
king figure as a scapegoat. "Gee-Gee was an advocate for the
lame, the diseased, the poor, for those who through no fault of
their own live out their lives in misery and pain." (*Aidos* "is the
feeling a prosperous man should have in the presence of the
unfortunate . . . a sense that the difference between him and
those poor wretches is not deserved.") Because he envisioned the
suffering in life, because it seemed "necessary to suffer oneself
in order to accept his message," and because he reminded "the
happy," "the well born," and "the rich" of a side of life they did
not wish to see, he and Peaches are forced to move from every
new home, their goods being transported in the scarlet van.
"We've moved eight times in the last eight years," says Peaches,
"and there's never been anyone to say goodbye to us" (pp. 44–
45). They move from "B___" in November, a time that does not
appear to be without meaning as far as the scapegoat is concerned. Says Sir James George Frazer, "Before entering on a
new year, people are anxious to rid themselves of the troubles
that have harassed them in the past; hence it comes about that in
so many communities the beginning of the new year is inaugu-
rated with a solemn and public banishment of evil spirits."[29]
Cash Bentley jumped over the furniture at the drunken parties
in an attempt to be a hero again, to regain his youth—a wish of
the fisher king—but Gee-Gee swings on the chandeliers and puts
on his performances not to try to be heroic or youthful again but

to remind others of their failures as humans, an act for which he must also be punished.

But, as it develops, Gee-Gee is not alone in his alienation. Living in "Y____" alone—his family had gone to Nassau for Christmas—Gee-Gee falls from a child's wagon which he propels with his crutch. He calls his old neighbor in "B____," Charlie Folkestone, and asks him to come help, telling him that he is all alone and that no one else will come. It has been snowing and Charlie, noting that his place is with his children, "and not with the succoring of drunkards who had forfeited the chance to be taken seriously," refuses the call. Almost immediately he is struck with guilt, remembering that Gee-Gee must once have been "fair, high-spirited, generous and strong," and his recriminations increase. He becomes irritable with his family and others, loses his job, and finally, like Gee-Gee and Peaches, begins his wanderings with his family in "the scarlet-and-gold van." Gee-Gee recovers from his injury but remains a scapegoat; Charlie, however, becomes more of a Wandering Jew for refusing the call.[30]

A different type of scapegoat is seen in J. Lasky Proctor of Wright Morris's *The Huge Season,* but in order to arrive at any understanding of Proctor it is first necessary to examine his relationship to the hero, Charles Lawrence, and to the other members of the comitatus. This might best be done by application of D. H. Lawrence's "theosophical myth," according to which, life is constituted by a system of electrical circuits.

There are three groups of circuits: those which run between one center and another within the individual; those which run between individuals; and those which run between an individual and the nonhuman cosmos. The Lawrentian theory of the hero should now be more exactly comprehended. The hero is a necessity because most people lack the third kind of circuit, that which runs between a man and the cosmos. The hero is the man who is most fully alive because he possesses all three groups of circuits. He is necessary because other people do not. Carlyle said that while the law of master and man is inexorable, every man may be in his degree heroic. The act of worshipping a master puts a man in a vital rapport with the heart of the cosmos. "Give homage and allegiance to a hero," says D. H. Lawrence, "and you become yourself heroic, it is the law of men."[31]

Huge Season illustrates well this "law of men." At Colton College, the setting for several of the "captivity" chapters, Lundgren, the scientist, plays with a magnet and iron filings, thereby providing the novel's basic metaphor. The hero, Charles Lawrence, all-conquering tennis champion and heir to a fortune, is the magnet attracting or tending to attract the "filings": Proctor (writer), Foley (professor), Lundgren (scientist), and Lou Baker (female witness). (Note the parallel between the occupations of the male witnesses here with those of characters in *Strange Interlude*.) But not all are drawn with the same degree of force. Lundgren is scarcely attracted at all, and both Foley and Lou Baker receive their charges through Proctor, the most magnetized of all. Since the force of attraction varies inversely with the distance between the charges, Proctor, closest to the hero, receives the greatest current.

While Lawrence's satellites regard him not as sun but as a constellation, he does not look upon himself as such. Rather he seems to depend upon Proctor and possibly even considers Proctor to be the hero. But Lawrence cannot fool anyone, including himself, for he seems to sense the burden that goes with the role of hero. He is lonely and, like Proctor, deliberately seeks suffering, burning his hand on a smudgepot because that is one act which is not "bullshit." Further he feels only contempt or unconcern for standards of conduct. Where most boys settle for "pimples," Lawrence catches "a dose of clap"; and as for term papers, he "didn't seem to care where they came from, who wrote them, or even who saw through it."[32] He simply does not care, for he feels that very little is important. On the matter of winning he obviously agrees with Quentin Compson's grandfather in *The Sound and the Fury*, that "victory is an illusion of philosophers and fools." "Nobody wins," Lawrence says, "at any game." He is a defeatist but, ironically, also a perfectionist, in tennis, bullfighting, virtue, or whatever he deems worthy of his attention. His involvement with perfection accounts for his suicide. Since he will have nothing to do with imperfection, he becomes "Saint Lawrence" and "so goddam good there isn't anybody left but Lawrence and God." "Pity," thinks Foley, "had led Proctor, pity and imperfection, to put an end to the great quarter-miler, but it was perfection, the terror of it, that had killed Lawrence. The knowledge that he might be caught with perfection on his hands and still be discontent."

Twenty years later Proctor gives a different version of why he shot himself in the heel. He did so, he tells Foley, not to prove to Lawrence that a Jew can take it—"any Jew can take it"—but "to show him a Jew who could give it up." Had he not shot himself, he implies, he would have degaussed Lawrence and taken away his own charge. This is why Proctor cannot kill Lawrence; it would leave him without a *querencia* (the place in the ring where the bull feels most at home). But after Lawrence's suicide the charge is gone, and for the witnesses the problem becomes one of living in a world from which the hero has departed. The bullet in the heel had only crippled Proctor physically, but "the shot that killed Lawrence had crippled all of them." For the next twenty years Proctor, Foley, and Lou Baker appear to be asking themselves the question from Arnold's *Obermann Once More:*

> Poor fragments of a broken world
> Whereupon men pitch their tent!
> Why were ye too to death not hurled
> When your world's day was spent?

After Lawrence's suicide Proctor tries to find a *querencia* by other means. He fights in the Spanish Civil War, becomes an "importer of Jews," "The Laureate of the Age of Bullshit," and, as a member of the Communist party, "the masked voice" of America. At the investigation of the McCarthy committee on Un-American Activities, Proctor is cited for contempt, having stated that if he were a good American, like Thoreau, he would be in jail. It is as a figure on trial, not so much as a communist but as a *revolté*, that Proctor becomes an unmistakable scapegoat.

Proctor on trial and "throwing open his shirt to show the public his wounds" is still more than a disillusioned idealist and persecuted *revolté:* he is the mutilated all-round man. Having been a fine but amateur athlete and an engaged intellectual, he was destined for tragedy, to become crippled and eroded, from the start.

With Lawrence dead and Proctor worn down what does Foley the professor decide about "the question"? There is, as he realizes, cause to go and fear that he might: "Who would be next? The steady erosion of the liberal mind. Winant, Matthiessen, Forrestal, and—Foley paused, swallowed the name that next rose to his lips" (p. 291). Perhaps Foley lacks the guts, as Lou Baker says, but ironically he finds that he has no choice, that he must live. He himself has been gaussed by all that transpired in his "captivity."

A lover like Lou Baker, a saint like Lawrence, a martyr like Proctor, and a witness like Foley. So much fire and water, so much fear and wonder, so much smoke and sprinkling of soot. But in the burning they gave off something less perishable. How explain that Lawrence, in whom the sun rose, and Proctor, in whom it set, were now alive in Foley, a man scarcely alive himself. Peter Foley, with no powers to speak of, had picked up the charge that such powers gave off—living in the field of the magnet, he had been magnetized. Impermanent himself, he had picked up this permanent thing. He was hot, he was radioactive, and the bones of Peter Foley would go on chirping in a time that had stopped. No man had given a name to this magnet, not explained these imperishable lines of force, but they were there, captive in Peter Foley, once a captive himself. (pp. 305–6).

The magnetization of Foley is another example of D. H. Lawrence's "law of men." Not heroic himself, Foley had remained faithful and given homage in his own quiet way. Thus, at last, he became charged and, though "scarcely alive," found a *raison d'etre.*

James Dickey's *Deliverance* is a story of an adventure into wildness and also a trip into the human psyche; accordingly the characters are highly symbolic, especially Lewis Medlock, the athlete and all-round man who is permanently maimed by the very nature he seeks so earnestly to conquer. Lewis is a sports nut, but he is not at the outset a good example of *homo ludens,* man at play. "Play," says Johan Huizinga, "demands order absolute and supreme. The least deviation from it spoils the game and robs it of character." This is not to imply that Lewis is not a fair player. Indeed, he is, but he foresees a time when, after the machine stops, all rules will be cast to the winds and everyone will be thrown back upon skills of survival. Lewis thinks he understands nature, but he learns that nature is more violent than he had realized and that he had been presumptuous to think that she could ever be conquered or understood. Lewis goes into the Appalachian wilderness not to commune with nature but to dominate her, an attitude that is reflected in the sports with which he is most involved, weight-lifting, archery, hunting and fishing, and, of course, canoeing. He is really too serious to be involved with play, hence a more appropriate term for Lewis would be *homo faber,* man the maker or artist, one who heroically attempts to sculpt a life and meaning by overcoming nature. In the praise he sings of nature and in his celebration of wildness he is Dionysian, yet in the discipline he seeks to maintain he is Apollonian, a son of light and order, a semidivine being with the body perfect, at least to his admirers on the trip. He is a grail hero in search of the golden eye, "another life," transcending the absurd routine of life in a modern tidewater city.

For all the physical prowess and beauty that allow for a facile comparison with the grail hero, Lewis has only a dim understanding of what his task of deliverance entails. In spite of his self-assured manner, Lewis does not know all the answers or even the right question to ask of the obvious fisher king, Tom McCaskill, the hermit of the mountain wood. Lewis had learned something about this figure on a previous fishing trip in which he was also crippled, but he had not learned enough.

In relating the earlier experience to Ed, Lewis says:

"Well, let me tell you. You come up here camping in the woods, on the river in some places, or back off in the bush, hunting or whatever you're doing, and in the middle of the night you're liable to hear the most god-awful scream that ever got loose from a human mouth. There's no explanation for it. You just hear it once, and sometimes it keeps on for a while." "What is it, for the Lord's sake?" "There's this old guy up here who just gets himself—or makes himself—a jug every couple of weeks, and goes off in the woods at night. From what I hear he doesn't have any idea where he's going. He just goes off the road and keeps going till he's ready to stop. Then he builds himself a fire and sits down with the jug. When he gets drunk enough he starts out to hollering. That's the way he gets his kicks."[33]

On the earlier trip Lewis had "fished," but he had not even suspected the meaning of the hair-raising scream. It is, of course, the primal one, the same that Bobby emits when he is sodomized by the mountaineer. What does it mean? It means that nature is unbearable, that there is a terror in the heart of darkness beyond all comprehension, that civilization is therefore built on a series of fictions. The Hermit is trapped in nature and so is Bobby when he is at the mercy of his attackers. For them there is no "beyond"; hence, they scream. Thus in a single blood-curdling sound both refute Rousseau convincingly. Without the law that Drew wishes to uphold there is only the chilling terror of the howling ape or the maddening silence of the grinning cat. Hence law, as Justice Learned Hand once observed, is superior to justice since law provides us with rules to play the game while justice is a subjective response to any situation. But law and justice do not tell the whole story either. There must always be awareness of the mystery inherent in the scream of Tom McCaskill. Else we will face a future like the one Norman Mailer sees as a real possibility, that is "one devoid of sin, guilt, choice, and the claim of the isolated screaming ego demanding to be counted, valued, and loved."[34]

Like Adonis, Lewis is wounded in the thigh, not by a wild boar but by a wild river, which amounts to the same thing. It is the river too and not the mountaineer that kills Drew, the river with "its incredible brutality and violence." Drew has been allowed to peep behind the curtain of Maya and thereafter cannot endure. "The best of the lot," he gives credence to the belief that the only people worth a damn in the world are those that go crazy or kill themselves or both or yell drunkenly in the night by a campfire in the wilds. Rather than killing himself, Drew sacrifices himself to a belief in a "beyond" that transcends the democratic vote establishing the lie of their condition. To argue that Drew is shot would rob the novel of its meaning and rich ironic complexity, which James Dickey obviously intended it to have. Drew is the Christ figure, the sacrificial victim who suggests a "beyond" that does not rest upon the denial of truth of nature, whatever that may be, but instead upon the denial of death or law of the jungle, eat or be eaten. Drew tells us what we should do: Lewis, the supreme athlete and body beautiful, merely what we cannot do. Lewis is human, but Drew is divine. The wound in Lewis's thigh and the consequent limp for life testify to one simple truth: Man cannot control nature or even come close to the core of it without paying the price for the violation of limits known as hubris. The perceptive observer can learn a lesson from Lewis's limp, but Lewis himself has learned nothing. "He is a human being, and a good one," Ed says, but he also says that the changes are not obvious. They certainly are not. He has merely gone from one extreme to the other, as is the case of obsessive athletes and compulsive personalities in general. With obvious reference to Eugen Herrigel's *Zen in the Art of Archery,* Lewis says, "I think my release is passing over into Zen. . . . Those Gooks are right. You shouldn't fight it. Better to cooperate with it. Then it'll take you there. Take the arrow there." Just as Lewis did not understand the midnight scream of Tom McCaskill, neither does he understand the self-sacrifice of Drew, the plainly writ lesson that man is not only a being but a becoming as well. Nor does he show any regret over all he has previously been and done. Just as Ed was, in the beginning, a slider on the surface of life, so Lewis is at the end.

Admittedly, Ed probably does learn something from the encounters in the hills. He is not so easily bored as he once was, and he acknowledges the power and mystery of the river. He will remember his "friend there who in a way had died for" him, but Ed is certainly not transformed. While he may have been delivered on the river, his deliverance is not permanent. He will not hunt anymore, but he still practices archery. The old Ed is still a lot like the new Lewis. In his apparent absence of guilt he is close to Zen. Mystery without guilt is as empty as mystery without manners. Nothing is wrong with Zen as long as it is integrated with something else. There is a gulf between Robert Pirsig's book and Herrigel's book in regard to philosophy. *Zen and the Art of Motorcycle Maintenance* is transcendental; Herrigel's *Zen in the Art of Archery* is merely behavioristic, as Arthur Koestler has clearly shown in his devastating criticism of Herrigel's work in the *Lotus and the Robot.* Indeed the words of Koestler on Zen are quite applicable to Lewis Medlock and his new approach to shooting and to life:

This impartial tolerance towards the killer and the killed, a tolerance devoid of charity, makes one sceptical regarding the contribution which Zen Buddhism has to offer to the moral recovery of Japan or any other

country. Once a balm for self-inflicted bruises, it has become a kind of
moral nerve gas—colourless and without smell, but scented by all the
pretty incense sticks which burn under the smiling Buddha statues. For
a week or so I bargained with a Kyoto antique dealer for a small bronze
Buddha of the Kamakura period; but when he came down to a price
which I was able to afford, I backed out. I realized with a shock that the
Buddha smile had gone dead on me. It was no longer mysterious, but
empty.[35]

Deliverance is a retelling of the story of the golden bough and
battle for king of the woods. The violence in the drama should
cause some recriminations in the mind of Lewis and prevent Ed
from bringing up the subject even in disguised form as a minor
conversation piece at parties and at lunch in "the city with strang-
ers." Since such is not the case, there is an implied indictment
of the ease with which Lewis and Ed deal with guilt and the clear
suggestion that such conduct, weird as it is, is typical of those
who, like Lewis, have turned their eyes to the East.

Perhaps now something can be concluded about the maimed
athlete as a cultural symbol. There are exceptions but generally
the crippled athlete is a twentieth-century figure, contrasted
with the crippled intellectual, more of a nineteenth-century
type, for example, Ahab, Chillingworth, Ben Halleck of *A
Modern Instance,* and Phillip in *Mill on the Floss.* There is in fact
something dated about the twentieth-century crippled intellectual, Squier in *The Petrified Forest,* Philip in *Of Human
Bondage,* Rickey in *The Longest Journey,* to name a few. Perhaps
the crippled athlete has also become a conventionalized fictional
type, but in any event he remains a more significant character
culturally than the maimed intellectual, usually born deformed.

Mythology provides a possible clue. Hephaestus, the archetype of the crippled artist-intellectual, is lame for reasons
that are comparatively simple and that seem to have evoked little
argument. Edith Hamilton says, "In one place in the *Iliad* he
says that his shameless mother, when she saw that he was born
deformed, cast him out of heaven; in another place he declares
that Zeus did this, angry with him for trying to defend Hera." By
contrast, the theme of the wounding, emasculation, and death of
Adonis has led to a number of psychological and anthropological
theories, some rather controversial. Taking exception with one

of the main points of Jessie Weston, Arthur Edward Waite says, "It is perfectly clear that an infirm King who, whether healed for the moment or not, dies subsequently and is in no case restored to life, has no relation to any Fertility Myth and is still less 'a deeply symbolic figure, . . . the essential center of the whole cult, a being semi-divine, semi-human, standing between his people and the land, and the unseen forces which control their destiny.' "[36] Whether this is true or not is quite beyond my ability to decide and beside the point here; what by now should be apparent is that some authors have used the maimed athlete, sometimes resembling Adonis and suggesting the fisher king, to point out the futility and frustration in the perpetuation of youth, to bring attention to certain wateland characteristics of society, and to illustrate, as it were, the truth of the Latin proverb *qualis rex, talis grex* (like king, like people). In other words, the maimed athlete through his resemblance to the central figure in the nature cult and the fisher king or by his role of scapegoat becomes a much more powerful cultural symbol than the crippled intellectual whose infirmity implies some aberration primarily within the soul. While both the crippled artist-intellectual and the crippled athlete represent the obverse of *mens sana in corpore sano* it is more or less expected that the artist-intellectual be maimed.

Art and scholarship themselves have a way of crippling even the hale and hearty who might pursue them, owing to the demands of the agon involved and to the endless wonders and terrors which they provide. Possibly the ratiocination which would find hope in the limping artist-intellectual is not unsound—for certainly he contributes to the consciousness of the race—but the maimed athlete or rather the number of maimed athletes in our fiction should be some sort of danger signal that the rules be altered not so much to make playing conditions on the field less hazardous but to make those off less mendacious and stultifying.

The Absurd Athlete

Perhaps what has plagued contemporary man more than all the tales of governmental abuses, riots, revolutions, and threats of annihilation is the sense of absurdity about everything. Says a character of André Malraux in a 1926 novel, "At the center of European Man, dominating the greater moments of his life, there lies an essential absurdity."[37] This, according to R. W. B. Lewis, is the first instance in which the word is used with its contemporary meaning. Through subsequent use and elaboration, notably by Camus, the word "has drawn to itself suggestions from the Latin words to which it is related: *absurdus,* which means harsh or grating and the root word *surdus,* which means deaf. An absurd universe is a tuneless universe—a universe that is tone deaf.... For Camus, ... discord has already followed; right and wrong have lost their ancient names, as the ancient order that named them has crumbled; and the task, as he has seen it, is not to restore but to create anew."[38]

But what are some of the more specific characteristics of the absurd hero and how would he "create anew"? The absurd hero, like Sisyphus, faces the night, scorns his condition, and finds or attempts to find meaning and joy in the struggle. He "is by definition a rebel because he refuses to avoid either of the two components on which absurdity depends: intention which is the desire for unity, and reality which is constituted by the meaninglessness of life. The hope which the absurd heroes offer to the secular societies of the West is that they may generate the values to replace those which are lost as once sacred traditions disappear."[39] Joseph Campbell seems to have the absurd hero in mind when he says that "the modern hero-deed must be that of questing to bring to light again the lost Atlantis of the coordinated soul" (p. 388). Because he does quest, the absurd hero rules out suicide and seeks instead freedom and fulfillment.

The folk hero either comes from a rural area to the city or, like Henry Wiggen and some of the other Mammoth players, is "a country boy from the city." Generally he is characterized by naturalness of behavior (or lack of sophistication), great strength in body and soul, and love of independence. Many of these qualities are also found in the modern absurd hero, his consciousness frequently being created by the environment in a metropolitan and industrialized culture. "'Only the modern city,' Hegel dares write 'offers the mind a field in which it can become aware of itself.' We are thus living in the period of big cities. Deliberately, the world has been amputated of all that constitutes its permanence: nature, the sea, hilltops, evening meditation. Consciousness is to be found only in the streets because history is to be found only in the streets—this is the edict."[40] Acutely aware of his own mind and surroundings and possessing the innate moral sense of his country cousin, the absurd hero rebels against his condition. In his refusal to ignore the facts of modern life, the absurd hero shocks us into a realization of the meaning of those facts; by his refusal of suicide he offers hope.

James T. Farrell's "Joe Eliot" is really more of a fragmentary character sketch than a short story, presenting as it does the oppressive thoughts of the titular hero, a Harvard graduate and Walter Camp All-American; but the piece is worth looking at briefly because of the picture it provides of the plunder of beauty and reason in the contemporary world.

While Joe Eliot had been in World War I in Europe, his wealthy father presumably had an affair with Joe's beautiful lower-class blond wife, resulting in a fatal childbirth. Later Joe's little girl is killed in an automobile wreck, leaving him without any purpose in life whatsoever. As he walks about the Loop in Chicago, he reflects on a world blacker than that of Schopenhauer, author of *A Pessimist's Handbook*. He wondered why men went on, "why generation after generation lived and suffered and died creating what would end in dust. Life became a horror of monotony. Men stood before his vision as so many creatures registering impressions, registering endless impressions, trying to build and order them, suffering and aching and agonizing, blundering, killing one another. He wondered why the race did not blot itself out."[41] Religion makes no more sense than anything else and offers no consolation. Somehow he feels that all chaos in his world can be traced to a loss of faith in the Presbyterian God, whom he can no more accept than he can the Catholic God. Neither is there anyting soul-restoring in the American City:

He looked about him. He was on Randolph Street, with all the lighted theatres. It was an ugly scene. Big electric advertisements, announcing cheap, sentimental shows and movies, glared at him. Heaped and tumbled store windows ran along the sidewalk. People passed him, crowds of them. They, too, seemed cheap and ugly. They were America, and this street, with its blazing lights and its stupid shows, was America.

He felt that not only was he going to hell but also Chicago and the country were going to hell. And it was not a merry journey, either, but merely a stupid one. (p. 69)

Standing at the corner of Madison and Wabash, Joe Eliot realizes that he wants to go to a whorehouse, but he does not, probably because he is an idealist. Instead he continues to move about the city like Hawthorne's Wakefield in London, seeing others without himself being seen.

He walked around, reflecting on how he was a stranger to all these little worlds in the city, and on how he only touched the edges of a few of them. He had no common bond with anything, it seemed. . . .

He walked around, and his thoughts welled around and around, tearing over familiar and much ploughed emotional ground. Finally he clenched his fists and, summoning forth all the disgust and loathing he could command, muttered through his teeth: "JESUS CHRIST!" (p. 75)

At this point Joe Eliot is near his wit's end, but having refused suicide there is for him the possibility of achieving what he had failed to achieve: "Something valuable—love, knowledge, something that would be significant and personal and worthwhile" (p. 68). He can yet attempt to exhaust the field of the possible by following the "really distinguished" code of ethics which the absurd hero must always do and do so consciously.

Another athlete pursuing the distinguished code of *mens sana in corpore sano* is William Faulkner's Labove of *The Hamlet:* unfortunately he is also pursuing the nymphet Eula. In fact, his satyriasis, in that it is an expression of a desire for a truth denied to man, becomes a form of pride. It is not Labove's rare form of hamartia alone, however, that makes him so inviting to analysis, but his total aspect, appearance, and meaning. He is at once Herculean hero in a nonheroic society, a comic figure, and an avatar of the warrior monk and the dark-vested introverts of Melville, Hawthorne, and Dostoevsky. He was

a man who was not thin so much as acutally gaunt, with straight black hair coarse as a horse's tail and high Indian cheekbones and quiet pale hard eyes and the long nose of thought but with the slightly curved nostrils of pride and the thin lips of secret and ruthless ambition. It was a forensic face, the face of invincible conviction in the power of words as a principle worth dying for if necessary. A thousand years ago it would have been a monk's, a militant fanatic who would have turned his uncompromising back upon the world with actual joy and gone to a desert and passed the rest of his days and nights calmly and without an instant's self-doubt battling, not to save humanity about which he would have cared nothing, for whose sufferings he would have had nothing but contempt, but with his own fierce and unappeasable natural appetites.[42]

Among Labove's natural appetites is that for learning. Labove's father tells Varner that his son wants to be governor, but worldly success really has no place in the young man's plans. He studies not so much to advance himself as to acquire knowledge that exists for no other reason than to be gained. He had the "hillman's purely emotionless faith in education, the white magic of Latin degrees, which was the actual counterpart of the Old Monk's faith in his wooden cross." He reads so much that he eventually requires glasses, and at the country school he teaches his students "all and everything." He is in fact a devoted student and an excellent teacher.

Not among Labove's appetites, however, is football. He plays it because it, like his job, is profitable, and possibly because, like knowledge, it is there. Basketball is another matter. This game he apparently loves, for he "hounded Varner into clearing a . . . court. He did a good deal of the work himself, with the older boys, and taught them the game. At the end of the next year the team had beaten every team they could find to play against and in the third year, himself one of the players, he carried the team to Saint Louis, where, in overalls and barefoot, they won a Mississippi valley tournament against all comers" (pp. 126–27).

Playing basketball in Saint Louis barefooted and in overalls, Labove is a comic figure, as he is on the Ole Miss campus in his "single unmatching costume." The entire Labove episode with the great grandmother sporting the Ole Miss letter sweater and making her way around on cleats vacillates between comedy and tragedy, and Labove himself falls into both. If he is an ascetic monk, he is also the Bunyonesque country boy who does not

know his own strength, who lays out one of the other players on
the first day of practice, and who has difficulty understanding
the "rules for violence" and the lucrativeness of a mere game.

"I ain't going to borrow money just to play a game on," he said.
    "You wont have to, I tell you!" the coach said. "Your tuition will be
paid. You can sleep in my attic and you can feed my horse and cow and
milk and build the fires and I will give you your meals. Dont you
understand?" It could not have been his face because it was in darkness,
and he did not believe it had been in his voice. Yet the coach said, "I see.
You dont believe it."
    "No," he said. "I dont believe anybody will give me all that just for
playing a game." (p. 122)

Labove despises even this incipient commercialism, but he
takes advantage of it and reveals to Varner how he tried to pin
down the coach if, presumably, he really played hard. "I knew
what the shoes cost. I tried to get the coach to say what a pair was
worth. To the University. What a touchdown was worth. Winning was worth."
    What is winning worth? Faulkner asked it, and American
coaches and alumni have answered it for him. Winning is worth
more than anything else on earth. "It is not the most important
thing; it is the only thing." As for the worth of a touchdown, it
cannot be computed, for touchdowns lead to bowls, advertisements, new cars, magazine feature stories, public office for the
asking, and even deification, all at the expense of *aidos*.
    While Labove expresses his contempt for overemphasis and
thinks that he is gaining materially by playing, it is he who is
being used. The shoes, letter sweaters, and other rewards are all
so much lagniappe. Labove is the exploited rustic, the strong-
armed boy who, when asked by the recruiting coach the way to
town, points with the plow, the same lad who throws rocks at
squirrels righthanded because he mutilates them too much with
the left. He is the prize catch from the boondocks about whom
coaches joke so much.
    Labove is comic not only because he is from the country but
also because he is from the past. While he is the warrior monk,
he is at the same time both the herculean and promethean hero,
herculean in the meaningless labors he has to perform, prome-

thean in his desire to discover what is forbidden man to know. Also in the intensity and madness of his search, he brings to mind Ahab, Raskolnikov, Ethan Brand, and other deranged questers and transgressors.

> He was mad. He knew it. There would be times now when he did not even want to make love to her but wanted to hurt her, see blood spring and run, watch that serene face warp to the indelible mark of terror and agony beneath his own; to leave some indelible mark of himself on it and then watch it even cease to be a face. Then he would exorcise that. He would drive it from him, whereupon their positions would reverse. It would now be himself importunate and prostrate before that face which, even though but fourteen years old, postulated a weary knowledge which he would never attain, a surfeit, a glut of all perverse experience. He would be as a child before that knowledge. He would be like a young girl, a maiden, wild distracted and amazed, trapped not by the seducer's maturity and experience but by blind and ruthless forces inside herself which she now realized she had lived with for years without even knowing they were there. He would grovel in the dust before it, panting: "Show me what to do. Tell me. I will do anything you tell me, anything, to learn and know what you know." He was mad. (pp. 135–36)

Like all curiosities and anachronisms, Labove is amusing. Whether he is pouring over books in the icy attic, bowling over tacklers, or wallowing his face on the bench where Eula has sat, he is pathetically humorous and thoroughly absurd. He expends great amounts of both physical and intellectual energy. His jersey has been retired, which is to say that he will always be remembered, first with a laugh and then with a pause, or vice versa.

The absurd hero, like the cripple, is invariably a *revolté* and scapegoat. He too has been maimed, only the wound is not physically visible. This is the point that Mr. Angstrom, in John Updike's *Rabbit, Run,* ironically makes when minister Eccles asks if he thinks his son Harry will come around. "He's too far gone. He'll just slide deeper and deeper now until we might as well forget him. If he was twenty or twenty-two; but at his age. . . . In the shop sometimes you see these young Brewer bums. They can't stick it. They're like cripples only they don't limp. Human garbage, they call them. And I sit there at the machine for two months wondering how the hell it could be my Harry, that used to hate a mess so much."[43] The terms *bums* and *cripples,* of course, recall numerous fictional athletes, but it is Biff Loman of *Death of a Salesman* with whom Rabbit has most in common. Both run or try to run from their situations. Biff goes west, and Rabbit wants to go both west and south. He gets as far as West Virginia; and while he has "a good time," he appears to conclude that he needs "another map," mainly because "the land refuses to change. The more he drives the more the region resembles Mount Judge. The same scruff of the embankments, the same weathered billboards for the same insane products" (p. 32). Both are "loved" by another, Biff by Bernard, and Rabbit by Eccles; neither has prepared for a profession, and neither "matures"— "it's the same thing as being dead," Rabbit says—and while each is either a "bum" or a "restless cripple," both are something more, Biff being a "poet" and an "idealist," and Rabbit a "saint." The big difference is that Biff goes west and stays. Rabbit runs, but he comes back home to face the dissonant music of urban life. "Consciousness," Hegel says, "is found only in the streets," and Rabbit, the old jump shooter, is certainly conscious and will not flee for long the pain of consciousness.

The world of Mount Judge, where Rabbit returns to live, is caught in the throes of change, as is Rabbit himself. An aging ex-athlete, he feels one world crumbling beneath him, another powerless to be reborn. Nowhere is his predicament better illustrated than in the scene with Ruth, his girl friend, and Tothero (probably pronounced "to-ther-o" though meaning "dead hero" from *tot-hero*), his old coach, the memory of whom "still disposes him to listen."

The old man's thin lips are wet with whiskey, and saliva keeps trying to sneak out of the corner of his mouth. "The coach," he says, "the coach is concerned with developing the three tools we are given in life: the head, the body, and the heart."
"And the crotch," Ruth says. (p. 54)

Ruth's remark hits the unsuspecting reader like a thunderbolt. Obviously what Ruth is denouncing is the sentimentalism and hypocrisy of Tothero, "a vile old bum" and one who corrupts and dirties, but there is also an implied savage indictment of the ideal itself, of the much-heralded code of the student-athlete, the all-around man, the creed of the Boy Scout, and in sum, the Greek concept of strength and beauty, music and gymnastic. That Ruth is on target with her remark in the case of Tothero is indisputable, but she has not really added a new dimension to the athletic ideal. The "crotch" was always accounted for in Hellenic idealism; the Greeks advocated not the death of Dionysus but his partnership with the god of order, Apollo. Walt Whitman, "the teacher of athletes," knew as much, which is why he regarded himself not only as the poet of "body and soul" but of "crotch and vine" as well.

Just as Whitman tried to find the middle way, so in his own fashion does Rabbit; after his return to Brewer he finds himself threatened on both sides by the contending social forces of the sixties, the familiar pattern of life on the one hand and the seemingly irrefutable arguments of the counterculture on the other. There is no mistake about it—Rabbit, especially in *Rabbit Redux,* is the man all parties warned us against, and he is under attack. As Rabbit, a "natural," tries to weave a way of sanity between Jill, Skeeter, Janice his wife, Stavros, his Mother and Father (the original Archie Bunker), his Boss and friends, the question becomes: can the center hold? To each and all he is an anomoly. With Whitman he might well ironically say,

> Do I contradict myself?
> Very well then I contradict myself
> (I am large, I contain multitudes.)

Actually, Rabbit does not contain multitudes; the multitudes attempt to contain him or to drown him either in mindless mechanical order automating every act of life or in an equally mindless flood of chaos. Rabbit simply wants what any sane person always wants, beauty with freedom. In his case the words of Camus could not be more appropriate: "All those who are struggling for freedom today are ultimately fighting for beauty." He could not be more correct when in defense of his position to his family toward the end of the novel he refers to himself as a virtual "statue of liberty" for having befriended the refugees of

the counterculture, Jill and Skeeter. But he is not a statue. He is
man in motion and is still on the run. He is also a fighter, one
who has accepted the agon of life but one who wishes to fight
fair. Everywhere he looks in his suburban environment he sees
the uglification of life, "Helen's exile," to use Camus's phrase,
but he will not bring Helen (or Janice) back at any price. Rabbit
has a "love of the law"⁴⁴ and hence rules, order, beauty, but he
prizes individual rights just as dearly. When old friends and
neighbors complain about what has been going on in his house
with Jill and Skeeter, he replies that that is the type of thing one
might expect to see when peeping in others' windows. He defends the war in Vietnam against the liberal arguments of Stavros and gives succor to Skeeter, a veteran, who ironically also
defends the war but only because it is another sign of his (Skeeter's) coming reign of glory when all will lie in ruins. Rabbit
wants no part of Skeeter's prophesized glory, but he gives him
aid because it "felt right" (p. 358) to do so. Toward Skeeter, a
dying and suffering Dionysian god, who feeds upon the bleed-
ing heart of Jill, herself a dying conscience of a WASP Apollonian order, and toward Jill too Rabbit has "a sense of duty." He
has *aidos,* the innate feeling that the difference between him and
those less fortunate is not deserved. He is moved to pathos and
near paralysis of will when he reflects upon the past suffering of
the blacks as he reads aloud to Skeeter from *The Life and Times of
Frederick Douglass,* yet he tells Skeeter bluntly that he wants no
part of Skeeter's millennium when it arrives. In sum, Rabbit, the
aging athlete and veteran, nonetheless symbolizes the ancient
athletic ideal of strength and beauty in unison.

To understand fully how this middle ground is held, it is
necessary to draw some analogies between terms and to note
how they are employed in the novel. The essence of the athletic
ideal was strength and beauty but these are merely other names
for chaos and cosmos (the Greek word *cosmos* meant beauty),
Dionysus and Apollo, Id and Superego. Skeeter promises Chaos
and is its high priest as he proclaims over and over, "Chaos is
God's body. Order is the Devil's chains" (p. 275). Jill is beauty,
but an emaciated beauty, as her own body suggests. She has
become conscience without strength; Skeeter, for those who ac-

knowledge him, strength without conscience, which is why he spits in Rabbit's hand at the end. He feeds upon himself and upon others who care enough to look and listen. At one point Rabbit calls him "a *baad* Nigger" and Nelson, Rabbit's son, finally agrees. When Rabbit expresses the belief that Skeeter would have saved Jill, Nelson exclaims, "He *wouldn't* of, Dad! He wouldn't *care*." Nelson is closer to the truth here than Rabbit, for Skeeter is beyond caring, willing to sacrifice all to the inevitable anarchy he predicts and foreshadows. He is like Jill's chicken livers with "burned edges and an icy center." He is a modern version of Bartleby the Scrivener, and Rabbit, like the Lawyer in that first story of absurdity in American literature, goes as far as he can, as far as we could expect a human being to go with another. These limits are defined by Skeeter's own hero, Frederick Douglass, about whom Rabbit, upon insistence by Skeeter, reads aloud: "A man without force . . . is without the essential dignity of humanity. Human nature is so constituted, that it cannot honor a helpless man, though it can pity him, and even this it cannot do long if signs of power do not arise" (p. 282). At the end of this passage of heroic resistance Rabbit looks at Skeeter and finds him, naked on the couch, responding autoerotically to the voice of Rabbit and Douglass's pen, his long arm feeding. Skeeter, like Douglass, has overcome the fear of death but in what perverted form? The response, if any at all, can only be a paraphrase of Melville's lawyer, "Ah, Skeeter, Ah Humanity."

The symbology of the characters is underscored throughout the novel by the subtle use of colors, the constant interplay of whites, blacks, and greens. Jill is fleeing the Establishment's sterile whiteness, offering herself in expiation to Skeeter who equates nature not with the greenery of summer or the flush of autumn but with black madness. To Rabbit he says: "Friend, you are wrong. You are white but wrong. We fascinate you, white man. We are in your dreams. We are technology's nightmare. We are all the good satisfied nature you put down in yourselves when you took that mucky greedy turn. We are what has been left *out* of the industrial revolution, so we are the *next* revolution, and don't you know it? (p. 234) Green is the symbol of life, remembered by Rabbit when he takes Nelson to a baseball game:

But something has gone wrong. The ball game is boring. The spaced dance of the men in white fails to enchant, the code beneath the staccato spurts of distant motion refuses to yield its meaning. Though basketball was his sport, Rabbit remembers the grandeur of all that grass, the excited perilous feeling when a high fly was hoisted your way, the homing-in on the expanding dot, the leathery smack of the catch, the formalized nonchalance of the heads-down trot in toward the bench, the ritual flips and shrugs and the nervous courtesies of the batter's box. There was a beauty here bigger than the hurtling beauty of basketball, the beauty refined from country pastures, a game of solitariness, of waiting, waiting for the pitcher to complete his gaze toward first base and throw his lightning, a game whose very taste, of spit and dust and grass and sweat and leather and sun, was America. (p. 83)

It is the green too that is the victim of too much order, society ("the lawn looks artificial, lifeless, dry") and too much chaos ("There is no green in her eyes, the black pupils have eclipsed the irises").

The concepts of play lie at the heart of Jill's tragedy and the plot of the book. Soon after she moves in the Angstrom house she tells Nelson:

The point is ecstasy . . . Energy. Anything that is good is in ecstasy. The world is what God made and it doesn't stink of money, it's never tired, too much or too little, it's always exactly full. The second after an earthquake, the stones are calm. Everywhere is *play*, even in thunder or an avalanche. Out on my father's boat I used to look up at the stars and there seemed to be invisible strings between them, tuned absolutely right, playing thousands of notes I could almost hear. (p. 159)

Rabbit is entranced by Jill when he hears her going on like this, perhaps loves her for it, but knows through experience and observation that she, like so many romantics, oriental and otherwise, is on this subject wrong or half wrong or partly self-deceived. To Rabbit "where any game is being played a hedge exists against fury." An unforgettable line this, and its meaning is clear. It is fury that is everywhere and play only in those places where rules are clear. Instead of play and ecstasy in the observable universe, there is what Ernest Becker calls "a nightmare spectacle" which Rabbit sees in everything: "Rabbit wonders how many animals have died to keep his life going, how many more will die. A barnyard full, a farmful of thumping hearts, seeing eyes, racing legs, all stuffed squawking into him as into a black sack. No avoiding it: life does want death. To be alive is to kill" (p. 311).

Jill may have misjudged the nature of the world that led to her death, but she did not misjudge Rabbit, as seen in the "cute" crayon sketches she made for Nelson.

Also from the same night, some drawings by her, in crayons Nelson found for her; her style was cute, linear, arrested where some sopho-more art class had left it, yet the resemblances were clear. Skeeter of course was the spade. Nelson, his dark bangs and side-sheaves exagger-ated, the club, on a stem of a neck. Herself, her pale hair crayoned in the same pink as her sharp-chinned face, the heart. And Rabbit, there-fore, the diamond. In the center of the diamond, a tiny pink nose. Sleepy small blue eyes with worried eyebrows. An almost invisible mouth, lifted as if to nibble. Around it all, green scribbles she had to identify with an affectionate pointing arrow and a balloon: "in the rough." (p. 265)

In the case of Rabbit, the metaphor could not be more appro-priate nor could Jill's choice of colors.

The Secret Christian

"Religion . . . was now an old gown, grown thin and with all the colors washed out of it. People still wore the old gown but it did not warm them any more."[45] These statements appear almost in the form of a thesis on the opening page of Sherwood Ander-son's *Beyond Desire,* and for the rest of the novel, Red Oliver, an athlete and the main character, attempts to find for himself not so much a new religion as the lost meaning of the old one. Being naturally religious, Red, a star shortstop in high school, for a mill team in Georgia—"the best player ever in the town"—and for his New England college, must have a dedication to something, but that something he finds cannot be traditional Christianity, par-ticularly in America. "Suppose . . . you were a man in America who really wanted God—suppose, you wanted to try really to be a Christian—a God man. How could you do that? All society would be against you. Even the church wouldn't stand that—it couldn't" (p. 319). Since he cannot accept orthodox religion in industrialized America, he keeps the Sabbath, not like Emily Dickinson by staying at home, but by going to the woods. "The young man had gone out of town along the railroad track and had turned from the track some miles out of town and had got into a pine forest. He wrote words about the forest and about the red Georgia land seen beyond the pine forest through trees. It was a simple little chapter of a man, a young man alone with nature on Sunday when all the rest of his town was in church" (p. 117).

Too engaged in the affairs of the world and too idealistic, too saintly almost, to shut himself off from it, Red makes a religion of communism, but it does not end his loneliness ("Red Oliver was alone") or remedy his feelings of ridiculousness. "I'm a silly ass," is his last thought as he steps forward from the striking workmen at Birchfield, North Carolina, to face the troop commander who had vowed that he would shoot the first to move from the crowd of strikers.

The young man who shoots Oliver is also an athlete. Ned Sawyer too had gone to college and had been a pretty good pitcher. "He had a fast ball with a little hop on it and a tantalizing slow ball. He was a rather nice, steady curve ball pitcher" (p. 332). Like Oliver he is an idealist but one who has taken an opposite approach, reading Emerson instead of Marx. But he too feels ridiculous. He too "had got himself into an absurd position" and he has the same thought as the man he shoots: "I'm a silly ass." By having the pitcher and the shortstop experience the same emotion at the same time, Anderson suggests that the sense of absurdity, like love, hate, and envy, is almost infectious, especially for those who have not been made immune by pills and innoculations.

The affiliations of Red Oliver and Ned Sawyer with large groups of men present a common theme in Anderson, the plea for brotherhood and faithfulness. He asks, "Wouldn't it be strange if this individualism we Americans love to talk so much about was something we don't want after all?" "There is a gang spirit in America, too" (p. 332). Ned Sawyer and Red Oliver are completely taken up with "gang spirit," which their athletic backgrounds had helped to form. Ned Sawyer, a pitcher, de-

pended upon his teammates for support, and through his teamwork with other members of the infield, Red makes friends for
life. Throughout the novel he maintains a correspondence with
Neil Bradley, the second baseman. "Neil at second base and Red
at shortstop. Oliver to Bradley to Smith. Zip! They had been a
good double play pair together" (p. 6).

But Anderson best expresses the sense of camaraderie and
teamwork in athletics by telling of his own days on the Clyde
baseball team.

On the ball field during the afternoon, there was a certain play made.
You had nothing to do with it. You were playing the right field and but
one fly ball came your way during the game. You muffed that. At bat
you did nothing. There was a ball shot down through the infield, very
hot, a hard hit one, and little Shorty Grimes raced over. He got it with
one hand, turned a quick pivot. He shot it to second . . . a double play.
All of the bases full, our side but one run ahead. At that moment you
felt something . . . something of Shorty's quick and so beautifully
graceful movement was also in your own body. You felt no jealousy, no
envy. There was a strange gladness in you.[46]

Such "strange gladness" Anderson found missing in life off the
ball diamond, and it disturbed him a great deal, particularly
after the suicides of Hart Crane and Vachel Lindsay. He expressed himself on the subject in a letter to Dreiser.

In your play, *American Tragedy,* the play ends by the pronouncement
that we can forgive a murderer but that society cannot be forgiven. To
tell the truth, Ted, I think it nonsense to talk this way about society. I
doubt if there is any such thing. If there has been a betrayal in America
I think it is our betrayal of each other. . . . I feel so strongly on this
matter that I am thinking of trying to get my thoughts and those of
others who also feel this thing into form. I think even of a general letter
or pamphlet that I might call "American Man to American Man." I
think it is our loneliness for each other that has made most of us throw
too much on woman. . . . I think this need of man for man in the imagi-
native world is more important. I think that if it had existed, men like
Crane and Lindsay would not have committed suicide. I would like to
issue a pamphlet, or a general letter, on this subject . . . where it might
reach out to all sorts of men needing what I am talking about here.[47]

What Anderson wished among his colleagues was the spirit of the Clyde baseball team or that of the double play combination of the "New England college" in *Beyond Desire,* or in the terms of Martin Buber, an I-thou relationship. Among writers he wanted a comitatus, the hero and leader of which would have been Dreiser, in whose presence Anderson "sometimes had the same refreshed feeling as when in the presence of a thoroughbred horse."

Possibly because of his fascination with the potential beauty of the human body and his belief in the mystical attraction between people, especially between sexes but within the same sex as well, Anderson endowed his athletes with inordinate sexuality. Indeed the popular image of the athlete as a sort of sexual potentate is in no way allayed in the fiction of Anderson. Either his athletes chase women, like the cow-pasture pitchers, or are chased by them, as is the case with the idealistic, college-educated Red Oliver of *Beyond Desire.* Ethel Long, who works at the library where Oliver stops after practice in his baseball suit to read Karl Marx (no wonder Oliver feels absurd), thinks of him at night as she has seen him, not at study but at play. "He was running furiously. . . . His body fell into balance. He was like an animal, like a cat. Or he was standing at bat. He stood poised. There was something in him delicately adjusted, delicately timed. 'I want that,'" she tells herself (p. 203). So much in fact does she desire the young, red-headed athlete that she seduces him on a table in the library, the same table where earlier he had been reading Karl Marx!

It might be remarked that such sexual attraction is not always the case of fictional athletes, and one notable exception is Ring Lardner's bushers. Many uncomplimentary remarks can be made about them, but they are not adulterous. Often his stars imagine themselves to be lovers and are forever looking at females in the stands; but their eyes never turn gray from passion as do those of the characters in Anderson. Jack Keefe, Harry Kane, Alibi Ike, Danny Warner, and others are all stupid, but they would have been shocked had they been witness to the scene in the library in Georgia. When Anderson said that Lardner and Mark Twain had no sensitive understanding of the "fellow in the street, in the hooch joint, the ball park and the city

suburb" one is inclined to agree with him, particularly in the case
of Lardner. One can easily imagine the "fleshy" and uninhibited
Anderson consorting with types who would have caused the
puritanical Lardner to take refuge in the nearest ball park.

In 1924, in *A Story Teller's Story,* Anderson made the intrigu-
ing comment that for him "the athlete, poor innocent one, has
become a symbol." Since Anderson wrote about the athlete so
much, it is in order to ask just what the athlete did symbolize to
him.

Through the athlete Anderson depicts the presence or the
absence of those qualities which constitute ancient and eternal
ideals, specifically strength and beauty and *mens sana in corpore
sano.* The innocence of the athlete is underscored either by his
ignorance as in the case of the Clyde and Bidwell pitchers in his
autobiographical writings or by naive idealism in the case of Red
Oliver and Ned Sawyer. All are representative of a type of
vitalism which always fascinated Anderson and which won his
applause when channeled in graceful and determined efforts,
Pop Geers making his move, Red Oliver at bat, Joe Louis on the
the attack. Vitalism and nobility of spirit, however, are easily
vitiated by those sports, namely football and golf, which in Anderson's view had come to demand a certain conformity of behavior and which had become means for social advancement in
an establishment characterized by commercial interest.

At the deeper level the athlete in Anderson's work represents
a synthesis of art and nature, subjects that engaged his interest
throughout his creative career. "It is only through nature and
art men really live."[48] Like Whitman he was a poet of the body
and a poet of the soul. Also like Whitman he was a creator of
beauty and a lover of beauty in its myriad forms. In his descrip-
tions of the special skills, instincts, and ordered energy required
of athletes, Anderson was one of the first American writers to
suggest that sports are art forms and hence means of supplying
relief from the world of commerce. He also saw, like Johan
Huizinga, Arnold Toynbee, and others, the reverse occurring,
the world of business encroaching upon the domain of sport.
Anderson knew too that the hero was being transformed into a
celebrity, but he himself remained faithful to the Lawrentian

dictum: "Give homage and allegience to a hero and you yourself
become heroic. It is the law of men." Some of the heroes that
Anderson gave allegiance to were athletes (and horses) and
through them and their contests he illustrated much of what was
still right in America as well as what was going wrong. The
renaissance that he hoped for and predicted does not appear to
be on the horizon; if it does come, it will be because men will
have rediscovered not only their minds but their bodies and
souls as well.

Another southern athlete not apt to be found in church on
Sunday, at least in his youth, is Sonny Joiner, hero of James
Whitehead's remarkable novel *Joiner*. To Joiner, a six-foot,
seven-inch, 265–310 pound NFL tackle from Mississippi who is
also a murderer, grade-school teacher, and avid student of history and art, the trouble with ideals is that they are often too
harsh and uncompromising, especially when not moderated by
sensualism; and "the devil in all the myths" of a better world, he
thinks, is Plato. If Plato had had his way, Joiner believes, the
world would never have had to put up with Southerners (blacks
and whites), Jews or Mongolians.[49] He also discredits the Greeks
because of the way they treated women, and certainly would
have sided with Cordelia in *The Rector of Justin* in her assessment
of the faults of her father. Yet when as a youth Joiner is asked to
speak before civic clubs, he talks more about classical ideals,
about *paideia*, than about Christ, mainly because if there is anything on earth Joiner abhors it is the public Christian, an attitude
that explains his demolishing a pulpit at a Billy Graham service
in Jackson, along with his ire over the poor construction of that
same unlucky pulpit. Later the Jackson Christians place a plaque
where the pulpit had stood on the football field, and during a
high school all-star game Joiner uses the memorial to clean his
cleats. Like Lancelot Lamar, Joiner does not think highly of the
Reverend Mister Graham.

Among the many objections Joiner has to proselytizing Christianity is the simplistic alternatives held up to potential converts.
In the biggest football stadium in the state Billy Graham is telling
"the peoples, nobody in the whole freaking place will be alive in
a hundred years, and where *will* you be in a hundred years? In

Heaven Brother? In Hell, Brother, Sister?—waving the floppy
red Bible and driving off the rain with his left hand" (p. 296).

Anyone who has ever so much as burned his fingers cannot
believe in Graham's hell, Joiner argues, but there is a hell, which
he finds expressed in the third soldier in the Resurrection picture of Grünewald's *Isenheim Altarpiece*. Intermittently dozing in
the tub and looking at the picture, he contemplates the scene in a
state that is neither wake nor sleep: "It's the helmet plus the legs
that bring on the horrors, because . . . those legs have lost control. They are almost muscleless and *are* boneless, and . . . the
delicate slippers hardly touch the ground at all . . . when he tries
to get up he won't have any legs to stand on. They'll have been
wiped away like something insubstantial as cotton candy. . . . His
pretty slippers are not touching the ground, are not dug in, and
in my bickering sleep I screamed—cried out—howled and rose
like a drenched weeping whale—THIS IS HELL—" (p. 356). In a
letter to John Adams, Thomas Jefferson stated that hell would
consist of body without mind; to Sonny Joiner the solipsistic
opposite would be equally true.

There is more to the Resurrection picture for Joiner, especially on the principal subject: "He's jumped out of the tomb
with perfectly articulated winding sheets strung out below and
behind, and the halo he's flying in looks like apotheosis of
Magee's Good Gulf sign, and his face is as wholesome and smug
as an eighteen-year old Dutch center's, and He's holding up his
arms and hands like a faggot official proclaiming the ultimate
Platonic touchdown: or Takeoff. I know my Redeemer liveth
but I hope to heaven he don't look like that" (pp. 354–55).

Joiner believes in hell, resurrection, and Christ, but not in any
conventional or shallow sense. What kind of Christian is he
then? He is, I think, a secret Christian which he obviously could
not claim to be but which he says one must be. Unlike Elmer
Gantry, Joiner is not a hypocrite and unlike Frank Prescott he
does not have an overriding sense of duty. He acts decisively
only in what seems to him extreme situations, when the center is
threatened, when Foots Magee, punched-out ex-Detroit Lion
and hopeless segregationist, feels "*obleeged*" to shoot Negroes,
and when Stream, a former teammate and fastidious abstrac-
tionist, who gives him such "squirrelly stuff" to read as D. H.

Lawrence and Wallace Stevens, chides him about his conduct.
Joiner kills Foots and tries to kill Stream and remains, it seems,
the only character in the novel of the southern civil-rights
movement in the sixties who has compassion without any compelling moral obligations, unless it is Sheriff Davis, the only good
southern sheriff perhaps in all literature.

Where does Sonny Joiner derive his views of the secret Christian? Not in the virtual library of impressive books on history
and art that he discusses, but possibly from a book not mentioned, Dietrich Bonhoeffer's *Letters and Papers from Prison*. This
argument is based not only on the use of "secret Christian" in
Joiner but also on the term *metanoia,* both of which are crucial to
Bonhoeffer's last view of the world. Admittedly Joiner mentions
metanoia in his discussion of Luther but its thematic importance
in the novel cannot be fully appreciated unless looked at in
connection with the idea of the *secret* Christian in the manner
of Bonhoeffer, who prophesied a day "when men will be called
again to utter the word of God with such power as will change
the world. . . . Until then the Christian cause will be a silent and
hidden affair, but there will be those who pray and do right
and wait for God's own time."[50] Until then the Christian must
practice *arkandisziplin* ("secret discipline") but not the discipline
manifested by the clean collar and a shined shoe. This secret
Christian must

plunge himself into the life of a godless world, without attempting to
gloss over its ungodliness with a veneer of religion or trying to transfig-
ure it. He must live a worldly life and so participate in the suffering of
God. He *may* live a worldly life as one emancipated from all false religions and obligations. To be a Christian does not mean to be religious in
a particular way, to cultivate some particular form of asceticism . . . but
to be a man. It is not some religious act which makes a Christian what he
is, but participation of the suffering of God in the life of the world. This
is *metanoia.* (pp. 222–23)

This definition of *metanoia* appears to be slightly different
from that applied to Luther by Joiner: Change of heart. Luther
did experience change of heart without question, but he
changed again, in Joiner's view, in turning on Muntzer's revolution, the irony of which is captured in Luther's own words.

"Strange times, these, when a prince can win heaven with bloodshed, better than other men with prayer!" (p. 345) The applicability of these words to Bonhoeffer's case is evident: a "prince" and his followers establishing a heaven on earth, the Third Reich, by bloodshed, and other men, a few men, praying in their last days. Bonhoeffer saw that in the name of duty German was killing German and Jew. Similarly Joiner saw white killing black in Mississippi out of the same sense of obligation. Nevertheless, Bonhoeffer argued, one must love life and participate fully in it even in the apocalypse, and this Sonny Joiner does, quite unlike the legions of self-pitying heroes in American literature who flee the world rather than involving themselves in it. Like Thoreau, Joiner came into the world not to reform it but to live in it, though much of his living carries him into dens and corners of American life that would have scandalized Henry David. To many people of Bryan, Mississippi, Sonny Joiner is so involved in the world as to be a public nuisance, but to the careful reader he will emerge as the opposite, a secret Christian.

Joiner, thus, is a repudiation of public muscular Christianity whether that of Elmer Gantry or of Frank Prescott. As different in intention and aims as these two are, the one self-serving, the other God-serving, they are nevertheless Christian soldiers in the army of the Lord. Not so with Sonny Joiner. Though a violent player on the field and at times off, he belongs to a less militant tradition and hence a much more silent one, a silent tradition articulated by Walt Whitman in "To Him That Was Crucified," which opens as follows:

> My spirit to your dear brother,
> Do not mind because many sounding your name
>   do not understand you,
> I do not sound your name but I understand you.

Sonny Joiner would appreciate this poem, but not Frank Prescott, the old WASP Ideal, nor Elmer Gentry, the leatherheaded evangelist.

In his biography of Luther, Richard Marius writes:

Jesus has become a name we apply to any current ideal of man. In our own century Jesus has been depicted as a soldier sighting down the barrel of a rifle in a World War I poster. He has been a great scoutmaster for the Boy Scouts, and he has been a kindly rotarian in the minds of the business classes. He has been a rather vacuous-looking shepherd in thousands of picture books for city children who have never seen a sheep, and he has been a rock singer in several stage productions that have attempted to translate the New Testament into the language of beats and hippies. . . . But all this is to say that we take him no more seriously than we take a billboard along the highway.[51]

To the list of Jesuses Marius mentions I would add the ones mirrored back to Frank Prescott, Elmer Gantry, and Sonny Joiner, and I would add that we do not take them seriously either. There, however, is a caution here to be noted. Marius says that "we can hardly grasp the meaning of the name of Jesus to Martin Luther," who, as Marius shows, was profoundly anti-Semitic. Neither can we grasp the meaning of Jesus to Dietrich Bonhoeffer who, of course, was anything but anti-Semitic. What we can grasp from the meaning of both men's views, different as those views are, is the danger of uncritical acceptance of the way that masses worship and reveal their loyalties. To have a secret discipline means anything but an indifference, as Bonhoeffer demonstrated, to the religious and political climate of one's own time.

5. The Wrap-up

IN his discussion of "American Demigods" F. O. Matthiessen states that George Washington Harris's Wirt Staples is the blood brother of Melville's Bulkington of *Moby Dick,* who in Ishmael's eyes "stood full six feet in height, with noble shoulders, and a chest like a coffer-dam. I have seldom seen such brawn in a man. His face was deeply brown and burnt, making his white teeth dazzling by the contrast; while in the deep shadows of his eyes floated some reminiscences that did not seem to give him much joy. His voice at once announced that he was a Southerner, and from his fine stature, I thought he must be one of those tall mountaineers from the Alleghenian Ridge in Virginia."[1] Continuing, Matthiessen says, "Melville symbolizes in him the natural seeker for the open independence of truth's sea, and his last words to him are: 'Bear thee grimly demigod! Up from the spray of the ocean-perishing—straight up, leaps thy apotheosis!'" Wirt Staples has many of the same distinguishing features, though differently described.

"His britches were buttoned tite round his loins, an' stuffed 'bout half into his boots, his shirt bagg'd out abuv, an' were as white as milk, his sleeves were rolled up to his arm-pits, an' his collar were as wide open as a gate, the mussils on his arms moved about like rabbits onder the skin, an' ontu his hips an' thighs they play'd like the swell on the river, his skin were clear red an' white, an' his eyes a deep, sparklin', wickid blue, while a smile fluttered like a hummin' bird round his mouth all the while. When the State-fair offers a premium fur *men* like they now does fur jackasses, I mean to enter Wirt Staples, an' I'll git it, if there's five thousand entrys." (p. 643)

Both Bulkington and Wirt, as Matthiessen shows, are fine examples of "the central man" of the Smoky Mountains, of the great American natural, the myth of whom continues to persist in American culture, as seen in the athlete, though Bulkington's apotheosis has not leaped and is not likely to leap from the ocean spray.

Both Melville and Harris obviously held faith that the ideal of the Natural Man would endure, but the ideal is in many ways *passé* and, as a literary theme, rather dated. This is not as tragic as it may first appear. We can live without the Natural Man such as Bulkington and Wirt just as we can live without epic and royal heroes so long as fools do not seriously try to fill the vacuum. We might do well to remember in fact that following the descriptive passage of Wirt Staples there is a scene in which Wirt throws a little Negro boy through a glass window! This essentially is the same type of naturalness or Chaos symbolized by Skeeter in *Rabbit Redux* and is, whether in Skeeter or Wirt, black or white, a characteristic to be abhorred.

As civilizations become more sophisticated and urbanized—not necessarily better—certain ideals become antiquated, a fact well recognized by Thomas Jefferson. The ideal of Jefferson, Matthiessen says, "is not quite" the same as that personified by Wirt and Bulkington. Neither is it the type of Natural Aristocrat that William Wirt made of Patrick Henry: "The qualities stressed were natural strength, natural endurance, natural eloquence and natural courage. Patrick Henry was characterized, Wirt added, by 'strong natural sense.' 'In short,' he concluded, 'he was the Orator of Nature: and such a one as nature might not blush to avow.' 'In a word, he was one of those perfect prodigies of nature, of whom very few have been produced since the foundations of the earth were laid.' "[2] It is no wonder that such an image of a grand American prototype gave Jefferson a case of nausea.

Though Matthiessen is not explicit about what Jefferson "had foreseen," there is little doubt that it was not so much the ideal of Natural Man but one of strength and intelligence classically combined, not man as he is in his natural state but what he may become, as can be seen in what Henry Adams imagines Jefferson saying:

If we can bring it about that men are on the average an inch taller in the next generation than in this; if they are an inch larger around the chest;

if their brain is an ounce or two heavier, and their life a year or two
longer,—that is progress. If fifty years hence the average man shall
invariably argue from two ascertained premises where he now jumps to
a conclusion from a single supposed revelation,—that is progress! I
expect it to be made here, under our democratic stimulants, on a great
scale, until every man is potentially an athlete in body and an Aristotle
in mind.[3]

Whereas Melville's and Harris's folk ideal was from the first
incompatible with growth in art, education, and even industri-
alization, Jefferson's classical ideal was not. Though divine and
eternal, strength and beauty is in a sense an artificial and urban
ideal, one that presupposes transforming our minds and bodies
(and hence our environment) from what they naturally are to
something more desirable. Considering the response of "the
New Englander" to Jefferson's views, "What will you do for
moral progress?" Henry Adams remarks that "Jefferson held
the faith that men would improve morally with their physical
and intellectual growth." Considering all that has happened
since Jefferson's time, one cannot say that his trust has been
wholly betrayed, but one feels that were he alive he would be
appalled by the fragmentation of the ideal and by the estrange-
ment between mind and body, thought and feeling, though he
hinself was not particularly athletic and felt that the "game of
ball" did little toward forming character, a view shared incidentally by a number of contemporary psychologists.

    There is a subtle danger involved in Jefferson's ideal, which is
thoroughly Socratic, and even an element of fatuousness, just as
there is in the blind adoration of naturalness which has frequently been a distinguishing characteristic of the American experience. The danger is inherent in the easy blinking of John
Adams's question, "What will you do for moral progress?" Possibly Robert Penn Warren was unfair in his treatment of Jefferson
in *Brother to Dragons,* but he made a number of important points,
one being that optimistic clichés betray us in the glare of stark
terror or tragedy. We know too from our time, from the atroci-
ties of Nazi Germany and Stalinist Russia to the horrors of dicta-
tors in power today, how easily strength and beauty or *mens
sana in corpore sano,* or their equivalents, can be exploited for
inhuman means. What we have seen in the examination of the

athlete in American literature is the unmistakable view of authors that while body and soul must be held together, no man can dictate or should be able to dictate to another even generally how that union is to be achieved. Quality, the coming together of mind and body, or the third event, cannot be defined but we know, as Robert Pirsig has argued, that Quality, in infinite degrees, exists, and central to "high" Quality or "high" heroism is freedom. To overlook the significance of the athlete in literature and life is to ignore a prevalent and predominant symbol of heroism in the modern world, is to overlook the various combinations of body and soul in our society, the patterns of conformity and instances of revolt.

This study has shown that in the view of American authors, most publicly applauded representations of beauty, prowess, or versatility are suspect if not fraudulent. In twentieth-century American literature there is the unmistakable conviction that strength and beauty, the athletic ideal, must forever be sought but can never be defined or achieved. It is a view soundly confirmed in indictments of stereotyped Apollonian models and caricatures, the dumb athlete, the leisure-class gentleman, the southern knight, the WASP ideal, the muscular Christian, the booster alumnus, the Hollywood model, and the brave new man, blonde and right at the middle-weight limit. Just as strongly and just as significantly there is the rejection of the mindless return to adolescence and nature as seen in the treatment of the darling and the beast, or Dionysus as the curly-headed babe or wild bull. In sharp distinction with this Dionysus is the Dionysus of tragic contrast or Adonis. Adonic types include the folk hero, or the natural (rural and urban), the cripple, the absurd athlete, and the "secret" Christian. They are the rebels with a cause and in some cases the crucified, those caught in a divided world between culture and nature. It is Adonis who points to "beyonds" even if it means self-sacrifice, which in history it often has, a fact that in itself confirms the eternal necessity of the heroic act.

It is finally a sign of hope that writers, in their treatment of the athlete, have indicted the same nemeses of fifth-century Greece as strongly as did any of the classical writers. There is hope too in the struggle that the Adonic figure undertakes in an attempt to achieve a higher beauty. It is a beauty inclusive of the sublime, to borrow a phrase from Poe, a beauty ever beyond the reach of man like that Keats equates with truth and Camus with freedom. Though the athlete is at times reprehensible as a stagnated model of self-proclaimed beauty, he is just as often a symbol of noble aspiration toward an eternal ideal, reminding others of a sense of duty not to a school, country, or particular religion, but to Quality itself. It is in this role especially that he is gloriously redeemed in literature and in life as well.

Notes

1. Game Plan

1. *Republic.* Book III, *Five Great Dialogues,* trans. Benjamin Jowett (New York: Walter J. Black, 1942), pp. 298–300.

2. *Anti-Intellectualism in American Life* (New York: Vantage Books, 1963), p. 25.

3. *Apocalypse* (New York: Viking Press, 1960), p. 25.

4. *Sex in History* (New York: Vanguard Press, 1970), pp. 236–37.

5. "Self and Ideal," *Myth of the Birth of Hero and Other Writings,* ed. Philip Freund (New York: Vantage Books, 1932), p. 293.

6. John B. Noss, *Man's Religion* (New York: Macmillan, 1974), p. 54.

7. Walter F. Otto. *Dionysus: Myth and Cult,* trans. Robert B. Palmer (Bloomington: Indiana University Press, 1965), p. 28.

8. Ibid., p. 85.

9. Jane Ellen Harrison, *Themis: A Study of the Social Origins of Greek Religions,* (Cleveland: World Publishing, 1912), p. 129.

10. Ernest Junger, "Drugs and Ecstasy," in *Myths and Symbols: Studies in Honor of Mircea Eliade,* ed. Joseph M. Kitagawa and Charles H. Long (Chicago: University of Chicago Press, 1969), pp. 327–28.

11. *The Freud-Jung Letters,* ed. William McGuire (Princeton, N.J.: Princeton University Press, 1974), p. 265.

12. *Athletics of the Ancient World* (London: Clarendon Press, 1930), p. 70.

13. *Mythology* (Boston: Little, Brown, 1942), pp. 37–38.

14. *Paideia: The Ideals of Greek Culture,* trans. Gilbert Highet (New York: Oxford University Press, 1945), 1:7.

15. "A Day of Prowess," *Selected Prose of Robert Frost,* ed. Hyde Cox and Edward Connery Lathem (New York: Collier Books, 1956), p. 91.

16. "It Is Not Strength, but Art, Obtains the Prize," *Yale Review* 56 (June 1967): 608.

17. For a discussion of the ideal of *sapientia et fortitudo* see Robert E. Kaske, "*Sapientia et Fortitudo* as the Controlling Theme in *Beowulf,*" *Studies in Philology* 55 (July 1958): 423–57; reprinted in *An Anthology of Beowulf Criticism,* ed. Lewis B. Nicholson (South Bend, Ind.: Notre Dame University Press, 1963).

18. Gardiner, *Athletics of the Ancient World,* p. 102.

19. See Alexander C. Judson, *Sidney's Appearance* (Bloomington: Indiana University Press, 1958), plates 1–32, pp. 83–87.

184 NOTES TO PAGES 15–28

20. Bruce Haley, "The Cult of Manliness in English Literature: A Victorian Controversy, 1857–1880" (Ph.D. diss., University of Illinois, 1963), p. 235.

21. *Billy Budd*, ed. Harrison Hayford and Merton M. Sealts, Jr. (Chicago: University of Chicago Press, 1962), p. 44. Strength and beauty, as F. O. Matthiessen points out, are also the qualities of Jack Chase and Pierre. *American Renaissance* (New York: Oxford University Press, 1941), p. 501.

22. "Gods" in "By the Roadside," *Complete Poetry and Selected Prose by Walt Whitman*, ed. James B. Miller (Boston: Houghton Mifflin, 1959), p. 195.

23. *Roughing It* (New York: Books, Inc., 1913), p. 132.

24. *The Stories of F. Scott Fitzgerald* (New York: Scribners, 1951), p. 70.

25. "A Horse's Tale," in *The Complete Short Stories of Mark Twain* (Garden City, N.Y.: Doubleday, 1957), p. 525. Throughout the ages the horse has symbolized different things to different people; see J. E. Cirlot, *Dictionary of Symbols*, 2d ed. (New York: Philosophical Library, 1972), but in America, in addition to whatever else he represents, the horse is the embodiment of strength and beauty.

26. Dixon Wecter, *The Hero in America* (Ann Arbor: University of Michigan Press, 1941), p. 362.

27. Gilbert Patten (Burt L. Standish), *Frank Merriwell's "Father": An Autobiography* (Norman: University of Oklahoma Press, 1964), p. 178.

28. *Sport—Mirror of American Life* (Boston: Little, Brown, 1963), p. 241.

29. Patten, *Frank Merriwell's "Father,"* p. 181.

30. Boyle, *Sport—Mirror of American Life*, p. 243.

31. *The Stories of F. Scott Fitzgerald*, p. 351.

2. Apollo

1. Gilbert Seldes, *The Seven Lively Arts* (New York: Sagamore Press, 1957), p. 114.

2. Quoted in Donald Elder, *Ring Lardner* (Garden City, N.Y.: Doubleday, 1956), p. 123.

3. "Lineup for Yesterday: An ABC of Baseball Immortals," in *Sprints and Distances*, ed. Lillian Morrison (New York: Crowell, 1965), p. 25.

4. As far as I can determine there are only two football stories by Lardner, "Oh, You Bonehead," *Saturday Evening Post* 188 (March 25, 1916); 20–23, 78, 81–82, and "A One-Man Team," *Redbook* 28 (November 1916): 93–103.

5. Stuart Sherman, "Ring Lardner: Hard-Boiled Americans," in *The Main Stream* (New York: Scribner, 1927), p. 170.

6. *The Portable Ring Lardner*, ed. Gilbert Seldes (New York: Viking Press, 1946), p. 170.

7. *The Real Dope* (Indianapolis: Bobbs-Merrill, 1919), p. 81.

8. *The Hero* (New York: Vintage Books, 1956), pp. 209–11.

9. Maxwell Geismar, *Writers in Crisis* (Cambridge, Mass.: Houghton Mifflin, 1942), p. 7.

10. "Ring Lardner Confidential," *Provincial* 1 (October 1956): 3.

11. *Lose with a Smile* (New York: Scribner's, 1933), p. 79.

NOTES TO PAGES 29-43185

12. *Civilization in the United States: An Inquiry by Thirty Americans,* ed. Harold E. Stearnes (New York: Harcourt, Brace, 1922), p. 461.

13. Wecter, *The Hero in America,* p. 480.

14. For definition and discussion of these terms see respectively Orrin E. Klapp, *Heroes, Villains, and Fools* (Englewood Cliffs, N.J.: Prentice Hall, 1962), pp. 102-3, and Daniel J. Boorstin, *The Image or What Happened to the American Dream* (New York: Atheneum, 1962), pp. 45-46.

15. *Lose with a Smile,* p. 2.

16. "American Fiction," *The Moment and Other Essays* (New York: Harcourt, Brace, 1948), p. 123.

17. "Ring," in *The Crack-up* (New York: J. Laughlin, 1945), p. 36.

18. "The Point of It," *The Collected Tales of E. M. Forster* (New York: Modern Library, 1968), p. 222.

19. James Thurber, "University Days," *The Thurber Carnival* (New York: Harper and Brothers, 1945), p. 225.

20. *Sport—Mirror of American Life,* p. 256. Concerning Frank's actions, Boyle adds, "Of course, having Frank be a party to cheating and kick(ing) a dog may have been Patten's way of humanizing him."

21. *Meat on the Hoof* (New York: Dell, 1972), p. 71.

22. F. Scott Firzgerald, *The Great Gatsby* (New York: Scribner, 1925), p. 154.

23. "It's Baker! . . . Going for Another Touchdown!" *Esquire* 66 (September 1966): 135.

24. Donald A. Yates, "Fitzgerald and Football," *Michigan Daily,* January 15, 1956.

25. F. Scott Fitzgerald, *The Crack-up* (New York: J. Laughlin, 1945), p. 84.

26. *This Side of Paradise* (New York: Charles Scribners, 1920), p. 285.

27. Ernest Hemingway, *The Sun Also Rises* (New York: Scribners, 1954), p. 142.

28. Count Baldesor Castiglione, *The Book of the Courtier,* trans. Leonard Eckstein Opdycke (New York: H. Liverright, 1929), p. 30.

29. *Theory of the Leisure Class,* p. 170. For a diametrically opposite view of sport, see Paul Weiss, *Sport: A Philosophic Inquiry* (Carbondale: Southern Illinois University Press, 1969). I can find no evidence that Hemingway read Veblen, but Harold Loeb, on whom Cohn is based, certainly did. See *The Way It Was* (New York: Criterion Books, 1959), pp. 32, 48, 213. Hemingway almost certainly would have known of Loeb's attitudes toward the leisure class which were quite different from Hemingway's own.

30. *The Web and the Rock* (New York: Harper, 1939), p. 201. If Fitzgerald in *This Side of Paradise* patterned Allenby and Amory, in part, on Hobie Baker and Hemingway patterned Cohn on Harold Loeb, there is evidence that Wolfe based Jim Randolph in part on the life of Augustine William Folger, star athlete at the University of North Carolina in 1916 and 1917. For parallels see Manly Wade Wellman, "Tom Wolfe's Own Football Hero!" *Durham Morning Herald,* November 13, 1960. The significance of Randolph, however, goes far beyond any similarities to Folger, as is the case with the fictional athletes of the other authors.

31. *Lancelot* (New York: Farrar, Strauss, and Giroux, 1977), p. 14.

32. *Le Morte d'Arthur: King Arthur and the Legends of the Round Table* (A Rendition in Modern Idiom by Keith Baines with an Introduction by Robert Graves) (New York: Bramhall House, 1972), p. 391.

33. Book III, *Five Great Dialogues*, p. 299.

34. Nathan N. Pusey, "Introduction," in *A Turning Point in Higher Education* (Cambridge, Mass.: Harvard University Press, 1969), p. 17.

35. *The Rector of Justin* (Boston, Mass.: Houghton Mifflin, 1964), p. 57.

36. Cordelia calls Charley "Billy Budd," she says, "in revenge for his indifference but he was too unlettered to know what I meant" (p. 141). Charley could not have read *Billy Budd*, since Melville's novel was not published until 1924.

37. *Abortion, Lost Plays of Eugene O'Neill* (New York: New Fathoms Press, 1950), p. 16.

38. *Strange Interlude, The Plays of Eugene O'Neill* (New York: Jonathan Cape, 1953), pp. 9-10.

39. *The Hero*, pp. 178-79.

40. Wade Thompson, "My Crusade against Football," *Nation* 188 (April 1959): 314.

41. Gelett Burgess, *Are You a Bromide?* (New York: Viking Press, 1907), p. 18.

42. *Elmer Gantry* (New York: Harcourt, Brace, 1927), pp. 39-40.

43. (New York: Harcourt, Brace, 1943), p. 179.

44. *Theory of the Leisure Class* (New York: New American Library), p. 196.

45. *Windy McPherson's Son* (Chicago: University of Chicago Press, 1965), p. 126.

46. *Kit Brandon* (New York: Scribners, 1936), p. 45.

47. *Babbitt* (New York: Signet, 1961), p. 158.

48. *Twnetieth-Century American Writings*, ed. William T. Stafford (New York: Odyssey Press, 1965), pp. 112-13.

49. *A Study of History* (New York: Oxford University Press, 1939), 4:238-39.

50. Ibid.

51. Afterword, *Babbitt*, p. 327.

52. James Thurber and Elliott Nugent, *The Male Animal* (New York: Random House, 1941), p. 30.

53. Burgess, *Are You a Bromide?*, p. 25.

54. *The Troubled Air* (New York: Random House, 1951), p. 239.

55. The similarity of theme in the two stories is noted by Stewart Rodnon, "Sports, Sporting Codes, and Sportsmanship in the Works of Ring Lardner, James T. Farrell, Ernest Hemingway, and William Faulkner" (Ph.D. diss., New York University, 1961), p. 72.

56. *The Life Adventurous* (New York: Vanguard, 1947), p. 194.

57. *Side Street and Other Stories* (New York: Paperback Library, 1961), p. 13.

58. *Farewell to Sport* (New York: Knopf, 1930), p. 209.

59. *Goodbye, Columbus* (Cambridge, Mass.: Houghton Mifflin, 1959), pp. 21-22.

60. *Mr. Sammler's Planet* (New York: Knopf, 1970), pp. 148-49.

61. *Come Back, Little Sheba* (New York: Random House, 1950), p. 71.

62. *Picnic* (New York: Random House, 1953), p. 55.

63. *All the King's Men* (New York: Bantam Books, 1963), p. 365.

64. *Who's Afraid of Virginia Woolf?* (New York: Pocket Books, 1966), p. 192.

65. Albert Camus, "An Absurd Reasoning," in *The Myth of Sisyphus and Other Essays* (New York: Knopf, 1955), p. 42.

66. Goethe, *Faust, Parts I and II* (Abridged Version), trans. Louis McNeice (New York: Oxford University Press, 1960), p. 142.

3. Dionysus

1. *The Best Short Stories of Jack London* (New York: Premier Books, 1964), p. 76.

2. *The Game* (London: P. F. Collier and Son, 1905), pp. 112-17.

3. *Golden Boy: Six Plays of Clifford Odets* (New York: Random House, 1939), p. 225.

4. *The Hero with a Thousand Faces* (Cleveland: World Publishing, 1965), p. 342. The boxing darling might also be regarded as the hero as lover who, according to Campbell, learns the art of combat from a warrior-woman (pp. 343-44).

5. See "The Great Game," *Undream'd of Shores* (New York: Brentano's, 1924), pp. 288-89.

6. (New York: Random House, 1947), pp. 332-33.

7. With Ed Linn, "What Baseball Means to Me," *Look* 30 (July 26, 1966): 33.

8. *Guys and Dolls* (New York: Grosset, 1934), p. 214.

9. Sir Walter Scott, "Football Song," in *Sprints and Distances*, ed. Lillian Morrison, p. 28.

10. *All the King's Men* (New York: Bantam Books, 1963), p. 204.

11. William R. Taylor, *Cavalier and Yankee: The Old South and American National Character* (Garden City, N.Y.: Anchor Books, 1950), p. 125.

12. "The Eighty-Yard Run," *Mixed Company* (New York: Random House, 1950), p. 16.

13. *The Troubled Air* (New York: Random House, 1951), p. 36.

14. *Burning Bright* (New York: Viking, 1950), pp. 44-45.

15. Robert Sherwood, *The Petrified Forest: Representative American Dramas*, ed. Montrose J. Moses and Joseph W. Krutch (Boston: Little, Brown, 1941), p. 936.

16. Kent Ladd Steckmesser, *The Western Hero in History and Legend* (Norman: University of Oklahoma Press, 1965), p. 57.

17. The pioneer himself has had problems of identification. Says Henry Nash Smith, "From the time of Daniel Boone, the popular imagination has transformed the facts of myth. Boone himself lived to resent the popular image of him as an anarchic fugitive from civilization, and successive biographers tried in vain to correct what they considered a libelous distortion of the hero's real character. Davy Crockett of Tennessee, made the hero of a quite different cycle of southwestern humor, was likewise completely transformed." *Virgin Land: The American West as Symbol and Myth* (Cambridge, Mass.: Harvard University Press, 1950), p. 114.

18. "Champion," *How to Write Short Stories*, p. 178.

19. "Baseball Hattie," in *A Treasury of Damon Runyon*, ed. Clark Kinnard (New York: Random House, 1958), p. 329.

20. *A Feast of Snakes* (New York: Ballantine Books, 1976), pp. 5-6.
21. "Self and Ideal," pp. 293-94.

4. Adonis

1. Lord Raglan, p. 187.
2. *Abysmal Brute* (New York: McMillan, 1913), p. 5. Subsequent references are to this edition. Sometime before he himself was established as a writer, Sinclair Lewis sold Jack London plots for a number of stories, of which that of *The Abysmal Brute* is one. See specifically Franklin Walker, "Jack London's Use of Sinclair Lewis's Plots," *Huntington Library Quarterly* 17 (November 1953); 59-74. Just which ideas in *The Abysmal Brute* are London's and which Lewis's is difficult to say. London, however, appeared willing enough to take credit for all. In a letter to Lewis dated December 20, 1911, he writes, "Personally, despite the fact that I did not make a financial killing, I'm darned glad I wrote *The Abysmal Brute.*" Mark Schorer, *Sinclair Lewis: An American Life* (New York, 1961), pp. 186-87.
3. *Abysmal Brute*, p. 135. Closely related to the folktale described by Lord Raglan and bearing a basic resemblance to the plot of *The Abysmal Brute* is the story of Rishyacringa, found in the *Rig-Veda.*
4. Frederick Lewis Allen, *Only Yesterday* (New York, 1931), pp. 210-11.
5. Arnold Toynbee, *A Study of History* (New York: Oxford University Press, 1939), 4:239.
6. John Lardner, *White Hopes and Other Tigers* (Philadelphia: Lippincott, 1951), pp. 20-21.
7. *Jack Johnson Is a Dandy*, intro. by Dick Schapp and the Lampman (New York: New American Library, 1969), p. 16.
8. *The Ultimate Athlete* (New York: Viking Press, 1975), p. 142.
9. *You Can't Go Home Again* (New York: Harper and Brothers, 1941), p. 64.
10. *The Letters of Thomas Wolfe*, ed. Elizabeth Nowell (New York: Scribners, 1956), pp. 722-23.
11. It might be well to recall that Indians were originally referred to as "naturals." Standard advice of the Virginia Company, for example, was: "In all your passages you must have great care not to offend the naturals, if you can eschew it." D'Arcy McNickle, *The Indian Tribes of the United States* (New York: Oxford University Press, 1966), p. 14.
12. Bernard Malamud, *The Natural* (New York: Dell, 1965), p. 26.
13. Damon Runyon, "The Big Umbrella," *More Guys and Dolls* (New York: Garden City Books, 1951), p. 214.
14. *Death of a Salesman* (New York: Viking Press, 1963), p. 132.
15. "Human Side Is Out of Sports—Miller," *Knoxville News Sentinel*, February 13, 1968.
16. *The Web and the Rock*, p. 122.
17. *The Southpaw* (Indianapolis: Bobbs-Merrill, 1962), p. 306.
18. *A Ticket for a Seamstitch* (New York: Knopf, 1957), p. 85.
19. *Bang the Drum Slowly* (Garden City, N.Y.: Doubleday, 1962), pp. 73-74.

20. *Bang the Drum*, p. 27. Bruce's farm is "about 300 yards up the road" from Bainbridge, the number three being significant. Nebraska Crane and Herman Youngberry in *The Natural* want to go back to three-hundred-acre farms. There is evidence, according to Freud, that the number three is a symbol of masculinity. Says Cirlot, "It is the number concerned with basic principles and expresses sufficiency, or the growth of unity within itself. Finally it is associated with the concepts of heaven and the trinity." *Dictionary of Symbols*, p. 222.

21. See Fiedler, *No! in Thunder* (Boston, 1960), 9, 15, and Farrell, "Baseball as It's Played in Books," *New York Times Book Review*, August 10, 1958, p. 5.

22. *The Southpaw*, p. 337.

23. The sports-war metaphor that Henry objects to so strongly is at least as old as *The Odyssey* where, according to Gardiner, the word *athlete* is used for the first time. Stung by the taunt of the Phaeacian spielman that he is "no athlete," Odysseus proceeds to prove that he is (see VIII, 97-384).

24. Jessie L. Weston, *From Ritual to Romance* (New York: Doubleday, 1957), p. 119.

25. *Cat on a Hot Tin Roof* (New York: Signet Books, 1955), pp. 111-12.

26. *The Presidential Papers* (New York: Putnam, 1963), p. 243.

27. *New Yorker*, August 22, 1953, p. 20.

28. Ibid., March 21, 1959, p. 45.

29. *The Golden Bough*, Part 6, *The Scapegoat* (New York: Macmillan, 1935), p. 225.

30. For a discussion of "Refusal of the Call," see *The Hero with a Thousand Faces*, pp. 59-68.

31. Eric R. Bently, *A Century of Hero-Worship* (Philadelphia: Lippincott, 1944), p. 246.

32. *The Huge Season* (Lincoln: University of Nebraska Press, 1954), p. 135.

33. *Deliverance* (Boston: Houghton Mifflin, 1970), pp. 50-51.

34. Amos St. Germain, "Norman Mailer's Meditation on Popular Culture and Technology," paper presented at Popular Culture Association in the South, October 8, 1976, Knoxville, Tennessee.

35. *The Lotus and the Robot* (MacMillan, 1961), p. 274.

36. *The Holy Grail: The Galahad Quest in the Arthurian Literature* (New Hyde Park, N.Y.: University Books, 1961), p. 434.

37. Quoted in R. W. B. Lewis, *The Picaresque Saint* (Philadelphia: Lippincott, 1959), p. 61.

38. Ibid., p. 61.

39. David D. Galloway, *The Absurd Hero in Contemporary Fiction* (Austin: University of Texas Press, 1966), p. 18.

40. Albert Camus, "Helen's Exile," in *The Myth of Sisyphus*, p. 36.

41. "Joe Eliot," *The Life Adventurous* (New York: Vanguard, 1947), p. 72.

42. William Faulkner, *The Hamlet* (New York: Vintage Books, 1940), p. 110.

43. *Rabbit Run* (New York: Knopf, 1960), p. 138.

44. *Rabbit Redux* (New York: Knopf, 1971), p. 326.

45. *Beyond Desire* (New York: Liveright, 1932).

46. *Sherwood Anderson's Memoirs*, ed. Paul Rosenfeld (New York: Harcourt, Brace, 1942), p. 14.

47. *The Portable Sherwood Anderson,* ed. Horace Gregory (New York: Viking Press, 1949), pp. 607-9.

48. *Sherwood Anderson's Memoirs: A Critical Edition,* ed. Ray Lewis White (Chapel Hill: University of North Carolina Press, 1969), p. 554.

49. *Joiner* (New York: Knopf, 1968), pp. 114-15.

50. *Letters and Papers from Prison* (New York: Macmillan, 1953), p. 188.

51. *Luther* (Philadelphia: Lippincott, 1974), pp. 46-47.

5. *The Wrap-up*

1. *The American Renaissance* (New York: Oxford University Press, 1941), pp. 643-44.

2. William R. Taylor, *Cavalier and Yankee,* p. 63.

3. "American Ideals," *History of the United States during the Administration of Thomas Jefferson* (New York: A. and C. Boni, 1930), 1:179.

Index